Casanova's Life and Times

Casanova's Life and Times

Living in the Eighteenth Century

David John Thompson

PEN & SWORD HISTORY

First published in Great Britain in 2023 by
Pen & Sword History
An imprint of Pen & Sword Books Limited
Yorkshire – Philadelphia

ISBN 978 1 39905 205 4

A CIP catalogue record for this book is
available from the British Library

Typeset by Mac Style
Printed in the UK by CPI Group (UK) Ltd, Croydon, CR0 4YY.

Pen & Sword Books Limited incorporates the imprints of After
the Battle, Atlas, Archaeology, Aviation, Discovery, Family History,
Fiction, History, Maritime, Military, Military Classics, Politics,
Select, Transport, True Crime, Air World, Frontline Publishing, Leo
Cooper, Remember When, Seaforth Publishing, The Praetorian Press,
Wharncliffe Local History, Wharncliffe Transport, Wharncliffe True
Crime and White Owl.

For a complete list of Pen & Sword titles please contact

PEN & SWORD BOOKS LIMITED
47 Church Street, Barnsley, South Yorkshire, S70 2AS, England
E-mail: enquiries@pen-and-sword.co.uk
Website: www.pen-and-sword.co.uk
or
PEN AND SWORD BOOKS
1950 Lawrence Rd, Havertown, PA 19083, USA
E-mail: Uspen-and-sword@casematepublishers.com
Website: www.penandswordbooks.com

Contents

Acknowledgements

Special thanks to the inspiration, encouragement, advice and help from Ian Kelly, Lisetta Lovett and Chris Booth, and, of course, to Kev, Jan, Vincenza and Richard. But most of all to chance.

Introduction

'I will leave it to others to decide if my nature is good or bad.'
Giacomo Casanova, *History of My Life*

This book is part of a two-book project that is centred on Casanova's wonderful *History of My Life*, a life woven unlike any other into the story of eighteenth-century Europe. Although *Casanova's Life and Times* ranges much further than the memoirs, it has been shaped by the events, ideas and concerns that impinge upon them. The second book explores his intellectual development in the context of the Enlightenment.

Casanova opens a window into the daily life and mindset of European society, but for a modern audience, at a distance of over 200 years, to understand the man and the place he inhabited requires more than *History of My Life* alone can provide. European culture; the social networks by which society operated; the Enlightenment; the public sphere; key events such as the Seven Years War; the position of women in society; the political environment – these were aspects of the times that Casanova did not need to explain to his contemporaries. Likewise moral values. Attitudes that seem reasonable today can be misleading when applied to a different era. On-screen fictional representations are in reality people of today dressing and behaving according to the historical assumptions of the twenty-first century. Actions that we may find odious but which were regarded as acceptable or even virtuous by our forebears are unlikely to be legitimised in modern portrayals of character motivation. In order not to offend, the past becomes sanitised.

Running to almost 1,250,000 words and written in French, *History of My Life* is twice the length of Tolstoy's *War and Peace* and covers Casanova's life to the year 1774. He began writing it around 1789 or 1790 when he was in his mid-60s, ostensibly to cheer himself up during a period of illness, and was still writing it when he died. It is a record not just of his love life but of what he ate; what he read; how he dressed; how he travelled; his gambling; his duelling; his business and financial dealings; medical treatments; the theatre; the Church; the political, intellectual and cultural preoccupations of the time; and morality. Casanova was an accomplished writer and a tremendous storyteller who loved to entertain his audience, which make his memoirs a joy to read.

Casanova wrote this monumental work during his time as a librarian in Dux castle in Bohemia, where he lived from 1787. In exile for a second time, ageing, homeless, unemployed and not in the best of health, he was offered the position of librarian by Count Joseph Charles de Waldstein. Casanova's pleasure-seeking days were behind him, and the attempts of this overreaching son of an actress to get the literary and scholarly world to take him seriously met with little success. He wrote ten to twelve hours a day and his output was prodigious. Casanova died on 4 June 1798, his memoirs beside him. Carlo Angiolini, Casanova's nephew-in-law, organised his burial, and it was he who inherited the many volumes of loose manuscript that comprised *History of My Life*. These volumes were bought in January 1821 by the German publisher FA Brockhaus, and Casanova, the forgotten adventurer fell, under the gaze of the European public. Over the next several generations, numerous abridged, censored, 'improved', pirated and poorly translated versions came on to the market. Some were little more than approximations of the original. The Busoni pirate edition (1833–1837) included fictitious additional material. The successful Laforgue version (1826–1838), based upon the original manuscript, had been censored and rewritten by Jean Laforgue, a French teacher employed by Brockhaus to edit the text prior to publishing.

Editions produced from 1838 until 1960 were based upon these unreliable versions rather than the original manuscripts which were kept hidden by Brockhaus to prevent further pirating. They included the 1894 Arthur Machen translation, which long remained the standard English version. This was later revised a few years later around the turn of the century by Arthur Symons who recognised the flaws in the Laforgue edition upon which the Machen translation had been based. The originals narrowly escaped being destroyed in the Second World War (1939–1945) by the Allied bombing of Leipzig. In 1960 Brockhaus finally published a faithful and unabridged edition. This became the basis for the main translations that followed, including Willard R Trask's authoritative English version (1966–1971) which is used here, supplemented with the recent Bouquins French edition (2013–2018) as discussed in the opening of the notes and bibliography. In 2010 the original manuscripts were bought by the Bibliothèque Nationale de France and made available online.

The editions prior to 1960 undermined faith in the veracity of Casanova's memoirs and the reputation of the man himself. Those who found his attitudes and behaviour objectionable saw in these inconsistencies evidence of his unreliability, and drew the conclusion that he was a fantasist or a self-serving propagandist (or both). The fact that his memoirs sold well did not mean that people took Casanova's adventures seriously. In every age there has been a market for scandal and a rollicking good story, true or false. The boundaries between fact and fiction in the public arena can become notoriously ill-defined. A 2011 survey uncovered that 21 per cent of people believed that fictional characters such as Sherlock Holmes and Miss Marple were historical figures. By a similar process but in reverse, the Venetian has become fictionalised, an archetype of the amoral playboy.

Casanova saw himself as a philosopher and had a particular interest in moral philosophy which he studied during the time he was at university in Padua. In his *Critical Essay on Science, Morals and the Arts* (1785) he explores foolishness and its intellectual and moral implications, asserting his own expertise on the subject: 'This [teacher of morals] must know the story thoroughly, and must have the deepest judgement to extract the moral from it, for the story itself is only a real labyrinth; he must be old, wry, gentle, complacent, eloquent, and learned from his own experience.'[1] In his pamphlet *The Soliloquy of a Thinker* (1786) he observes, 'It is difficult to arrive at the science of the moral world without a very useful map which represents it to us in miniature.'[2] The map he had in mind was 'the good comedy, the one that corrects morals by making people laugh.' He is referring to Molière but it appears that he had a similar purpose in mind for *History of My Life* which he was to begin writing a couple of years later. In it, Casanova is explicit about wanting to make people laugh at human folly, particularly his own. He had made the same point in Venice after his return from exile. In *Thalia's Messenger* (1780) he writes how parodies help a person to 'make moral reflections on the vanity of this poor world.'[3] The morally-educative value of the theatre was not a new idea. The Venetian playwright Carlo Goldoni, whom Casanova knew, has one of his characters in *The Comic Theatre* (1750) declare, 'Comedy was created to correct vice and ridicule base customs; when the ancient poets wrote comedies in this manner, the common people could participate, because, seeing the copy of a character on stage, each found the original in himself or in someone else.'[4] It had also been a defence employed in the seventeenth century for the risqué and subversive buffoonery of *commedia dell'arte*.

Casanova may describe human foolishness but he does so more in the spirit of the anthropologist than the preacher. The Venetian is sceptical of religious and philosophical systems. When combined with humanity's numerous shortcomings they are more likely to inflame the disease than to cure it. He tends not to be judgemental of specific behaviours in and of themselves; it is not the act in isolation that matters so much as the context, intention and consequence. He is more critical of the cast of mind that leads people to do stupid things, such as superstition, lack of self-awareness and poor judgement. Casanova is particularly damning of those he labels fanatics: people who push behaviours to the extremes whether that be piety or libertinism. In his book

Refutation (1769) he declares that 'moderation is recognised as the first virtue of the Venetians,'[5] and elsewhere that the success of England 'needs nothing but moderation to maintain its advantages.'[6] This is an Aristotelian ideal that is consistent with Casanova's own pursuit of moral and personal freedom. Extremism, either self-imposed or imposed externally, tends to restrict the liberty of the individual and the range of moral choices available to them. Consonant with this outlook, *History of My Life* has a habit of problematising moral assumptions and absolutes.

Casanova was keenly aware of the currents of thought that engaged Enlightenment thinkers and was a participant in the debates that took place. Through *History of My Life* he uses his own experiences as a way of exploring philosophical ideas. Ivo Cerman comments: 'He [Casanova] investigated human nature in order to discover the limits of human capacities to act morally… [*History of My Life*] was supposed to be a true record of his own past actions, which should have shown Casanova what kind of person he really was.'[7] Unlike Jean-Jacques Rousseau (1712–1778), who believed that man was innately virtuous but corrupted by society, Casanova's vision was of a being who was morally free to act for good or ill, at least up to a point. *History of My Life* provides him with the evidence. It may be Casanova who takes centre stage but this human comedy is populated by numerous others whose moral character is exposed to the light, from the highest in rank to the most lowly. As Tom Vitelli astutely observes: 'Moreover, his narrative strategies are designed to bring his readers along with him in his adventures in such a way that they can discover, within themselves, their own similar impulses and understand how an action ordinarily deemed abhorrent can, under certain circumstances, seem reasonable and even virtuous.'[8] Casanova highlights this complexity early in his 1797 Preface to *History of My Life*: 'My misfortunes as well as my happiness have shown me that in this world, both material and moral, good comes from ill as ill comes from good.'[9]

History of My Life in particular allowed Casanova to explore whether libertinism possessed genuine moral value. Was the search for pleasure, based as it was upon the naturalness of human emotions and needs, a legitimate moral goal? What was the relationship between virtue, pleasure and happiness? What part did marriage and religion play in these equations? Several times the seriousness of Casanova's love for a woman is attested by his avowed wish to marry her. This was itself an Enlightenment impulse, if not a particularly libertine one, elevating love and happiness above more conventional grounds for marriage that were rooted in pragmatic and patriarchal family interests.

Casanova uses personal experience to explore the nature of the soul. His earliest memory was from the age of 8, and he takes the lack of any memory prior to that age as empirical evidence that the soul is dependent upon the material body of its host. It is clear to him that memory and self-awareness, essential to what it is to be a human being, are the consequences of a biological process of maturation tied to the physical world. The concept of a materially-dependent soul, leaving open the possibility that the soul itself was material, while not orthodox, was consistent with other streams of thought and did not exclude the intervention of God as its designer. For Casanova, the universe was composed of matter that, like God, was eternal. This had moral implications. A common belief was that mankind would not behave morally without the promised reward of heaven and the punishment of hell. It was a position adopted by Voltaire. But from Casanova's perspective, in a letter he composed for Emperor Joseph II, he observes that 'after the death of my organs I will no longer have memory, since without the cabinet in which the impressions are made it can't exist.'[10] Without memory or bodily sensations it is difficult to see how a heavenly incentive could work. And anyway, he adds, 'Miserable, most miserable, and worthy of the deepest contempt the man who to be just in this world needs to believe in reward or punishment after death.' Instead, he argues, the true incentive for moral behaviour lies in the value that an individual places on their reputation in posterity and their desire to protect it.

Although Casanova calls his memoirs a history, the notion of 'history' in the eighteenth century and previously was different to how it is now understood. We would not usually associate science with history but this was the case in the eighteenth century. The meaning of 'history' was broader than simply human affairs over time. It was the domain that concerned itself with things as they were. Thus science could be known as 'natural history' as well as 'natural philosophy'. Writers about the past such as Voltaire were relatively unusual with regards to the extent of their concern for factual accuracy. Even David Hume, famous in his day as an historian, was criticised for historical inaccuracies, yet was preferred to other historians due to his engaging narrative style. Accounts of the past in previous centuries had been even less reliable, as much myth as fact. Virgil's *Aeneid* (19 BCE) ingeniously blends myth with historical fact in his epic poem on the origins of Rome. Neither did a text's factual inaccuracy necessarily undermine faith in the truths it purported to convey, as in the Bible. Classical, Medieval and even Renaissance historians would happily make things up to fill gaps in whatever narrative they were composing. Cerman observes: 'They invented descriptions of battles, and inserted direct speeches which gave moral lessons to the reader and many other things which are unacceptable in modern critical history.'[11] Moral and rhetorical priorities were more important than an objective interrogation of source material. From the Renaissance, scholars began to turn away from this mythologizing of the past although it continued to persist, for example in the work of the French bishop and theologian Jacques-Bénigne Bossuet (1627–1704), and history was subject to considerable polemical bias for much of the eighteenth century.

From this point of view, *History of My Life* should not be judged according to the standards of accuracy that we would apply to a history text today. Casanova makes claims that he knew to be false, perhaps sacrificing fact for narrative interest or some deeper truth he wished to highlight. He writes that during his stay in London in 1763 one of his patrons, the Marquise d'Urfé, had died.[12] In fact she died in 1775. There are doubts that he ever met Rousseau as he claims. In an encounter with a surgeon at Orsara, a port on the Istrian peninsula, Casanova discovers that he himself was the source of an outbreak of the pox as a result of a visit the previous year. But the description Casanova ascribes to the surgeon bears a suspicious resemblance to the account of a similar event told by Dr Pangloss in Voltaire's *Candide* (1759). Unsurprisingly in such a gigantic work spanning four decades, there are mistakes, while the numerous conversations he recounts are best treated as reconstructions rather than transcriptions. Referring to this technique in *The Duel* (1780), he explains that 'he [that is, himself] who is writing this feels the need to become dramatic in order to be faithful and clear in his account.'[13] Casanova's keenness to engage his audience no doubt influenced what he wrote, maximising coherence, tension and interest, at least within particular narratives, possibly at the expense of accuracy. It is also clear that he shaped his memoirs to focus upon certain aspects of his life over others; he could have given far more attention to Casanova the man of letters. Instead it is Casanova the libertine and picaresque adventurer who hogs the limelight; the story of a free man who makes his own moral choices.

One of the quirks of the memoirs is that some of the names of Casanova's lovers and their relations are anonymised in forms such as Marchese F..., MM, CC, Countess AB, and so on. There has been plenty of speculation as to whom they are, and the identity of some are known with certainty. For the sake of simplicity, I have used the labels that Casanova has provided unless there is a reason to do otherwise.

Chapter 1

A Different Country

'I have written my history...but am I wise to give it to a public about whom I know only that which is to its discredit?'

Giacomo Casanova, *History of My Life*

History of My Life supplies the reader with a great deal of information, particularly on the *minutiae* of eighteenth-century life. Casanova drew upon a voluminous stock of notes, correspondence and administrative records that he had accumulated since his teens, supplemented by an impressive memory. Early scepticism about the credibility of the memoirs has markedly softened. Sufficient corroboration has been unearthed to suggest that we should accept Casanova's references to particular events unless we have reason to believe otherwise. Fundamentally supporting Casanova's account are letters; court records; police reports; newspaper articles; advertisements; receipts; passports; descriptions of people, places and happenings confirmed by other travellers. The ageing Venetian is a man who is making an honest attempt to record his life, albeit subject to his own biases and agenda. Indeed it is astonishing the degree to which he is willing to expose the intimate corners of his past to the judgement of others, including incidents which he knows are liable to reflect upon him badly. The old librarian is himself frequently critical, if forgiving, of the younger adventurer. Casanova was an historian and philosopher who treats his life as the subject of rational examination. As his memoirs are a study of human behaviour and morality, it made sense for him to describe in detail his relationships with women.

Nonetheless, dangers do lie in wait for the reader despite Casanova's openness. As touched upon in the introduction, we may know that the past is a different country but unless we know in what ways it is different, we are likely to apply a modern bias to what we read. To guard against this presentism as best we can, it is worthwhile exploring some of the differences between how Europeans in the eighteenth century experienced life compared to today. Typically we live in societies where our economic and social well-being has been transformed. Few of us have direct experience of scarcity of food, war or the death of a young child – commonplaces for people during Casanova's time. Life and livelihoods were precarious for the majority of the population; small misfortunes could leave families facing heart-rending decisions. It is important for us to understand what choices people faced. Inevitably we will be guided by values we hold today. However, not only have the material conditions of our lives changed but so have our ethics. We also need to be sensitive to changes in the meaning of language. We may think we know what the implications are of words such as 'devotion', 'honour', and 'love' but there are contemporary subtleties which can mislead us.

We will take a brief look at nine areas in which the conditions, attitudes and perceptions of the time were different to today: making ends meet; pragmatism; law enforcement; violence; superstition; personal freedom; sexuality; medicine; and taboos.

Making ends meet

During the eighteenth century, Europe was transitioning from economies which were still to some extent barter systems to ones which were primarily cash-based. Most people were in debt and struggled to subsist. In societies in which workers did not receive a regular income, many resorted to credit. Food insecurity was commonplace, especially in the spring, and occasionally there was famine. It has been estimated that an English household would on average spend more than half of its income on food and drink.[1] Food riots were common. Life was unpredictable, with even families of rank being pushed into destitution by some misfortune or other. One such was the family of Count Bonafede.

Casanova met him in Venice while the two were incarcerated in the fortress prison of Sant'Andrea, Bonafede there for non-payment of debts. Casanova was smitten by the count's beautiful teenage daughter when she visited one day, along with her mother, both dressed in their finery. But the family of nine were penniless. They survived on charity and Bonafede's small government salary. When Casanova later called on them, he found that the house was dilapidated and the women dressed in tatters. Their clothes were in pawn. To keep up the appearances of their rank, they would go without eating in order to redeem their clothes for when they went to church, the charity from which they would lose if they did not attend. Casanova was to meet Bonafede and his daughter ten years later. The family were still living hand-to-mouth and the question arose over whether the daughter would sell her virtue. Up to that point she had refused but matters were getting desperate. Bonafede's meagre pension had been stopped and they were about to be evicted. Father and daughter tried to lure Casanova into what appears to have been a plot to extort money from him. The awfulness of the family's position eventually took its toll on the daughter who had some sort of break down and spent five years in an asylum. When she was released, she was reduced to begging on the streets along with her brothers. Probably the majority of beggars across Europe at the time were women and their children, often those who no longer had menfolk to help to support them for various reasons. It is estimated that at the end of the eighteenth century 90 per cent of beggars in London were women.[2]

The dilemma facing Bonafede's daughter was one which many women faced: to trade their virtue for more tangible benefits. Those benefits could involve far more than money. Louis XV's chief mistress from 1745, Madame de Pompadour (1721–1764), was one of the most important figures in France, actively involved in the country's politics, economy and culture. A woman who obtained the support of a nobleman could benefit those around her, notably the men in her family for whom lucrative financial and job opportunities might be found. She could also become a hub of influence more generally. But the risks were high. Women could be misled by false promises, their reputation and the reputation of their family injured, and the chances of finding a successful marriage undermined. Casanova came to the aid of several such women.

Money is ever present in *History of My Life*. It was not just a preoccupation of Casanova's but of society as a whole. As with sex, people's attitudes were less inhibited than today. Haggling was the norm, except for Casanova, that is; it was a matter of honour that he refused to haggle. But generally if you did someone a service, you expected compensation unless you were comfortably well-off. Taking one of his lovers back to her convent one night by boat, the two are caught in a perilous storm. Seeing another boat approaching, Casanova calls out, 'Help!', then prudently adds, 'For two zecchini!'.[3] The gondoliers come to their rescue, but only on condition that they receive one of the zecchini up front. This concern about money was a reflection of the rockiness of people's lives and how even small sums were important to most. An eighteenth-century Venetian knew the value of a soldo (one four hundredth of a zecchino, to be precise).

Casanova regularly informs his reader of the state of his finances. He tells us that when he was 20 and embarking for Corfu his clothes, jewellery and cash made him well-off. Having hit legal and financial problems, towards the end of 1759 he hotfoots it out of Paris to the Dutch Republic taking with him 200,000 French livres in bills of exchange and jewellery. Notice that he includes jewellery and clothes in estimating his worth. Such assets were particularly important for women who would often receive them as gifts. 'Women's consumer goods, clothes in particular, became, in effect, an alternative currency,' notes Margaret Hunt.[4] In an uncharacteristically cruel act, Casanova once bartered a 1000 zecchini dress with a hard-up noblewoman for sex so that he could enjoy her humiliation. The court dress of the Countess of Strafford cost £100 in 1711.[5] To put that into perspective, in the middle of the century Samuel Johnson estimated that he needed £30 a year to live in London.[6] Such was the immense value of the wardrobe of Empress Elizabeth of Russia, she was willing to sell half of her 15,000 dresses to help fund the Russian war effort during the Seven Years War.[7]

Casanova records everything: the costs of dowries; gambling; contracts with mistresses; a military commission; expensive gifts; his daughter's boarding school in London; setting up his silk fabrics workshop; accounts of the financial arrangements of the Paris lottery; his dealings on international bond and currency markets; and his estimate of how much a year he needed to maintain his Parisian life-style (apparently 100,000 livres). But it is not just big-ticket items he includes. Numerous smaller ones are mentioned. In ascending order of value here are a number of them: one zecchino a month for a squalid lodging house; one zecchino to a go-between; one zecchino a day for a cooked meal; two zecchini for a box at the theatre; one louis to distract a hounding mob with the offer of breakfast; fifty paoli for one hundred oysters; three zecchini a month to rent a casino; six zecchini for sex with a virgin; three guineas for a night with a high class prostitute; ten zecchini for a fine gun; six louis to bribe a servant; six guineas to charter a packet boat from Calais to Dover; eighteen zecchini for a dozen shirts; ten guineas for a parrot; fifty louis for a steel sword. He even tells us how he 'spent a soldo on a good stick' to beat up one of his enemies.[8] It is a hopeless task trying to convert prices to modern values. Instead, I have related sums of money to more meaningful measures. That steel sword, for instance, cost around the average yearly wage of two Parisian workers.

Paradoxically, people's sensitivity to the value of money explains Casanova's unwillingness to strike bargains. A person of high status or, like Casanova, someone who wished to be perceived as such, was likely to incur reputational damage if they were a 'pinchpenny'. Generosity was less to do with personal ethics and more to do with public performance. It indicated that you were a person of means, someone who could be trusted, someone who rose above the narrow pecuniary mindset that dictated the lives of most. Casanova records overhearing a Spanish Cardinal berating one of his servants for economising: 'It will be said at Versailles, at Madrid, and at Rome…that the Cardinal de la Cerda is a beggar, or a miser. Know that I'm neither. Either stop disgracing me or leave.'[9]

Debt was the brooding menace that threatened to up-end the lives of both poor and rich. Casanova experienced it from a young age. He recalls falling into debt trying to keep up appearances with his peers when he was 14 and a student in Padua: 'In this new life, not wanting to appear less wealthy than my new friends, I indulged in expenses that I could not afford. I sold, or pawned everything I had, and incurred debts that I couldn't pay.'[10] He fled England in 1764 to evade his creditors: 'I saw before my eyes the inevitable gallows.'[11]

On that occasion he was also accused of passing on a forged bill of exchange. This was a last-ditch measure to get out of a tight spot. He was accused of it several times. It was a high-risk strategy carrying as it did the death penalty across much of Europe.

Gambling was another source of debt. When Casanova was 21, to cover his losses, he pawned a diamond worth 500 zecchini that had been lent to him. In *History of My Life* we regularly come across those who are either trying to avoid debt or are in debt and trying to escape from it, both types desperately searching for fresh sources of funds. A friend reported to Casanova how a common acquaintance called Baron don Fraiture had written to him for money and was threatening to kill himself. Casanova discovered in London that he had a son called Daturi who had been put in prison for being unable to pay back ten pounds. Teresa Imer, mother of his daughter Sophie, spent much of her adult life struggling with debt. Under the name of Cornelys, she became a well-known London society figure staging dinners and balls for the well-to-do. She was never able to free herself of her liabilities and died in Fleet prison in 1797 at the age of 74. With so many destitute or teetering on the edge of destitution, the power of money was immense.

Pragmatism

In the context of the economic fragility of most people's lives, attitudes which today may appear cynical and hypocritical, particularly given the dominance of religion, would be regarded by many as no more than pragmatic. Moral principles were luxuries that most could not afford. Society was not, after all, meritocratic. Your life chances were dictated far more by privilege, access and luck. Casanova was typical of this pragmatic mindset. Those in need whose scruples prevented them from taking advantage of some piece of good fortune, such as their beauty, Casanova regarded as foolish. If you were the secretary to an important official and somebody wanted to contact them urgently, why not accept a small sum to hurry things along? If you were a servant who could earn some money by acting as a go-between for two lovers, what was the harm? If you had witnessed a card sharp cheating, why not accept a cut of their winnings to keep quiet? If you were a woman, one of the ways you could repay a debt was through sex. On various occasions when Casanova had been of help in some way to an attractive woman, whether she was married or single, he felt that he had a legitimate claim to her 'favours' in return, and if they were not forthcoming would feel slighted.

More than today, relations between men and women had a transactional nature to them. Although love matches were increasing in the eighteenth century, traditional marriages resembled business deals or political alliances, particularly in the case of those of higher rank. Contractual arrangements between noblemen and courtesans were common and under certain conditions men would pass on their lovers to other men. Shortly before leaving Russia, Casanova declared to a Parisian actress who was out of favour with the Empress that he wanted to have an affair with her. If she were to consent to travel with him and become his lover then he would help to obtain the Empress's permission for her to leave the country. She agreed, with the proviso that in addition to a passport Casanova would pay for her journey to Paris.

Law enforcement

Pragmatism, too, was conspicuous in the exercise of policing and the law. It will surprise no-one that justice was not immune to the realities of power, status, money and poverty. One incident illustrates this clearly.[12] At an inn and about to set off to Paris, Casanova is informed that the lanterns on his carriage are not fastened properly and he will need to employ a lantern maker to fix them. He then discovers that it was a lantern maker who had deliberately loosened them in order to charge for the repair. Furious at the delay this will cause, Casanova speaks to the innkeeper, offering two louis if the innkeeper can get the man sent to prison. The innkeeper goes off and comes back ten minutes later with the chief of police who pockets the two louis, writes out a fine for twenty louis and organises the man to be sent to prison until he pays it. Additionally, one of Casanova's fellow travellers has falsely testified in writing that he was an eyewitness to the crime (the employment of false witnesses, often for payment, was common across Europe). Given the lantern maker's poverty, he has now essentially been handed a lengthy prison sentence – as we know, the fine was roughly the equivalent of the average annual wage of a Parisian worker. An hour later the man's family appear (mother, wife, babe-in-arms and four small children) to plead with Casanova. As was characteristic of him in the face of a personal appeal, he relents and drops the charges. He also gives six livres for the children. All of this, of course, bears little resemblance to due process as we understand it today. What we see is deference to those of higher status, private payment to pursue a complaint, police taking on the role of judge and jury, and the devastating impact that punishment could have upon the lives of the poor even for relatively minor offences.

Casanova himself frequently experienced the vagaries of eighteenth-century justice. Twice he was imprisoned in Venice without being made aware of any accusation, trial or length of sentence. The first, briefly, at Sant'Andrea fortress, the second under the Leads in the Doge's Palace. There was a similar lack of transparency when Casanova was incarcerated in Barcelona for six weeks. In Paris, London and Stuttgart he became embroiled in legal actions that either involved false witnesses being procured against him or the threat of them. In Naples, apparently notorious for 'chicaning lawyers', a baseless claim was made against him in order to extort money. Foreigners, in particular, seemed to be more vulnerable to exploitative treatment at the hands of local authorities. The chief constable of Lugano was running something of a protection racket. He assured Casanova that upon payment of a small sum of money 'either per week, or per month or per year' he should have no fear for his safety in the streets.[13] If not, the chief constable made clear, then there could be no guarantee. Several times Casanova's influential friends came to his aid. Imprisoned on accusations of financial misconduct in Paris, he was bailed out by Madame d'Urfé after only a few hours. In another case, the influential Madame du Rumain was able to arrange a private meeting for him with the powerful lieutenant general of the Paris police, Antoine de Sartine. In Naples the threat of extortion mentioned above was seen off by Aniello Orcivolo, a wealthy lawyer and husband of one of Casanova's ex-lovers.

Throughout Europe criminal punishment had always had a public dimension. Shame, humiliation and ostracism simultaneously accentuated the suffering of the guilty while offering the chance for people to unite against those who were threats to their community. In societies blighted with crime and with limited resources to deal with it, it was hoped that cautionary tales would act as a deterrence to some degree. This tradition continued through the eighteenth century and into the nineteenth. The last public hanging in Britain was in 1868. Executions could be great social events, especially when the perpetrator or the crime was notorious. To curry favour with one young woman and her aunt, Casanova rented a window for three louis overlooking the grisly execution of Robert Damiens, would-be assassin of Louis XV (1715–1774). He records the punishment of a midwife in Bologna involved in abortions and supposedly substituting living babies for stillborn. She was paraded through the streets half naked on an ass, being whipped by the executioner and jeered by the crowds.

Flogging, as here, and the pillory, were two other common forms of public reckoning. Even an arrest could be turned into something of an occasion. When Casanova was imprisoned in Venice in the Leads, he estimated that thirty or forty constables were involved in his arrest, making it clear to everyone in the locality what was going on. In an interesting reversal, thirty constables escorted him back to his hotel when he was released from his wrongful imprisonment in Buen Retiro in Madrid, sending out a public message that he had been exonerated.

Violence

Direct experience of violence is rare for most Europeans today. The reverse was the case in the eighteenth century. Despite the fact that, outside of war, society had become less violent, rough justice was still the norm. Punishment meted out by a figure of authority for the purpose of moral correction was regarded not only as legitimate but essential for the maintenance of social order. Children could be beaten severely for minor transgressions. Rousseau received several severe beatings as a child for breaking the teeth of a comb, a crime he claimed not to have committed.[14] At the Jesuit college Louis-le-Grand, attended by Voltaire, corporal punishment was employed frequently and could be brutal. Casanova was beaten when a student in a seminary college: 'I then felt rain down on my back seven to eight blows from a rope or stick'.[15] Violence perpetrated outside these hierarchal norms or, worse still, that undermined them, was treated very differently. If a servant assaulted their master, or a child their parent, the penalty could be severe. For a wife to murder her husband was classed as petty treason.

Mechanisms of law and order were slow and inadequate, throwing people back on to their own resources. Casanova generally carried with him either a knife, a sword or a pistol, without which he felt vulnerable. He also refers to women who carried weapons. One of his mistresses, the nun, MM, sported a brace of pistols. He himself would not have been regarded as an overly aggressive man by the standards of his time. Yet although Casanova disliked cruelty, if he felt he was being insulted, swindled or threatened, he would willingly resort to violence. He was certainly prepared to kill. While a prisoner in the fortress of Sant'Andrea, Casanova engineered an ingenious escape and alibi in order to revenge himself upon a man called Razzetta. He cudgelled him (with the 'good stick' he bought for a soldo), threw him in a canal and fled back to prison. A couple of years later, he left a man stretched out on the ground and covered in blood for having passed himself off as a high-ranking nobleman, and worse, for having used this invented status to publicly insult him. Rather dramatically, the episode culminated in Casanova fleeing to Casopo, a peninsular on the north shore of Corfu, where single-handedly this still young man put together a local militia ready to defend himself against any backlash from his superiors. As it turned out, the man whom Casanova attacked was revealed to be a fraud, and Casanova was exonerated.

On one occasion Casanova received a summons for allegedly attacking and raping a woman's daughter. His response to the accusations was to explain how the mother was selling her daughter to him for sex and charging him a premium rate as she was a virgin. The mother, he claimed, took his money but then the daughter refused to have sex. Seeing that he had been deceived, and annoyed with himself for handing over money in advance, he had punished the daughter by beating her with a broomstick.

On another occasion, when Casanova was staying at an inn, he struck, kicked and threw downstairs a young serving boy, the nephew of the innkeeper, who had innocently addressed Casanova as the husband of a woman who was the mistress of another man. Casanova had been furious at the insult. When he discovered that the boy and the innkeeper, who had now armed himself with a knife, had been deliberately misled by the mistress's lover (in what was to turn out to have been a scam) Casanova went on to attack the lover and had to be restrained by the innkeeper from breaking the man's head open with the butt of his pistol. When the man maintained his innocence, the innkeeper in turn hit the hapless lover in the face with the inn register. Casanova made amends to the nephew by giving him two zecchini, a significant sum for an inn boy. Casanova was also willing to get others to do his dirty work. He paid his Spanish manservant, Leduc, to beat up a Jewish impresario for breaking his word to him.

Casanova was in danger of being murdered on an alarming number of occasions. He fought at least nine duels and in the most famous of these, his duel with the Polish nobleman Branicki, he was within a whisker of being butchered by his opponent's men. Plots were hatched to assassinate him several times. He avoided one, fought off another, and a third he escaped by jumping out of a window overlooking Piazza San Marco in Venice. He was attacked by sailors during a storm on a ship bound for Corfu. They attempted to throw him over the side having been convinced by a priest that the bad weather would not relent as long as Casanova, whom the priest had denounced as a malign influence, remained on board. The Spanish Countess he had humiliated (she of the 1000 zecchini dress) employed a witch to try to kill him by supernatural means.

As well as local violence there was, of course, violence between nations and states. For most present-day Europeans, experience of war is largely non-existent except amongst its oldest generation and those caught up in the tragic events of ex-Yugoslavia and Ukraine. By contrast, war in the eighteenth century was a regular occurrence. The size of armies was to increase several-fold between the late-seventeenth century and the late-eighteenth century, and huge numbers were killed. The Revolutionary and Napoleonic wars (1792–1815) were particularly destructive. Tim Blanning notes: 'Twenty-three years of fighting had probably killed around 5,000,000 Europeans, or proportionally at least as many as the First World War.'[16] Wars were a cause of terrible hardship. Compounding the emotional trauma was the economic cost to families of the death, injury or absence of so many men. Then there was the destruction of food supplies and property, the spread of disease, the general impoverishment of communities, the social disruption and the political instability.

Judicial violence became less prevalent and extreme after 1600. States were more organised and did not need to rely so much on the inhibitory warnings of gruesome public spectacles. Alternative punishments were increasingly used, such as incarceration, fines and banishment. But that said, judicial violence remained quite common, particularly for the poor. Flogging; branding; mutilation; hanging; burning; being buried alive, impaled or broken on the wheel, all remained ugly facts of life. Torture or the threat of torture was still used on occasion to investigate crimes.

Superstition

The eighteenth century may have been the age of the Enlightenment but religion and superstition were as ingrained as they always had been for the overwhelming majority. This was the case even in Venice, and the Venetians were amongst the most educated and worldly people on the planet. This is not a surprise. Science was in its infancy and there was only the sketchiest understanding of the physical causes of phenomena, such as extreme weather, illness or violent geological disturbances, when harm could descend from out of a clear blue sky. But ignorance has never stopped people speculating. An implausible explanation is more reassuring than no explanation at all. It allows the possibility that you can exert influence by placating or bribing a divine being. It is well understood that the more uncertain an event, the more superstitious the participants in it are, whether they be sports fans, gamblers or war combatants. The less you can exert tangible control over an outcome, the more likely you will pin your hopes on methods that are intangible. And the more desperate you are or the greater the importance of the outcome, the more willing you are to follow the teachings of priests and traditional folklore or the advice of local healers, magicians and occultists. Add all that to the insecurity of life in general, if you were a citizen of the eighteenth century you would regularly seek the intervention of supernatural forces to do you favours and keep you safe. If you were a gambler, you might send up a prayer to the

Virgin Mary to influence the throw of a dice. If you were a woman, you might invest in a love potion to hang on to a wealthy lover. If you were a farmer, you might leave a plot of land uncultivated where the devil could grow his docks and thistles instead of amongst your corn.

Casanova saw himself as a philosopher guided by reason but he was religious all the same and admitted that he was superstitious. He records numerous examples of superstitious behaviour, of his own and others. He believed that at times his actions were guided, usually for the better, by a supernatural being (variously labelled his 'angel', 'daemon', 'oracle' and 'genius'). He constantly refers to providence and fate. He practised the occult art of cabbala, derived from Jewish mysticism. Sometimes he did so sincerely, more often he did so to take advantage of the gullible (amongst whom were some of the wealthiest and most influential members of society). Casanova's first love, Bettina, convinced the family that she was possessed, and her mother blamed it on an old servant whom she accused of being a witch. Following the death of a lay-sister, a peasant woman informed Casanova that she had put guards over the body to prevent witches disguised as cats from making off with an arm or a leg. He convinced a farmer that he was a magician who had the power to retrieve buried treasure. Casanova refers to an occult force which prompted him to approach a woman who was standing alone having just disembarked at Venice from a Ferrara packet boat. One of the reasons he was imprisoned by the Venetian Inquisition was for the possession of occult books. The list goes on.

Personal freedom

Privacy and personal freedom were notable by their absence. Women in particular were closely supervised. Casanova was astonished to discover that his housekeeper, Madame Dubois, had travelled unescorted from England to Lausanne. He was equally amazed by the more liberal attitudes of the Dutch when he was allowed to accompany a respectable young woman alone to the theatre. Urban living spaces in particular tended to be small, crowded and boisterous. Households were filled with the comings and goings of extended family members, servants, lodgers, neighbours, tradesmen, clergymen and an assortment of visitors. Sharp eyes, keen ears and ready tongues ensured little passed unnoticed. It would be a naive hope to expect doctor-patient confidentiality. The private and the public were very permeable. Non-matrimonial bed sharing and communal sleeping were common. Travelling companions and strangers could expect to share a room or a bed while on the road. One time Casanova had taken a fancy to a respectable peasant girl who had travelled to Venice with her old uncle. The three of them ended up sleeping in the same room at an inn despite Casanova's offer to pay for another room. The girl and uncle slept together, she naked. 'I have found this common among good people in every country in which I travelled,' Casanova reports.[17]

One consequence of this congested private space was that personal intimacy was less inhibited. The actress Toscani and her young daughter were more than happy for Casanova to check with his own hand their boast that the daughter was still a virgin. Moreover, the mother and Casanova made love while the girl watched. On another occasion he was staying with a noble family. The countess was suckling her new-born while travelling in a carriage with Casanova and the countess's sister who was his love interest. When the baby finished suckling, Casanova, larking around, took over at the countess's breast with the mother's good-humoured acquiescence.

This was a society of roles with their sets of expectations about where you should be and when, what you should be doing, saying, behaving, dressing, and whose company you could, should or should not be keeping. People possessed an acute awareness of each other's position in society; how they should seem; how they should behave towards others, and others to them; and of all the signs of status and place that went along with it. Were you male, female, legitimate, illegitimate, the oldest sibling, of marriageable age, married, mother, father, an aunt, uncle, in-law, cousin, widow, widower, patriarch, matriarch? You were in possession of social capital, consolidated in words like 'honour' and 'reputation', that you could grow and nurture or that you could squander. You could bankrupt your social capital as easily as your financial capital with consequences that would be just as dire. Most people existed at the centre of their own tight web of relationships. They were mindful that their actions could affect the opportunities of others, especially family members, such as those of Madame de Pompadour mentioned above. The further up the social scale the more rigid and demanding these duties and expectations became. If you were the patriarch of a powerful noble clan then your behaviour had greater ramifications for far more people, including future generations.

Unsurprisingly, rituals of politeness, etiquette and deference, fine-tuned to one's social standing, acquired great significance. The slightest misstep could cause enormous offence:

In polite society, matters have reached the stage that if you want to be well-mannered you cannot ask somebody which country they are from, because if they are Norman or Calabrian they must, if they tell you, apologize to you, or, if they are from the Pays de Vaud, tell you that they are Swiss. You also don't ask a lord what his coat of arms is, because if he doesn't know the heraldic jargon, you'll embarrass him. You must refrain from complimenting a man on his fine hair, because if it's a wig, he might think you're making fun of it, nor praise a man or a woman on their good teeth, because they might be false. They thought me impolite in France fifty years ago because I asked countesses and marquises their baptismal names. They didn't know them. And one gallant who unfortunately was called Jean satisfied my impertinent curiosity but offered me a duel.

The height of rudeness in London is to ask someone what religion they are, and in Germany too, because if they are a Herrnhuter, or an Anabaptist, they will be reluctant to admit it to you. The safest thing in the end, if you want to be liked, is not to question anyone about anything, not even if they have change for a louis.[18]

Casanova's complaint is rather ironic considering how touchy he was himself about his honour and how regularly he felt slighted by others. Upon receiving a passport, he protests: 'I find my name without the slightest title, something that is noticed in Spain, because it is only a servant who is refused the *Don*, as we refuse them the *Signor*, and the French the *Monsieur*. ... Burning with anger because of this mark of contempt, I wrote a letter to D Domingo Varnier.'[19]

This extreme sensitivity invited abuse. Confident that they were unlikely to be openly challenged, travellers passed themselves off with titles, honours and lineages which were pure fiction. Casanova adopted the title *Chevalier* before he had the right to use it.

Beyond the communal intrusion into people's lives, the State and Church also took a close interest. Spies and opportunistic informants funnelled information to the authorities about their fellow citizens. In Spain, inn rooms had locks on the outside but not the inside. Innkeepers suspicious of some illegal moral impropriety could thereby prevent unmarried guests from leaving while allowing access to tipped-off authorities. Agents of the Spanish Inquisition were stationed in theatres to keep an eye on the actors and spectators. Unlike Venice and Paris, theatre boxes in Madrid were open to view to ensure that their occupants could not engage in illicit behaviour. Casanova was publicly shamed in the same city by being included on a list for the excommunicated for not attending mass (he had been ill).

Empress Maria Theresa (1740–1780) established a Chastity Commission in Vienna to crack down on adultery and loose morals. Noblemen could incur heavy fines and the loss of their military careers. Women adjudged to be promiscuous could be sent to convents or banished. Prostitutes could be whipped, fined and deported. On one visit to Vienna in 1766, Casanova and a newly-acquired mistress received a visit from the local police only the morning after their arrival, his mistress being ordered to leave the city within twenty-four hours. A police unit was employed in Paris to monitor courtesans and prostitutes who operated from protected brothels. They served higher status men such as Casanova, who frequented one such brothel called the Hôtel du Roule.

The lives of the nobility who made up the governing elite of Venice were tightly regulated and supervised. It was a serious offence, for instance, to socialise with a representative of a foreign power, however fleetingly. To be a member of this elite required not only your father to have been of patrician descent but that your mother did not come from a plebeian background. If she was an outsider bride (that is, not from a patrician family) careful investigations would be carried out to ensure that she and her family were of good social and moral standing. Restrictions were placed upon the French nobility with regards to engaging in commerce.

Movement was supervised for the majority of the population in Europe. It is estimated that around 80 per cent of women and 50 per cent of men required permission from someone to move somewhere else.[20] That someone could be an employer, a master, a superior officer, the head of a household or even the head of state. To a large extent this was to tie down labour. It was also a way to control certain religious and ethnic groups. Jews were sometimes confined to ghettos. Passports, visas and identity documents were required to travel across borders, internal as well as external. Both foreigners and the nobility required the permission of the tsar or tsarina to leave Russia. There were numerous regulations on what and when people could eat; how they could dress (in France rouge could only be used by noblewomen); what they could read; the religion they could practice; the kinds of pleasures they could pursue, and when. In London on the Sabbath, Casanova notes how spies would patrol the streets listening outside houses to detect whether some kind of entertainment was taking place inside.

Sexuality

One of the central preoccupations of all societies is sexuality. It has been claimed that the eighteenth century witnessed a transformation in sexual behaviour and attitudes. Casanova himself refers to 'the scandalous morals of the times'.[21] Given the inherently tricky nature of the evidence, the truth of Casanova's claim is up for debate. But what is clear is that alongside a major increase in population, there was a significantly higher proportion of both illegitimate children and women who were already pregnant when they got married. More people were getting married and at a younger age. As well as being indicative of an increase in fertility, this could suggest a change in attitudes towards sex, possibly a shift towards more penetrative and phallocentric sexual practice according to Tim Hitchcock.[22] Masturbation became increasingly stigmatised. Not only was it considered immoral but it was blamed for all sorts of social, psychological and physical ills: fainting fits; epilepsy; erectile dysfunction; infertility; hysteria; general weakness; gonorrhoea, and so on. In discussion with the Muslim Yusuf Ali in Constantinople, Casanova explains to him how masturbation for Christians is 'an even greater crime than unlawful copulation' and that 'we [Christians] claim that young men impair their constitutions and shorten their lives.'[23] He goes on to assert that masturbation is less risky for women than for men.

There was a growth in sex manuals and erotic literature, in particular pornographic novels, buttressed by mass printing and increasing literacy. It could be cheaply produced and read aloud in coffee houses and taverns, making it accessible across the social spectrum. Casanova refers to such literature in his memoirs on a number of occasions. Increasing secularisation and the spread of Enlightenment ideas challenged conservative religious norms. Enjoyment of sex, it was argued, was good in itself; it did not have to be in the service of procreation.

There seems to have developed an openness with regards to sexual behaviour (or, at least, heterosexual behaviour), particularly in cities such as Venice, Paris and London, an openness that went well beyond a libertine few. In their letters and diaries, men unabashedly recounted the sexual adventures of themselves and their acquaintances. Women had traditionally been regarded as more libidinous than men, and Casanova gives plenty of examples of sexually assertive females. He claims that it was the amorous attentions of the 63-year-old dancer La Binetti that killed off her last husband. As the century wore on, debates around the sexual biology of men and women emphasised the primacy of the male role, with women being viewed more as passive, albeit morally superior, recipients ('men give, women receive' as Casanova puts it). It was the male libido which was in the ascendance by the end of the century, and women who were perceived to be the victims of it. There also seems to have been something of an obsession with the penis and male virility. More than once does Casanova express his shame upon discovering that his penis is not as big as that of some other man's. But while masturbation was being deemed unhealthy (at least for men), there was a medical opinion that sex itself was essential for well-being. So what was an unmarried man to do? The answer for many was to engage the services of a prostitute.

Attitudes towards same-sex attraction changed dramatically over the eighteenth century. Prior to 1700, despite sodomy being a sin which could command the death penalty, it was recognised that men desired adolescent boys (ranging from around their early teens to early 20s) as well as women. Casanova refers to pederasty, or the so-called 'wristband game', on various occasions. At this time, homosexuality was perceived as a behaviour not an intrinsic identity. A sodomite (a term commonly used at the time) was somebody who engaged in sodomy. If they gave up the practice, they were no longer sodomites. Likewise, it was accepted that women could desire other women as well as men. Randlolph Trumbach explains how this attitude began to change from the beginning of the century: 'Europeans began to think that most men desired only women and that only a deviant minority of men desired other males.'[24] According to Trumbach this change started in northwestern Europe from 1700 to 1750, spreading to central Europe by 1800, and southern and eastern Europe by 1900. It was only later in the eighteenth century did the concept of homosexuality itself emerge as a recognized orientation that defined a segment of society.

One interesting but contested theory is that this shift was at least partly the result of an altered understanding of male and female biology. At the beginning of the century, it is claimed that a one-body, or one-sex, model prevailed in which it was hypothesised that women were underdeveloped men. Female genitalia were the same as the male's but internal and inverted. On this understanding, the sexual identities of males and females were not so fundamentally distinct and a certain sexual fluidity was comprehensible. Same-sex attraction was not entirely unnatural or surprising particularly – as seems to have been generally the case – if the older partner were dominant, mirroring the accepted hierarchy of male over female. It was considered wrong but not abhorrently so. It has been convincingly argued that Casanova was sympathetic to the idea of a one-sex model, and certainly the malleability of gender boundaries and roles is a recurring theme in *History of My Life*.[25] As the eighteenth century progressed, the two-body model displaced the one-body, and sexual identity became conceived as inflexible and immutable. Consequently, deviations from heterosexual practices and gendered norms of masculinity and femininity became increasingly policed and stigmatised, especially amongst men.

Casanova records a number of homosexual encounters as a participant and observer, and there appears to be evidence of others that he chose not to include in his memoirs. In addition, John Masters has raised the possibility that one reference to an affair with a woman may have been a disguised affair with a man, and that a number of his other relationships with men may have had a homosexual dimension.[26] Casanova's experience and point of view as depicted in his memoirs reflects his southern European upbringing, possibly influenced retrospectively by the emergence of homosexuality as a stigmatised identity.

In 1745 Casanova met Bellino and her family, with Bellino disguising herself as a castrato. The family included her supposed brother Petronio. Casanova observes: 'Petronio was a real Giton [male prostitute], and a professional. This is not uncommon in capricious Italy, where intolerance in this matter is neither unreasonable as in England nor fierce as in Spain.'[27]

As a 17-year-old enrolled in a seminary college, a fellow student sneaked into Casanova's dormitory bed and Casanova reciprocated a few nights later. From his telling, it was purely innocent, although he notes that had they been caught in bed together they would undoubtedly have been accused of sodomy. During his brief stay in Constantinople when he was 20, he rejected a proposition by an older, high-status man called Ismail because 'I didn't find it to my taste' and that 'I was not a fan of it.'[28] Ultimately, they did have sex together, while watching a group of naked women bathing. Perhaps the scene allowed Casanova to rationalise to the reader the behaviour that he had previously declared to be repugnant to him.

Fifteen years later, in 1760, having watched his friend Dolci have sex, Casanova records: 'He was a Ganymede [a beautiful youth with whom Jupiter fell in love] who could easily have made me Jupiter.'[29] He turned down the advances of a young male prostitute in the same year but in his account of the incident he implies that it was not something that he would necessarily have always ruled out. In 1761 he allowed himself to be pleasured by the hand of the Duke of Matalona in the presence of the duke's young mistress (who, it transpired a little later, was Casanova's daughter, much to Casanova's surprise). In 1764 in Russia, when he was 39, he engaged in pederasty with a young Russian officer called Lieutenant Lunin. The Venetian's warm praise for Lunin's sexual opportunism in his seduction of senior officers, and in his willingness to defy orthodox social norms, was consistent with Casanova's generally pragmatic approach to life. His sympathy may also have been underpinned by memories of his own youth, in particular his relationship with the trio of noble bachelors and friends Bragadin, Dandolo and Barbaro who we will meet in the next chapter.

Casanova's memoirs record various instances of same-sex intimacy between women, sometimes in three- or more-somes, of which he was one of the participants and none of which provoked any moral concern on his part. Of particular note were the nuns CC and MM who have affairs separately and together with Casanova, his future protector Abbé de Bernis (1715–1794), and between themselves. On one occasion CC and MM perform in front of the two men. In a revealing discussion with a nun from Chambéry, Casanova discovers that lesbianism was common amongst the sisters and, indeed, seems to have been tacitly condoned. The nun also makes it clear that having sex with a man out of wedlock is the greater sin. When Casanova was taking the baths at Bern with his mistress, Dubois, two bath girls entertain them, one of them playing the part of a man. One woman called Marcolina, whom Casanova rescued from his dead-beat brother, Gaetano, and who subsequently became his own lover, turned out to have had many affairs with both men and women.

Medicine

Casanova's memoirs contain numerous references to the medical ailments and treatments of the time. Within eight pages of the first chapter, he records how for the price of a silver ducat an old woman cured him of a chronic nosebleed by means of magic rituals, and also how his father died due to the incompetence of a trained physician who failed to treat properly an abscess in his head. Setting aside the irony that the old woman was more successful than the physician, the juxtaposition of the two events neatly illustrates the co-existence of a wide spectrum of medical beliefs and practices. Of the treatment of his father, he writes: 'The physician Zambelli, after having given the patient some oppilative remedies [medicine that blocks passageways from the body], thought to repair his error by Castoreum [an anal secretion from beavers], which caused him to die in convulsions. The aposteme [abscess] burst from his ear a minute after his death.'[30] In her valuable medical analysis of Casanova's memoirs, Lisetta Lovett explains that 'Casanova, in accordance with ancient medical theory, believes that the physician should have taken immediate measures to encourage, not prevent, the expulsion of the bad humours that developed in his father's brain.'[31] We are in a very different world.

Over the last three centuries there has been a transformation in our understanding of how the body works and how we should address illness, leading to a similar transformation in this regard to the mindset of the modern European. Let's take one example. Bloodletting, by lancet or leech, was a commonly accepted procedure practised across all social groups as a way of combatting numerous maladies. It had been around for over 3,000 years, and was still a thriving business in the nineteenth century. In 1833, France imported forty-two million leeches.[32] They would be attached to almost any part of the body, including the anus, the vagina, and the tonsils. In 1799, the day before his death, George Washington was subjected to a number of remedies in an attempt to cure a fever, including bloodletting. Casanova refers to bloodletting on various occasions and was bled himself. One of the aims of the practice was to manage the movement of blood around the body in order to restore a healthy balance as understood according to humoral theory, originally formulated by Hippocrates in the fifth century BCE. On the basis of the experience of individuals who self-harm, Lovett has speculated that a release of endorphins might have reduced anxiety in patients who were bled. If that is the case, it may explain in part why the practice endured for so long.

It is clear that Casanova possessed considerable expertise in medical matters, at least as understood at the time, which he used to inform his personal experience and actions. Perhaps the greatest turning point in his life was when he rescued Senator Bragadin from near death as a result of a mercury treatment prescribed for him following what was probably a stroke. Confident in his own judgement that the mercury was killing the senator, he countermanded the physician's instructions and Bragadin immediately began to recover. Twenty years later, in Warsaw, Casanova rejected the diagnosis of not one but three Polish surgeons who pronounced that he had developed gangrene after being injured in a duel the previous day. They insisted that immediate amputation of his hand was the only solution. Convinced they were wrong, he refused, and he was not prepared to budge even in the face of pressure from the Polish court and King Stanislas himself. But the surgeons persisted. In the evening of the same day, he was visited by no less than four of them who now determined that his condition had deteriorated to the point that his arm would have to be removed. Casanova stuck to his guns and refused to have any more to do with them. Eventually he recovered, hand and arm fully intact.

Where did this expertise come from? It may be that his fascination with medicine was sparked by his early childhood experiences. In addition to those already mentioned, one episode that was particularly striking occurred when Casanova was about 13. It involved Bettina, the sister of his Paduan tutor, Dr Gozzi. Bettina was several years older than Giacomo, who had become infatuated with her. Bettina contracted smallpox. In eighteenth-century Europe the disease is estimated to have killed around 15 per cent of those who contracted it.[33] It killed the majority of children who caught it. Young Giacomo stayed by Bettina's bedside for two weeks, along with her mother, while the other lodgers were sent to board elsewhere. By the tenth and eleventh days, he notes, 'all her foul pustules turned black and infected the air. Nobody could bear it except me.'[34] Curiously, he writes that he 'had no need to fear it,' and indeed he remained free of this highly contagious disease apart from being infected with eight to ten pustules.[35] Yet there is no indication that he had ever suffered from smallpox, and there is no mention elsewhere that he had been scarred – a common symptom. Lovett suggests that he may have had a benign variant, variola minor, that would have conferred immunity against its nastier sibling. It was also possible that he had been inoculated against the disease through the use of infected tissue from someone who had only been mildly infected. This would have been the late 1730s and inoculation, although generally uncommon in Europe, was becoming known and practised. In 1715 a work on the topic by the physician Jacob Pylarani was published in Venice. Bettina survived and the two remained good friends until she died many years later.

Although Casanova was forced by his family to read law, his true ambition had been to study and practise medicine, and it was an interest he continued to pursue. While working towards his degree, he took additional classes in medicine, physics and chemistry, and attended lectures by the renowned anatomist, Giovanni Morgagni. In later life he corresponded with Count Simeon Stratico, a professor of theoretical medicine. Furthermore, his degree entailed the study of philosophy, central to which would have been that of the ancient Greeks, from which professional medicine had drawn some of its most enduring beliefs. Like most of Casanova's contemporaries, it was these ideas from antiquity that dominated his understanding of how the body worked.

Fundamental was humoral theory. This theory paralleled the Greek notion that matter was constructed from four elements, with each possessing two qualities, each of the two qualities corresponding to one of the four seasons: air (hot and wet – spring), fire (hot and dry – summer), earth (cold and dry – autumn), and water (cold and wet – winter). Similarly, the health of the body was determined by the balance of four humours, or fluids, again with each possessing two qualities: blood (hot and wet); yellow bile (hot and dry); black bile (cold and dry), phlegm (cold and wet). If it was judged that a patient was suffering from an excess of blood, the symptoms of which were hotness and wetness, this could be counteracted by medicine that promoted cooling and drying, or through bloodletting. Galen in the second century CE developed humoral theory further to include phlegmatic, choleric, sanguine and melancholic temperaments. It was Casanova's conviction that from childhood onwards his personality at different stages of his life was dominated by one or other of these four humours moving in turn from the phlegmatic (relaxed), to the sanguine (optimistic), to the choleric (bad-tempered), and ending, in old age, with the melancholic (analytical).

Other ancient beliefs included the idea that illness was the result of an individual's constitution and lifestyle, and needed to be treated on that basis. Although external causes were recognised in contagions such as the plague, this was put down to underlying similarities in people's constitutions and behaviours rather than being spread from person to person. Miasma, or bad air, was one possibility that was put forward. As early as 30 BCE, individuals had suggested that tiny animals might be agents of disease, and in the seventeenth century the Dutchman, Antonie van Leeuwenhoek, coined the term 'animalcule' for the microorganisms he had observed in rainwater through the use of a microscope. But it was not until the nineteenth century that germ theory became established.

In the sixteenth century the influential medical alchemist Bombastus von Hohenheim, who was to take the name Paracelsus after a famous Roman physician called Celsus (adding 'para-' to signify that he was superior to the original), prioritised direct experience over the authority of the distant past. He emphasised specific herbal and, in particular, chemical treatments for specific ailments. One such was the use of mercury to treat venereal disease. This was to become known as iatrochemistry and, by the eighteenth century, followers of Paracelsus called spagyrists were well established. Alongside iatrochemistry developed iatromechanism, drawing on mathematics and physics, which considered the body in terms of mechanical laws. These more empirical approaches yielded discoveries like that by William Hervey of the blood circulatory system. While some academics and professionals saw such developments as a refutation of the ancient Greeks, others tried to reconcile the old with the modern.

Nonetheless, humoral theory retained its hold over people's understanding of the body. Having been around for a long time it was embedded in European culture and was well understood by both the lay person and specialist. New ideas were often little known or subject to dispute, while the medical profession itself was notorious for quacks and poor practice. How were people to distinguish what was genuinely beneficial from an ineffectual, or even dangerous, novelty? Casanova's own sentiment would have been echoed by most: 'those who die killed by doctors far outnumber those who are cured.'[36]

Taboos

We are now moving into sensitive and contentious waters. The attempt to understand behaviour that touches on issues such as consent, paedophilia and incest in the context of the past should never be construed as an effort to justify them. Neither should we assume that there was unanimity of attitude, practices and belief. Then, as now, and as always, the moral battleground has been a fiercely contested space. But if we do not try to address them or, at the least, try to improve our awareness of them, we are liable seriously to misread the past.

A strategy Casanova would not use in his seduction of women was to ply them with alcohol; he wanted willing partners whose consent was meaningful. This was all very laudable and as it should be, we might think. Yet in several sexual encounters with women consent appeared to be set aside. He coerced a newly-wed farmer's bride to have sex in a carriage. He made love to a nun when she slept. He was one of a group of men who abducted and had sex with a married woman. These all seem to be clearcut instances of rape. But what was understood by consent or a lack of it?

A woman's rejection tended not to be taken at face value but treated as little more than conventional social etiquette. To be believed, she needed to demonstrate sufficient resistance, particularly given that women, at least in the first half of the century, were regarded as sexually promiscuous by nature. Raphaelle Brin writes, 'The *Encyclopedia* entry for "Viol" (Rape) echoes this point of view. For there to have been rape, the plaintiff had to prove ... that there was "a strong and perseverant resistance until the end; had there only been efforts in the beginning, it would not be *rape*, and the prescribed sentence would not apply".'[37] To make matters worse, rape was seen, in part at least, as property theft. 'Evidence from rape trials in Scotland and England suggests that the theft of personal and family honour was considered more grievous than the physical assault upon the female victim.'[38] This was not unique to eighteenth-century Europe. Treating women as the property of others rather than self-governing individuals has been a feature of many societies prior to the twentieth century.

In each of Casanova's three sexual encounters listed above, Casanova obviates the charge of rape by portraying the women as ultimately having enjoyed the experience. In his telling, the incidents are stripped of all seriousness. The accounts involving the married women, in particular, are treated playfully. The reader is left to decide whether to go along with Casanova's framing, collude with it if you will, or to question its moral implications. Is each woman's happy reconciliation credible? Is it a reflection of an age where, as James Rives Childs has suggested, 'sexual intercourse had hardly greater significance than the act of eating or drinking; it was a bodily function to which scant importance was attached'?[39] Or is it a libertine fiction to justify sexual exploitation and abuse? More broadly, consent needs to be considered in a context in which autonomy, including the ability to deny or reject the demands of others, was limited. Rights were tied to status, hierarchy and communities. It was not an environment that was conducive to viewing the individual as an intrinsic object of respect. It is no surprise that the three women above were commoners.

For today's reader, the other two most troubling aspects of Casanova's libertine career were his commission of incest and his attraction to young girls. Of around fifty of his lovers whose ages he mentions, Casanova records about thirty-five of them as being aged from 11–18 (although the true ages of many of them were probably older). He also had sexual intercourse with his 26-year-old married daughter, Leonilda, and his 13-year-old niece, Guglielmina.

Today, Casanova's behaviour would be seriously criminal on both counts. This was not the case in the eighteenth century or, at least, not to the same degree.

With regards to age there was a different understanding of childhood, adulthood and appropriate sexuality. A child became an adult with the onset of puberty. The discovery of adolescence is of twentieth-century origin, and Lisetta Lovett notes how 'In the eighteenth century there was no concept of paedophilia.'[40, 41] The contrast between the past and the present can perhaps best be illustrated through a range of examples. From 1576 it was legal to have sex with a 10-year-old girl in England. In Shakespeare's *Romeo and Juliet*, Juliet's mother had conceived her daughter when she was 12. The play was written in 1595. Casanova was born only 130 years later, far closer to the age of Shakespeare than the present day. In 1800, 63-year-old Sir John Acton received papal dispensation to marry his brother's eldest daughter, 13-year-old Mary-Ann.[42] Not until 1861 was the age of consent in England raised to 12. A 12-year-old female and a 14-year-old male in eighteenth-century Scotland were legally married if they had agreed to marry and then had sex.[43] Across the rest of Europe and America during this period, the age of consent typically ranged between 10 to 12. Girls wore adult clothing starting at the age of 12 or 13 in eighteenth-century France. The bat and bar mitzvah for 12- or 13-year-old Jewish girls and boys marked their transition from childhood to adulthood. In 1836, 27-year-old Edgar Allan Poe married his 13-year-old first cousin Virginia Poe. Casanova's memoirs themselves refer to a number of young girls who were either married or mistresses such as the 13-year-old wife of Yusuf Ali and the 13-year-old mistress of the Duke of Albermarle.

How old Casanova's lovers were is in reality unclear, despite what he records. This is because he has a tendency to reduce their ages. Casanova claims that Miss XCV was 20 when he met her in Paris, in 1758 according to his memoirs. It turns out that this was Giustiniana Wynne, who was born in January 1737, making her 21. He states that Donna Lucrezia was the same age as himself when she was significantly older, perhaps as much as ten years older. 'Fifteen-year-old' Manon Balletti was 16 or 17. 'Fourteen-year-old' Esther of Amsterdam, appears to have been 17-year-old Lucia Hope. There are several possible reasons for the discrepancies: it could have been a strategy to disguise the identities of his lovers; the women themselves may have lied about their ages, particularly those who were performers; a sense of chivalry may have been a factor; it may also be that guesswork played a part.

Attitudes and responses towards incest across Europe varied but, as with age and consent, there was a different understanding of its moral significance relative to today. Incest was traditionally understood as sexual intercourse between individuals prohibited from marriage. Beyond that there was no universally agreed definition and certain relationships characterised as incestuous at the time would not be regarded as such today. During the eighteenth century there was an ongoing debate about definitions, degrees of relationship and prohibitions. A man who had sex with his wife's sister could be adjudged to have committed incest on the grounds that husband and wife were 'one flesh' (Genesis 2:24). In England a man could not marry his wife's sister, even if the wife was dead. The Catholic Church recognised the offense of spiritual incest. This was sex between a godparent and godchild or with someone who had taken a vow of chastity. To complicate matters further, although incest was forbidden by scripture, it was, at the same time, present in the biblical narrative. The offspring of Adam and Eve had populated the world; Lot was seduced by his daughters; Abraham married his half-sister; and there was some speculation that Joseph and Mary were first cousins. This could cast doubt on the idea that sexual relations between close kin was always inherently immoral, and might suggest that its sinfulness was relative to particular social contexts.

Different states and religious groups adopted different policies. In Russia, Austria, Hungary, Spain and Sweden there were prohibitions against first-cousin marriage throughout the eighteenth century and beyond, although dispensations were available.[44] In England, first-cousin marriage was not classed as incestuous by the state, although such marriages were banned by the Quakers until 1883.[45] As a consequence, first-cousin marriage in England was not uncommon, both in the eighteenth and nineteenth centuries. Queen Victoria and Prince Albert were first cousins. There were obvious benefits, not least the consolidation of wealth and power within close-knit social networks, both amongst affluent commoners and the aristocracy, and the forging of useful alliances. There was little interest in incest as far as English law was concerned; sexual relations between parents and their offspring were not a secular offence until 1908. It was left to the ecclesiastical courts where it was treated relatively lightly through the imposition of spiritual penalties such as the performance of penance. On the other hand, in early eighteenth-century Scotland it was punishable by death, where, as Brian Levack points out, it was seen as a 'violation of not only biblical but natural law', its seriousness often equated with bestiality.[46] It was also a capital offence in Sweden.[47] Later in the eighteenth century, incest prohibitions were abolished in France during the French Revolution (1789–1799), it being deemed largely a family matter.

Incest went to the heart of a number of Enlightenment concerns about authority, religion, the law and moral boundaries. Lovett explains how scholars engaged 'in open discourse about definitions of and attitudes towards incest that challenged the Church's position. Much of the debate questioned whether negative responses to incest arose from natural revulsion, that is, a contravention of natural law, or instead from widely accepted cultural norms.'[48] The view of the eighteenth-century moral philosopher Immanuel Kant was that 'in sexual intercourse each person submits to the other in the highest degree, whereas between parents and their children subjection is one-sided; the children must submit to the parents only; there can, therefore, be no equal union. This is the only case in which incest is absolutely forbidden by nature.'[49] Given Casanova's enduring interest in moral philosophy it is unsurprising that it should figure on a number of occasions in his writing. In 1787 he published his huge science-fiction novel *Icosameron* with which he expected to make his name and which is described by Laurence Bergreen as 'a free-flowing compendium of philosophical and theological arguments.'[50] In it Casanova envisages a new society built around the incestuous relationships of the siblings Edward and Elizabeth and their subsequent children. It would not likely be published today.

The central concern with sexual relations judged to be incestuous was not so much the transgression of an absolute incest taboo or biological disorders. The concern was with illegitimate marital and pre-marital sexuality, such as adultery, the undermining of parental authority, and the impact upon social cohesion, as understood according to traditional religious and social norms. To the eighteen-century mind, the maintenance of authority and its hierarchical structures were of paramount importance. Exceptional circumstances aside, the child owed unconditional obedience to the parent, and the wife owed unconditional obedience to the husband. The primary danger of incest for many was the threat it posed to this natural social order by destabilising parental authority and family relationships. The most egregious form of incest within this hierarchical conception would be between a mother and a son. A work with which Casanova was familiar, and which discusses the relationships between natural law, authority and incest, was Baron de Montesquieu's influential *The Spirit of the Laws* (1748). For Montesquieu, mother-son incest was more serious than father-daughter incest. The concern in the latter case was not the father's abuse of parental authority but the loss of the chastity of the daughter, the responsibility of which was for the father to protect. Mother-son incest, on the other hand, undermined the natural state of husband-wife, parent-child relations. In the hypothetical circumstances of a society in which a mother was allowed to marry her son, where would the authority reside, with the parent or the husband?

Sexual relations between close relatives which did not undermine the social order could be regarded, in themselves, as minor moral infractions or, indeed, as entirely benign, such as first-cousin marriage or even marriage between an uncle and niece, particularly, in the latter case, if there was little age difference. Voltaire had a concubinal relationship with his niece Madame Denis. Roger Pearson observes: 'such relationships were not uncommon, and if marriage was intended…one could even apply to the pope for special permission. As La Condamine, Pâris-Monmartel and the journalist Fréron, among others, could all attest on the basis of personal experience.'[51]

Casanova's own attitude is unclear. On one occasion he discusses his fatherly feelings towards several women, who happened to be sisters, despite Casanova himself having been their lover. He goes on to reflect that 'I have never been able to conceive how a father could tenderly love his charming daughter without having at least once slept with her.'[52] On another occasion he writes:

If the father seizes his daughter on the basis of his paternal authority, he exercises a tyranny that nature must abhor. The natural love of good order also gives reason to find such a union monstrous. The offspring of it are bound to be characterised by confusion and insubordination. In short, this union is abominable in every respect: but it's no longer so when the two individuals love each other and have no knowledge that reasons which have nothing to do with their mutual tenderness ought to prevent them from loving each other.'[53]

In this passage Casanova argues that if the relationship is based on love rather than authority, then it is morally acceptable. But what does he mean by 'reasons'? Is Casanova referring to the possibility that the individuals do not know they are related or, from a libertine perspective, is he referring to artificial social conventions?

Considering these eighteenth-century perspectives, the incestuous aspect of Casanova's relationships with his daughter and niece may not have provoked the uniformly visceral disgust to the degree they do now, even if they were still regarded as immoral and unnatural. Preserving the chastity of his daughter, Leonilda, was not an issue; she was already married, albeit to an ageing and now seemingly impotent husband. The adultery may have been a problem although, it would appear, it was not a concern for the marchese, and today, of course, is something that hardly raises an eyebrow. In discussing with Casanova the relationship between Leonilda and the marchese prior to Casanova's affair with Leonilda, Donna Lucrezia comments, 'He is not jealous either, and I am sure that if in the nobility of this city she could have found a man made to please her, the marchese would have made friends with him, and in fact he would not have been upset to see her become pregnant.'[54]

By discreetly providing a male heir, Casanova had done the couple a service, not least by securing Leonilda's status within the household and the 'good order' of society. It might also have been thought that it would help to give her mother, Donna Lucrezia, security in her old age. Research has revealed that Leonilda's husband had had a son by a previous marriage, but even if that was the case, and assuming the son was still alive, it may be that family politics had led the marchese to want a second child by Leonilda.[55] The marchese himself was on good terms with Casanova, who had been his guest while the affair was underway. The two were both freemasons, and it is possible that the marchese was likeminded in other ways as well, perhaps ways that were more transgressive and libertine. The marchese made a present to Casanova of the considerable sum of 5,000 ducati, and another 5,000 to Donna Lucrezia for having introduced the Venetian to him. Was this a thank you? Was this another example of the transactional character of social relationships typical of the time?

The incestuous nature of his relationship with Guglielmina, being uncle-niece rather than father-daughter, was even less of an issue. The concern in this case would have been for Guglielmina's pre-marital chastity, the moral implications of which, for the large majority of the population of modern Europe, are minimal.

The trap of applying modern values to the past is something to which it is easy to fall prey. This creates a problem. If we apply today's expectations regarding sex within marriage or the age of consent, how are we to make sense of pre-twentieth-century societies in which a large proportion of people were sexually abused without perceiving themselves to be abused, and were sexual abusers without perceiving themselves to be abusers? What's more, according to their long-established laws and religious beliefs they were neither. If we were to label Capulet a paedophile and Lady Capulet a victim of paedophilia would that help us better to understand in any meaningful way either the characters themselves or *Romeo and Juliet* as a whole?

Chapter 2

Giacomo Casanova: 1725–1798

'At dawn the following day Messr Grande came into my room. Waking up, seeing him and hearing him ask me if I was Giacomo Casanova was the business of just a moment.'

Giacomo Casanova, *History of My Life*

It was 26 July 1755. For the next fifteen months Casanova was to be held in the Leads, the prison of the Council of Ten, before engineering his dramatic escape to Paris and exile. He was 30 years old.

Early life

Giacomo Casanova arrived on 2 April 1725 in Venice. Just over one year earlier his then 16-year-old mother, Zanetta Farussi, had eloped with a penniless actor-dancer called Gaetano Joseph Jacques Casanova whom she later married. Giacomo was the product of this union, according to the official family version handed down to him by his mother. But as far as our adventurer-to-be was concerned, the origins of his paternity were less clear-cut; the beautiful Zanetta was known to have had influential admirers. Pointedly, Casanova refers to his father as 'my mother's husband'. That said, his suspicions may have been nothing other than wishful thinking; he would have found the idea that he was the son of an aristocrat rather appealing, and illegitimacy did not carry the stigma in Venice that it did elsewhere in Europe. Zanetta went on to have five more children while carving out a successful stage career. The responsibility for looking after Giacomo was handed over to Marcia, his maternal grandmother, shortly after his first birthday. Casanova's mother's husband died when Casanova was 8, and at the age of 26, Zanetta was a widow and the family's sole breadwinner. Gaetano had worked for the Grimani brothers, Alvis, Zuane and Michele, members of Venice's powerful patrician class, and had arranged for them to become protectors of his family after his death.

Casanova was born at a time when the 1,000-year-old, sea-borne empire that was Venice was no longer the political, military and commercial powerhouse that it had once been. By the end of the seventeenth century it was managing to hold its own against the existential threats of the Ottoman Turks and the Habsburg Monarchy but the current of history was running against it. Spain, France, England and the Dutch Republic were the dominant players at sea, including in the Adriatic. The Venetian navy and its legendary shipyards, upon which the glory of the Serenissima had been built, were out of date. Their ships were slow and more vulnerable to the Barbary pirates compared to the modern but far more expensive galleons of the northern and Atlantic nations. Merchants abandoned oared galleys, preferring foreign sailing ships, although the military persevered: the deficiencies of old-fashioned galleys were less exposed over the shorter distances and more benign sailing conditions of the Mediterranean. Venice did attempt to update its fleet through hire, purchase and manufacture but the number of modern warships at their disposal remained small.

But Venice was still wealthy, and in some ways thriving. 'For the greater part of the century,' notes John Julius Norwich, 'Venice was enjoying a period of unusual commercial prosperity and economic growth.'[1] In terms of trade, more tonnage was going through the city in 1783 than in its entire history.[2] The aristocrats of Europe were also going through the city in larger numbers than ever before. This centre of tolerance and sophistication was the destination *par excellence* in the age of the Grand Tour. Whether it be music, art, theatre, books, churches, sculpture, gambling or the pleasures of the flesh, Venice catered for the most demanding of tastes. If you had money, Venice would help you to spend it. The state was politically stable, and most importantly of all, in the eighteenth century it managed pretty much to stay out of the wars that were depleting the treasuries of the rest of Europe.

Casanova grew up surrounded by women in a tiny house in the Calle della Commedia. It was not far from the bustle and noise of the Grand Canal, and was part of the fashionable district of San Marco. When his mother was abroad Casanova lived with his grandmother in the miserable Corte della Munghe, located in the rather less reputable parish of San Samuele. Close by was San Samuele theatre. Casanova was a sickly, introverted child whose parents, it would seem, had little to do with him. They were of the view that their son was an imbecile destined for an early grave. Casanova's first memory was that of his grandmother taking him to Murano to see a witch to cure his worryingly persistent and profuse nosebleeds. A few months later his mother packed him off to a miserable lodging house in nearby Padua (a city that was part of the Venetian empire) where the air was regarded as healthier than that of Venice. 'That was how they got rid of me,' he reflects, the hurt lingering even into old age.[3]

In Padua the 9-year-old Casanova received tuition from Antonio Maria Gozzi, a priest, musician, and doctor in canon and civil law. Under Gozzi his hitherto unsuspected intellectual talents flourished. Then after almost six months Giacomo sent word to his grandmother about how unhappy he was with his lodgings. The food was poor and he slept on a filthy bed in an attic room which he shared with three fellow boarders and which was infested with rats and lice. Quickly his grandmother arranged for him to relocate to the Gozzi household instead. For the next several years Giacomo became part of the household.

The quiet imbecile turned into a quick-witted boy, street-wise, and with an inexhaustible thirst for knowledge. At 12 he enrolled at the prestigious University of Padua to read law, although he did much more than study, falling in, as he did, with some rather disreputable company. It was during this time that Casanova began what was to be a life-long interest in gambling. He claims to have graduated at 16 but this is disputed. Historian Federico di Trocchio argues that it is certain he never graduated whereas Ian Kelly, a more recent biographer, supports Casanova: 'The Paduan records make clear that he graduated in 1741.'[4]

Intended for a career in the Church, in 1740 Casanova became an abate (abbé in French), dividing his time between Padua and Venice. This was the first rung on the ladder towards the priesthood. It gave Casanova an enhanced status which allowed him access to more elevated social circles, including that of the 70-year-old Senator Alvise Malipiero. Malipiero was a grandee and wealthy bachelor who had enjoyed the high life. It is worth noting that well over half of the Venetian nobility were unmarried. This was to prevent the dispersal of family wealth and the dilution of the patrician elite. It was the custom for only one or two sons to marry and produce heirs. The senator took the 15-year-old abate under his wing and revealed to him a world of elegance, luxury and privilege that was much to the young man's taste. But the friendship was short-lived. Malipiero, besotted with a 16-year-old impresario's daughter called Teresa Imer, discovered that Casanova had himself become a rival for Teresa's affections, with plans similar to the senator's own.

Upon achieving his law degree in 1741 Casanova returned to Venice to continue his Church career. At this point, which was prior to his Malipiero disgrace, his virginity was still intact. Unsurprisingly this striking, intelligent and witty young man who had kept company with the cream of Venetian society had not been without offer or opportunity. At the age of 17 his struggle between priestly duty and carnal desire, highlighted by his refusal to take advantage of a 14-year-old caretaker's daughter, was finally decided through the intervention of two sisters. Nanetta and Marta Savorgnan, 16 and 15 respectively, were friends of a girl called Angela with whom Casanova was enamoured. Using the pretext of meeting up with Angela, who never appeared, the girls invited Casanova to a sleepover where a threesome duly ensued.

In March 1743 Casanova's grandmother died and the Grimanis enrolled him into San Cipriano seminary where he was expelled after being found in bed with another boy. He was imprisoned in the fortress of Sant'Andrea shortly afterwards, probably on the orders of his Grimani protectors. There he contracted his first of at least ten bouts of venereal disease from which he was to suffer over his lifetime; in the eighteenth century, syphilis and gonorrhoea were regarded as different stages of the same disease. Meanwhile Zanetta, who was working in Dresden, looked to advance her son's career by pulling some strings in high places. Her desire was that he should eventually become a bishop, and she managed to obtain employment for him as secretary to Bernardo de Bernardis, Bishop of Martirano in southern Italy.

After the Grimanis freed Casanova from prison he left Venice in 1744 (not 1743, as recorded in his memoirs) to meet up with Bernardis in Rome. Journeying to Ancona by ship, and then much of the rest of the way by foot, he paired up with a Franciscan monk called Brother Stefano. The two frequently quarrelled. Stefano was a seasoned traveller who knew how to procure supplies and shelter for free but he was coarse and loutish. Following an eventful journey Casanova arrived at Rome to discover that he had missed Bernardis who had gone on ahead. When finally Casanova arrived at Martirano, he encountered a see that was impoverished and backward. It was not going to be the route to success he had anticipated. Fortunately Bernardis was willing to release him from his service.

During his return journey to Rome from Naples, Casanova met the sexually emancipated Donna Lucrezia Castelli, who was to bear him a daughter, Leonilda. In Rome a letter of introduction secured him a position under the powerful Cardinal Acquaviva, and during this period he met Pope Benedict XIV (1740–1758). Casanova became embroiled in controversy when he tried to prevent a young woman being seized by the authorities, and Acquaviva, although sympathetic, dismissed him. It may well be that his affair with Lucrezia had also played a part in the cardinal's decision. Apparently on a whim, Casanova chose to make his way to Constantinople, the 19 year-old falling in love en route with a castrato called Bellino, mentioned earlier. Such 'musici' were highly paid opera singers who had been castrated before puberty to retain their unique prepubescent vocal range. 'He', in fact, turned out to be female; there were significant financial incentives for female singers to take the risky course of disguising themselves as men. Such was Bellino's effect upon Casanova that he had been tempted to marry her. It was not to be, but this episode did convince him that he was unsuited for an ecclesiastical career.

Casanova continued with his Constantinople plan, now in the service of Venice instead of the Church. He bought a military commission from a young lieutenant and armed himself with introductions from the Grimanis. In Constantinople his cultured intelligence and education impressed all around him, to the extent that one wealthy Turk, Yussuf Ali, offered his 15-year-old daughter in marriage, which Casanova reluctantly declined. His sexual education continued apace. He discovered that within this otherwise orthodox Muslim society the members of certain social circles enjoyed a freedom of sexual license which matched that of Venice.

Casanova's account of his experiences in Corfu and Constantinople was a composite of several trips he undertook from 1741 to 1745, possibly refashioned due to gaps in his records or memory; a housekeeper in Dux destroyed three of his notebooks that detailed his visits. He may also have wanted to combine different trips for the sake of a more coherent narrative. There is evidence of a similar reshaping of material elsewhere, such as in Paris, and his involvement in the Military School lottery.

Casanova left Constantinople rich with experiences but little in the way of a career. After a short and unrewarding stay at Corfu he returned back home to Venice in November 1745. Casanova was now 20 years-old, broke, and had acquired a reputation for being immoral and irreligious. He knew how to play the violin and obtained the poorly paid position of fiddler in San Samuele's small theatre orchestra. This was a humiliating reversal for a young man with such high ambitions. But less than a year later the fates smiled upon him in the form of Senator Matteo Giovanni Bragadin. The middle-aged senator was a wealthy and influential Venetian. He was also, and more importantly as far as Casanova's prospects were concerned, a cabbalist and believer in the occult.

It was March 1746 and the time of the Carnival. Casanova had accepted the offer of a lift in a gondola by Bragadin who shortly afterwards suffered a stroke. The young man organised a surgeon and got the senator back home but the surgeon's prescription of bloodletting and a mercury poultice only made matters worse. Seeing Bragadin deteriorate, Casanova, a young nobody, audaciously countermanded the surgeon's orders and the senator recovered. The nobleman immediately hailed Casanova as a natural healer, a part Casanova was only too happy to play, and in a short time he convinced Bragadin and the senator's two close friends, Marco Dandolo and Marco Barbaro, that he possessed occult powers.

The money and connections of these three patrons transformed Casanova's life. Once again, he found himself in the company of the great and the good and enjoying the best that Venice could offer, whether that be fine foods, clothes, the theatre, women, casinos or books of the most esoteric and illicit kind. But questions were raised about the nature of Casanova's relationship with the men. Kelly writes: 'The Inquisition files are pregnant with a couched but pointed insistence that at this time Casanova was something between a free-loader, a social climber and a rent-boy.'[5] It may be that when Casanova met Bragadin on the night of his stroke it was for purposes of prostitution. Venice liked to keep a close watch on its citizens and employed an army of informants. Of greatest concern were not so much issues relating to religion or morality, although they were of interest, but of social status, in particular, anything that might affect the standing of the ruling families. Inevitably they kept a close watch on this young man of questionable reputation who had so dramatically catapulted into the upper echelons of Venetian society, noting his various transgressions and disreputable company.

Over the next ten years Casanova enjoyed life to the full: gambling, duelling, swindling and conducting numerous affairs. He found himself particularly attracted to strong and unorthodox women, such as Henriette, whom he first encountered in Cesena in 1749. She was dressed as a soldier and was travelling in the company of a Hungarian officer. Casanova toured northern Italy and in 1750 visited Paris where he immersed himself in the city's intellectual sophistication, cultured cynicism and sexual freedom. Returning to Venice, in 1753 he met Teresa Imer for the first time since their Malipiero dalliance. They spent the night together and she became pregnant. He was also having an affair with another girl, CC, who likewise became pregnant. Casanova next found himself embroiled in a ménage-a-quatre, one of whom was the French ambassador. For the authorities matters were getting out of hand. Casanova's affairs, his gambling, his debts, his cabbalistic meddling, his public mocking of respectable figures, and fears that he was a corrupting influence upon aristocratic youth, were all weighing against him. Eventually the Inquisition decided to act. Bragadin, who had been a State Inquisitor himself, warned Casanova to flee Venice but he chose to ignore Bragadin's advice. 'His conviction,' writes Ioanna Iordanou, 'was the outcome of numerous denunciations by aggrieved husbands, zealous religious devotees, and upright city-dwellers, exasperated by Casanova's licentious behaviour. His crimes can be summed up as insatiable promiscuity, sensationalist religious sophistries, and a libertine lifestyle.'[6]

The wanderer

Casanova was imprisoned without trial. The Inquisition neither revealed to him his crime nor the length of his sentence (it was five years). He thought it would be a few weeks or months but as time passed he became desperate. He took matters into his own hands and on 1 November 1756 escaped. The prison was reputed to be impregnable so when Casanova and his side-kick, a disgraced patrician priest called Father Balbi, broke out – the first of its inmates ever to have done so – he became something of an international celebrity. Casanova was now an exile and for the next eighteen years toured Europe from Paris to London to Berlin to St Petersburg to Barcelona and to a bewildering array of towns and cities in between. His longest continuous stay was in Paris to where he had fled after his escape. He was to reside there more or less permanently for three years and made use of the city as a base of operations for another three. Casanova would generally remain somewhere for no more than a few weeks or months. The reasons behind this continuous movement were diverse. Sometimes he was pursuing a business opportunity (London) or was in search of formal employment (Berlin and St Petersburg on both counts). Sometimes he was fleeing because of his debts (London and Paris) or from arrest (Stuttgart) or on account of a duel (Paris). Sometimes authorities would expel him (Turin, Vienna, Paris and Florence). During these meanderings Casanova was incarcerated for short spells in Paris, Madrid and Barcelona.

It was unsurprising that Casanova initially made his way to Paris. It was a healthy distance from the Venetian Republic and he had already spent a happy couple of years there. He had not only established a useful network of friends and contacts but a reputation as a man possessed of occult powers. More importantly, the French ambassador he had befriended in Venice several years earlier was none other than Abbé de Bernis, now Louis XV's chief minister.

Drawing on his social connections, his celebrity status and his improvisational skills, Casanova lost no time in rebuilding his fortunes. He blagged his way into becoming the co-director of a lottery which was to make him a fortune. He befriended the wealthy Marquise d'Urfé (1705–1775) from whom he was to defraud huge sums of money. He worked as a French spy. And he was employed secretly by the French state to negotiate financial transactions on the money markets of the Dutch Republic, an operation which proved to be hugely profitable both for France and for himself. Casanova was briefly reacquainted with Teresa Imer on one of his trips to Amsterdam. There he met for the first time their 5-year-old daughter, Sophie, as well as Teresa's 12-year-old son, Giuseppe, whom he brought back with him to Paris and whose upbringing he took charge of.

With his purse overflowing and surrounded by the temptations of Paris, a city renowned in the mid-eighteenth century for its luxury, excess and sexual promiscuity, Casanova's old pleasure-seeking ways were supercharged. He indulged in an eclectic variety of love affairs, including actresses, a shopkeeper's wife, a Dutch heiress, a dancer and ladies-in-waiting. At one point he established a factory for the painting of silk fabrics employing twenty young women, all of whom he took as lovers. Each of the women demanded an apartment and furniture. The enterprise turned into a costly failure, with sales undermined by the on-going Seven Years War and Casanova's stock being stolen by one of his employees. Casanova's lifestyle was prodigiously extravagant. He rented two properties, one of which was particularly luxurious, employed servants, owned two carriages and a number of stallions, gambled, and lavished expensive gifts on lovers and friends.

The fiasco of Casanova's silk factory and the related legal proceedings that were brought against him took the shine off his enthusiasm for Paris. In 1759 he set off to Amsterdam on another mission to raise finances for the government but on this occasion he was unsuccessful. At the same time, an ongoing, unconsummated love affair with the actress Manon Balletti ended when she informed him that she was going to marry another man. As a consequence of these developments Casanova turned his attentions further east and south, spending most of the next three years out of Paris touring through the Holy Roman Empire, Switzerland, France and Italy. When he was in France, travelling between Pontcarré, Aix-la-Chapelle, Besançon, Marseille and Lyon, the main focus of his attention was the Marquise d'Urfé, whom he ruthlessly exploited to subsidise his gambling and lavish lifestyle. In Geneva he had a memorable encounter with Voltaire. It was to spark considerable animosity on Casanova's part towards the great man for many years afterwards. He also claims to have previously met Rousseau on a brief visit to where Rousseau lived near Montmorency. In Florence he came across his 16-year-old son Cesare Filippo for the first time, born to Bellino. While in Naples, Casanova discovered that he had a 17-year-old daughter he calls Leonilda. Fortunately he made the discovery prior to taking Leonilda as his lover, as he had been about to do, and instead provided her with 5,000 ducats for a dowry. Casanova stayed for a time in Rome where he got to know the illustrious painter Anton Raphael Mengs, frequented the Vatican library, and met Pope Clement XIII (1758–1769), from whom he received the Papal Order of the Golden Spur. It was this honour which allowed him legitimately to adopt the title of chevalier. In 1761 Casanova was engaged to undertake a diplomatic mission representing Portugal at the planned Congress of Augsburg (the Congress was cancelled before he could take part).

Meanwhile, Teresa Imer (now calling herself Mrs Cornelys) had settled in London. She was making a name for herself as a fashionable hostess, organising concerts, balls and suppers, and wanted to be reunited with her son Giuseppe. Prompted by letters from Teresa, the opportunity to see his daughter, and ambitions of his own to take advantage of an economically thriving London, Casanova sold up in Paris. In June 1763 he headed across the channel, furnished with jewels and cash thanks to the generosity of d'Urfé. Despite being introduced to George III (1760–1820) and Queen Charlotte (1761–1818), meeting Dr Johnson and generally mingling with the elite of English society, Casanova's trip was to be a chastening experience. Much to his annoyance, he received a cool reception from Teresa, perhaps concerned that the unpredictable Venetian might queer her pitch. His plan to establish a lottery along the lines of the Paris lottery did not lead anywhere. The Marquise d'Urfé finally lost faith in him, closing the lid on that particular treasure trove, and worst of all, Casanova was to be the dupe of an unscrupulous courtesan by the name of Marie-Anne Charpillon whom he had contracted to become his mistress. The machinations of La Charpillon and her mother plunged him into such despair that he came close to throwing himself off Westminster Bridge. He was saved by a chance encounter with a friend who happened to be passing. Casanova claimed that the affair cost him in the region of 2,000 guineas (£2,100). For comparison, in England a barrister would typically earn £230 a year, and a general labourer £21 a year.[7] As ever, his lavish spending had burned through his funds at an alarming rate. Casanova was also facing legal action for, wittingly or unwittingly, passing on a counterfeit 520 guinea bill of exchange. Very sick, having succumbed to another bout of venereal disease, in dire financial straits and depressed, Casanova fled from the courts and his creditors back to the continent. His stay in England had lasted nine months.

Once safely back across the channel, albeit ill and penniless, Casanova made his way to Brussels where he waited for the ever-reliable Bragadin to send him money. In 1763 the Seven Years War had ended, and Casanova hoped to find some profit in its aftermath, notably the need by authorities to raise funds for the reconstruction of those areas of Europe that were particularly hard hit, such as Prussia. But he was never again to recapture his glory days of Paris.

Making his way to Berlin, in 1764 Casanova stopped for a short time at Brunswick where he began work on his translation of the *Iliad*, which he was to publish in Venice over a decade later. On arrival in Prussia's capital, he met a couple of old acquaintances, including Jean Calzabigi, who had been involved in the Paris lottery. It was Casanova's intention to introduce a similar lottery in Prussia but Calzabigi had beaten him to the punch. He did meet Frederick II (Frederick the Great, 1740–1772) to discuss his project but the monarch decided to commission Calzabigi. Casanova hung around for a while in the hope of receiving some sort of preferment, during which time he dined with James Boswell. Frederick offered Casanova a position as a tutor but the Venetian felt it was beneath him and moved on.

Casanova decided to try his luck in St Petersburg, encouraged by the success of others who had travelled east and made their fortune. He arrived in December 1764 where he stayed until the September of the following year, the highlight of his visit being his meetings with Catherine II (Catherine the Great, 1762–1796). Notwithstanding his more impecunious circumstances, there were the usual amorous adventures, theatre going, gambling, balls, and rounds of socialising with entertainers, expats and the local aristocracy. But once again his hopes of advancement came to nought.

Wanting to avoid another Russian winter, Casanova moved on to Warsaw, arriving in the Polish capital in October 1765. Things went pretty well to start with. Casanova's letters of introduction had assured him of a warm reception. He received an audience with the king of Poland, Stanislas Poniatowksi (1764–1795), and began gathering material for his authoritative *History of the Polish Troubles* which he was to publish in 1774. As usual, Casanova hoped to make money with a lottery scheme or by gaining some other kind of employment at the court. On this occasion his plans were disrupted by an event which was to become famous across Europe. Count Branicki, a Polish general of considerable renown, engineered a confrontation with Casanova rooted in a rivalry between two Italian dancers, one of whom was the count's lover. The resulting duel left both men injured, and Branicki seriously so. Casanova had behaved honourably but nonetheless the incident aroused hostility towards him. For many, the most shocking aspect was that a nobleman countenanced a duel with a social inferior. While duels were common (even though illegal in a number of countries, including in Poland) they normally only took place amongst men of comparable status. Casanova may have recovered from this setback but for the unfortunate appearance in Warsaw of Madame Geoffrin, a famous Parisian hostess who was an old friend of the king and who appears to have spread unfounded but damaging allegations about Casanova. Any chance of advancement was now gone. Casanova had lost the favour of Stanislas and, to make matters worse, was heavily in debt. Several months after the duel he was instructed to leave. Fortunately he still had some allies and he received 1,000 ducats to pay off what he owed.

In July 1766 Casanova moved on to Dresden for six months where he visited his mother. He was now in his 40s, and since London he had become only too aware that he was past his prime. Ambition, curiosity and impulsiveness had previously dictated his travels but as he grew older and needed to find ways to make money, it was more necessity that directed him. This task was not helped by a growing reputation for him being a man of questionable character, amplified, albeit unfairly, by his duel with Branicki. Bragadin had always helped Casanova out but with his death in 1767 that support had dried up.

More and more he had to pull in his horns. The focus of his interest in the years ahead was to be literary. He was intellectually voracious and had always harboured literary ambitions but had not been prepared to devote himself entirely to study and writing while life offered so many distractions. Not for Casanova was the penury and isolation of a Rousseau.

From Dresden, Casanova travelled to Vienna but once more fell foul of local authorities, being expelled by the highly puritan rulership of the Empress Maria Theresa following false accusations of gambling. In Spa, near Liège in Belgium, he came to the aid of a young pregnant woman who had been abandoned by her lover after he had gambled away everything they had. Casanova took her back to Paris where he cared for her and was with her when she died in childbirth. The d'Urfé affair now came back to haunt him and he was temporarily banished from France by Louis XV. Casanova travelled south to Madrid where he became involved in a scheme to colonise Sierra Morena with Swiss and Germans but ultimately it did not lead anywhere. He wrote a libretto for one of the acts of a new opera for the Spanish court before moving on to Valencia and then Barcelona. There he was attacked by two men who were likely hired to murder him. He may have killed one of them, running him through with his sword. Casanova was imprisoned for forty-two days on grounds that were unclear but are likely to have been due to associating with a mistress whose madly jealous lover happened to be the Captain-General in command of Catalonia. Possibly it was the Captain-General who was behind the assassination attempt.

In 1769 Casanova left Spain, evading in the process another plot to assassinate him. He travelled across southern France, staying for several months in Aix-en-Provence where he convalesced from illness, and then carried on into northern Italy. Not long after his escape from prison in Venice, Casanova had begun to reach out to the Venetian authorities to see if they would let him return, and had been trying to find different ways of ingratiating himself. To that end he had composed his *Refutation* (1769), a treatise rebutting criticisms of Venetian systems of governance. In Naples occurred the notorious incident referred to in the previous chapter where Casanova made love to his own daughter Leonilda. Visiting Turin, Naples, Rome, Florence, Bologna (where he met Farinelli, the most famous castrato of his age) and Ancona, he finally made his way to Trieste, arriving in November 1772. Trieste was close to the border of the Venetian Republic and there Casanova continued to write his *History of the Polish Troubles* along with other works, while lobbying for permission to return to Venice. This finally arrived in September 1774.

Later years

Casanova was 49. He still had old friends and admirers in Venice and was warmly welcomed. A few years later he was to settle down with a humble seamstress called Francesca Buschini. A small allowance had been bequeathed to him from the estate of Marco Barbaro, who was now dead, along with Bragadin – but the allowance was insufficient. Neither was he able to raise much money from his literary efforts. Casanova brought out three volumes of his translation of the *Iliad* but had to abandon further publication due to a lack of subscribers. He began to produce a monthly periodical of his own writings, including essays, translations, theatre reviews and extracts from his Polish history. He managed a theatre troupe for a short period. Needing to generate more income to scrape by, in 1776 he became an informant for the Inquisition, and several years later the secretary to a Genoese diplomat. A dispute which provoked Casanova to write a satirical attack upon one of the city's leading citizens, Carlo Grimani, forced him to leave his beloved Venice yet again. This time he would never return. He was 58.

Travelling north-west from Venice across to the Dutch Republic and then southwards, Casanova reached Paris in September 1783 where he stayed for three months with his brother Francesco, a renowned painter of battle scenes. While Casanova was there, he met a son that he had had by Madame Dubois, who had been his housekeeper over twenty years earlier. He also met Benjamin Franklin, who was in Paris as a US diplomat. The brothers moved on to Vienna where Casanova obtained a position with the Venetian ambassador, Sebastian Foscarini. In Vienna at this time was Mozart's librettist, Lorenzo da Ponte, whom Casanova knew from Venice, and they now resumed their friendship. Several years later in Prague, Casanova's relationship with Da Ponte seems to have led him to participate in the production of Mozart's *Don Giovanni* although the fact and extent of his involvement is disputed.

In 1785 his employer Foscarini died and Casanova took up a previous offer made to him by Count Waldstein to become his librarian at the castle of Dux in Bohemia. Casanova was to live there for thirteen years until his death in 1798 where he wrote prolifically, partly to distract himself from melancholy. For many years the consensus was that this was a rather unhappy final resting place, a supposition that was largely due to a first-hand account of his life there by his friend the Prince de Ligne. Casanova was portrayed as a lonely and isolated figure, eking out a miserable existence persecuted by disrespectful servants, and all made worse by his own irascible temper. Helmut Watzlawick has punctured this myth.[8] He points out that of those thirteen years, the Venetian spent four of them away from Dux, travelling and visiting.

Within a short radius he was surrounded by many friends, relations and old acquaintances. Casanova lived just over a day's journey from the rich cultural hubs of Prague and Dresden, the latter home to the families of his siblings, Giovanni and Maria Maddelena, and close by was the fashionable spa town of Teplitz. Waldstein himself was a benevolent employer who paid him a respectable salary even when the old librarian was off on his travels. On top of this, Casanova corresponded regularly with a wide range of individuals.

In the decade before Casanova died, Europe was thrown into turmoil by the French Revolution. From Dux he witnessed a dramatic reshaping of the world that he had known, and affected most of all were the two cities closest to his heart, Venice and Paris. In the course of that reshaping, the Most Serene Republic and the Old Regime were swept away.

Chapter 3

Connections

'It was then that the pope laughed so much that he had a coughing fit, and after spitting he laughed some more. "We shall be pleased to know the outcome of this story without the world being informed of our simple curiosity".'

Giacomo Casanova, *History of My Life*

So here is our Venetian adventurer amusing Pope Clement XIII. One of the astonishing aspects of Casanova's life is the extent to which he was able to interact on a personal level with the most important figures of his time, whether rulers, philosophers, cardinals, soldiers, artists, writers or, indeed, anyone of note. He was born the son of an actress at a time when the acting profession was regarded as disreputable and actresses little better than prostitutes. How did Casanova pull this off?

Social networks

Much of the explanation for Casanova's success in this regard lies in the nature of the society inhabited by men and women of high status. Once you gained entry to its social circles you could move around it with a certain degree of ease. It was a more personal, less institutionalised world, where reputation and codes of respect, honour and reciprocity were important. Proof of who you were and what you did were carried by word of mouth and letters of recommendation. Formal qualifications such as degrees did exist but not on the scale of today. As with all more closely-knit societies, friend-of-a-friend relationships operated as a powerful mechanism through which an individual could obtain initial acceptance into any particular group which, in turn, might open up further opportunities elsewhere. An extraordinary feature of the period was the accessibility of even the most exalted individual. A ball at Versailles in 1745 to celebrate the Dauphin's marriage was open to the public as long as they were properly dressed. Some years later Robert Damiens was able to stab Louis XV by pushing forward from a small crowd of onlookers. Casanova requested a meeting with Frederick II simply by writing a letter to him. The King of Prussia's secretary responded two days later telling him when and where. Matters were even less formal with the Empress of Russia. Casanova took a morning stroll in the Summer Garden where she went for walks, and was able to catch her eye (although it is true that his freemason friend, Count Panin, was accompanying her).

Ironically, Casanova's first connection with this elite world may have derived from the rather shady origins of his birth. It is possible that his true father was Michele Grimani, a theatre owner and member of one of the most prestigious families in Venice. Casanova's supposed father, Gaetano, was able to secure the protection for his children of the three Grimani brothers, Alvise, Michele and Zuane, before he died. Gaetano is reputed to have been one of the Venetian nobility's favourite performers, so that might also have been the reason for the Grimanis' involvement irrespective of whether Michele was Casanova's actual father. Whatever the truth behind his paternity and guardianship, it does demonstrate a paradox which went back to antiquity: the fascination of aristocrats for public performers despite their contemptible status. Emperor Nero performed as a poet, actor and singer before the masses, and tried his hand at charioteering, much to the disgust of the senatorial class.

Given the high esteem in which actors are generally held today, it is perhaps worth pausing to consider why the reverse was the case. As early as St Augustine in the late fourth and early fifth centuries, acting was regarded as morally suspect by Christians despite the fact that theatrical performance was a part of Church culture. Deliberate falsification was at the core of acting: pretending to be someone you were not, expressing emotions you did not feel, asserting ideas you did not believe. The purpose of the theatrical experience was to give pleasure to the audience, something else with which Christian theology was not comfortable (Christ never laughed, it was pointed out). Instead of inculcating Christian virtues, the theatre promoted lust and envy, inflaming passions that were best kept under lock and key. It subverted respectable social norms, most notably sexual ones. It encouraged prostitution. It offered the degenerate spectacle of men dressed as women and *vice versa*, behaviour forbidden in the Bible. It created celebrities and inspired hero worship, displacing God from the centre of people's devotions. It could undermine the established social order through unflattering representations of those of high rank. Theatres themselves were castigated for being places of disorder and uninhibited fraternising between men and women. Criticism was directed at rulers who lavished resources sponsoring this iniquitous business, money that could have been better spent elsewhere. It was a long list of charges.

Anti-theatrical sermons and essays were commonplace. Rousseau's treatise, *Letter to M. d'Alembert on Spectacles* (1758), generated much public discussion. According to Rousseau he was impelled by duty to speak out against Jean le

Rond d'Alembert's suggestion that Geneva should establish a theatre. It was vain to believe, as far as he was concerned, that the theatre could improve people. 'These productions of wit and craft,' he observes 'have for their end only applause.'[1] They existed 'to please corrupt minds.'[2] Tragedy had little to recommend it but comedy was worse: 'the more the comedy is amusing and perfect, the more its effect is disastrous for morals.'[3] Rousseau refers to 'imbecile audiences' and abhorred the idea of women on the stage: 'I ask how an estate, the unique object of which is to show oneself off to the public and, what is worse, for money, could agree with decent women and be compatible with modesty and good morals?'[4,5] What's more, it was 'a perversion of natural relations' when women were portrayed achieving 'ascendancy' over men, as was not uncommon.[6,7] Likewise, old people who should have been venerated for their wisdom, experience and authority were always being seen as odious.

Nonetheless, this most infamous of trades was to prove useful in introducing Casanova to people in high places. A striking example was when he was 18. He was yet to pin down a solid career path for himself and had recently been in prison. His mother, Zanetta Farussi (Farussi was her maiden name), was now a successful actress. She had performed throughout Europe, and no less a figure than Carlo Goldoni, the most renowned Venetian playwright of the time, had written a short comedy for her. One of Zanetta's admirers was the Queen of Poland, whose daughter was the Queen of Naples. In 1743 Zanetta came to an arrangement with the Franciscan monk, Bernardino de Bernardis, that she would use her influence to obtain for him the bishopric of Martirano in Calabria, which was under the authority of Naples, if he would employ her son. As mentioned earlier, Martirano turning out to be a dead end, Casanova moved on, although not before receiving from Bernadis letters of recommendation to important figures in Naples. Having gained access to elite Neapolitan society, new influential acquaintances now supplied him with letters of introduction, one of which being for Cardinal Acquaviva. Once in Rome and in the orbit of Acquaviva, Casanova managed to organise personal audiences with Pope Benedict XIV. In the space of less than two years, thanks to his mother and the practice of personal recommendation, from being an inmate in Forte Sant'Andrea, this nonentity was hobnobbing with some of the most important people in Europe.

We find Casanova once again benefitting from the aristocracy's fondness for the theatre on his first trip to Paris in 1750. This time his circumstances were different: there was his close relationship with Bragadin, Dandolo and Barbaro, and he had recently made a small fortune from a gambling venture. Paris was gearing up for the birth of a new royal and the Comédie Italienne was to play a prominent part in the celebrations. An Italian star of the Parisian

stage who would be involved in those celebrations was Sylvia Balletti. Her son
Antonio – dancer, ballet master and actor – was about to travel up from Venice
with a troupe of actors to join his mother, and persuaded his friend Casanova
to come along.

The centrality of theatre to Paris and the court, along with the fame of
the Balletti family, gave Casanova entry into French high society, or *le monde*.
The theatre was an ideal place to socialise. Aristocrats, ministers of state,
influential courtesans, wealthy commoners, ambassadors, poets, painters,
all became part of his French milieu. Through the Balletti family Casanova
was introduced to the distinguished French poet and playwright Crébillon,
a favourite of Madame de Pompadour. Crébillon volunteered to tutor him
French, and for the following year the Venetian visited him three times a
week. At a performance of *Cenie* (1750) by Madame Graffigny, Casanova
struck up a friendship with Monsieur de Beauchamp, Receiver-General of
Taxes, and his wife. The next day he met the popular opera singer Le Fel. His
connection with the Ballettis, and his wit and self-assurance, quickly got him
noticed in court circles. For several weeks each year, the court of Louis XV
would migrate to Fontainebleau for the hunting season, taking entertainers
with them, including the Ballettis. Casanova was invited along. He was able
to make the acquaintance of Pompadour herself at the opera. A couple of
days later he visited the court, and while he wandered around unhindered, he
witnessed Louis XV and the entire royal family making their way to Mass. On
the same occasion Casanova came across the Queen dining alone at a large
table surrounded by a dozen courtiers.

Given that acting and the theatre was in Casanova's blood, it is no surprise
that he always felt at home amongst performers; on more than one occasion
he was an impresario. As French and Italian actors, singers and dancers were
the most highly sought after amongst the courts and theatres of Europe, there
was usually a network of contacts available to him wherever he travelled. Like
many communities disparaged for transgressing the norms of mainstream
society, its members developed strong loyalties to each other. This affinity for
semi-closed, mutually supportive groups with an international reach was to
be something of a feature of Casanova's life, and one which he used to his
advantage to gain access to those with money and influence as he travelled
across Europe. A notable example were the freemasons, which he joined
during a stop in Lyons on his way to Paris for the first time. Casanova is clear
about the practical benefits of being a member: 'Every young man who travels,
who wants to get to know the great world, who does not want to find himself
inferior to another, and excluded from the company of his equals in the times
in which we live, must be initiated into what is called masonry, if only to know

at least superficially what it is.'[8] Like academies and *conversazioni* (learned social gatherings), masonic lodges were convivial spaces that facilitated intellectual debate and the dissemination of ideas. They were places where Casanova could establish his reputation as a cosmopolitan man of letters and hone his sociability. The latter was both a key virtue for those who wished to be accepted by good society, and a notion of some philosophical importance, claimed, as it was, to be a cornerstone of the formation of human society.

Freemasonry

It was during Casanova's lifetime that freemasonry developed into the form with which we are familiar today. Despite heroic attempts in the eighteenth century to trace freemasonry back to figures such as, amongst others, Adam (of Garden of Eden fame), Egyptian pyramid builders, King Solomon and the Knights Templar, in reality its distant roots are obscure. Even the term 'freemason' has alternative explanations. It may have originally meant a worker of freestone (a form of sandstone or limestone used for ornamentation) but it may have meant a mason who was not indentured. They were organised around a lodge: a community of masons of a specific area. In the Middle Ages, masons could progress to become master masons, the architects of their day, acquiring wealth and status. In the seventeenth century, non-masons (speculative masons) were admitted to lodges. These non-masons were often educated and propertied men, men such as fellows of London's Royal Society, attracted by the mythology of masonic culture and the prospect of discovering ancient secrets. Eventually, entirely speculative lodges emerged and became dominant, founded upon an ethos of fellowship.

The first Grand Lodge formed to govern these speculative lodges was established in London in 1717. A fraternal movement such as freemasonry offered an opportunity to transcend the national, religious and dynastic rivalries that had been the cause of violent conflict for generations. In the 1720s, Jacobite refugees inspired the establishment of a lodge in Paris. Others followed across France. The movement quickly spread throughout the continent despite opposition from the papacy and the threat of excommunication (a threat which was in force until 1983). It was outlawed in Venice in 1751. But attempts to suppress freemasonry were futile. By the late eighteenth century, every major European town housed at least one lodge. In England there were more than 500. In France there were more than 700 by the time of the Revolution, with an estimated 50,000 members.[9] Unlike Catholic states, the Church of England was sympathetic to freemasonry, and in the second half of the century many Anglican clergy became freemasons. It was popular amongst merchants who consequently were instrumental in the dissemination of lodges. They valued the fellowship and practical support offered by its members on their travels away from home. This was particularly valuable in moments of adversity. Aristocratic supporters such as the future King of Prussia, Crown Prince Frederick, who himself founded a lodge, helped to give the movement respectability. Despite hostility from the Habsburg Monarchy's Maria Theresa, in line with the papal ban of 1738, by 1784 there were 66 lodges in the Monarchy's territories, and both her husband Francis, and son Joseph, became members.

Regular lodges were men only although a parallel system of mixed-sex lodges of adoption emerged which enabled female participation. In these mixed lodges women played an increasingly prominent role as leaders and participants in the election of officers. Freemasonry was a hierarchical, secret society that operated according to a formula of degrees of membership, initiations, oaths, codes and solemn ceremonials, and its members committed themselves to a number of core principles. These included the development of moral character, charity, a love of learning, investigating the mysteries of nature and science, and the promotion of each other's interests. Although members were drawn from a broad social spectrum, most were reasonably well off. It would be difficult for an unskilled worker to afford the fees and other costs, such as dress, that were involved. A belief in God was required but in no particular faith or doctrine.

In Paris at the lodge of the Duke of Clermont (the Grand Master of all the French lodges), Casanova advanced from apprentice to companion and then master mason. This gave him a point of contact with businessmen, politicians, aristocrats and people of letters all over Europe. These included Sir Horace Mann, British consul in Florence; the Duke of Matalona, one of the leading members of the nobility of Naples; Count Waldstein, Casanova's employer at Dux; Prince de Ligne, friend and memoirs confidante; Count Panin, political mentor to Catherine II; and Mozart. Two examples of these contacts in action will illustrate their value. Casanova's acquaintance with the Dutch freemason financier Monsieur DO gave him access to the Republic's richest men. After dining at the Burgomaster's Lodge, DO informed him that 'I [Casanova] had supper with company worth three hundred million.'[10] By the mid-1760s, Casanova's fortunes were in decline and, travelling east, he was hunting around in search of ways to revive them. In 1764 he reached St Petersburg, well provided with letters of recommendation. Through an Italian dancer, he was introduced to Ivan Perfilievich Yelagin, the city's leading freemason and the Empress's secretary of state, whom he came to know well, and it was through Yelagin that Casanova met Count Panin. It was this fellow freemason who encouraged him to make himself known to Catherine II. As a consequence of the support, advice and influence of the count, Casanova was to have no less than four audiences with one of the most powerful rulers in Europe.

The occult

It was not uncommon for members of freemasonry to be followers of the Order of the Rosy Cross, or Rosicrucianism, which consequently became established in many lodges. Casanova indicated to others that he was a Rosicrucian; it was another useful gateway whether or not he was a sincere follower. Rosicrucianism was a movement that arose early in the seventeenth century after the emergence of three anonymous texts that asserted the existence of a primeval wisdom derived ultimately from God, and which combined elements of alchemy, cabbala, mysticism and the occult. There were promises of spiritual transformation, a type of spiritual alchemy if you will, turning base souls into golden ones. Rosicrucianism would unify biblical and pagan teachings, it was claimed, and supersede Aristotelian scholasticism, the tradition of learning that had dominated Western thought for several centuries. There were rumours of a secret society dedicated to this advancement of human understanding, whose members could heal the sick by dint of their esoteric knowledge. There were also claims that freemasonry itself had been created by the leaders of the Order of the Rosy Cross. One figure of particular interest to the movement was the aforementioned Paracelsus. The Swiss, sixteenth-century physician and alchemist dabbled in prophesy through astrology and divination, and was the favourite author of the Marquise d'Urfé.

From his childhood, the occult had figured large in Casanova's life. Of the various occult and mystical doctrines swirling around Venice and Europe at the time, cabbala was particularly fashionable. For Casanova it was to become a lifelong pursuit. Kelly writes: 'the origins of his interest and possible belief in cabbala may have been deep-rooted and familial… Brought up by a folk-healer, Marcia Farussi, within an extended family of commedia [dell'arte] actors in eighteenth-century Venice, Casanova would almost certainly have ingested cabbalistic mantras and subsumed cabbalistic imagery with his mother's milk.'[11] His deep interest in the cabbala, along with occult practices generally, gave Casanova a point of commonality with high status and affluent fellow believers that was to prove immensely beneficial.

Cabbala sprang from a mystical strain of Judaism. It sought to explain the nature of creation and existence, and its relationship with its creator. Cabbalists investigated classical Jewish literature to find concealed inner meanings using a range of esoteric mathematical and linguistic techniques. Different schools and off-shoots evolved with contrasting aims: to understand and describe the divine; to become one with God; and to control the forces underpinning the universe. From the Renaissance onwards, these ideas moved beyond the confines of Jewish society and rooted themselves in the Christian world. Progress in mathematics and natural philosophy led to curiosity in cabbalistic formulae, the former lending legitimacy and credence to the latter. There was, after all, no clear division between the invisible forces of nature and those of the divine, nor between the material and the spiritual. If men like Isaac Newton (1643–1727) could use the methods and tools of mathematics and natural philosophy to understand and manipulate the one then why could not equivalent methods and tools be applied to the other? But cabbalists did not restrict their interest to spiritual enlightenment. They sought tangible benefits in the here and now, whether that be knowledge of the future direction of the bond market, a cure for a bad back or, more ambitiously as in the case of d'Urfé, reincarnation.

A typical cabbalistic technique might involve taking a word or phrase from a religious text and giving each letter a numerical value. These numbers could then be organised into the form of a pyramid comprising several rows. This would be the oracle that enabled the cabbala master to decipher the hidden meaning, usually the answer to a question which had been put by the cabbala master on behalf of another. The pyramid numbers could be worked in various ways according to the judgement of the cabbala master, for example, by subtraction or addition, and the resulting numbers constructed into new letters and words. This would be the answer, often a rather ambiguous one, to the supplicant's query. Somebody with the mathematical and linguistic skills of Casanova, who possessed a quick-witted intelligence, a love of word-play, and an ability to improvise on the spot, could pretty much come up with any response they fancied. On his trip to the Dutch bond markets mentioned above, Monsieur DO, the financier with whom he lodged, had an attractive daughter for whom Casanova provided a demonstration:

> I told her to ask in writing about something she didn't know, and about which she would be curious, assuring her that by dint of a calculation she would receive a satisfactory answer. She laughed, and asked why I had returned to Amsterdam so soon. I teach her how to arrange a pyramid with numbers drawn from words, and all the other ceremonies; then I have her pull out a numerical answer which I have her translate into the French alphabet, and she's surprised to read that what made me return to Amsterdam so quickly was love.[12]

Casanova often gives the impression that he was sceptical about supernatural forces and that his interest in cabbala was cynical. But it does appear that to some extent he was a believer. He notes on one occasion how his knowledge of cabbala had not helped him win at cards, suggesting that he was open to the possibility that it might have done so, and in old age his interest continued. Kelly records how Casanova's papers include thousands of cabbalistic calculations: 'Cabbala, its associated disciplines as well as its attachment to atavistic faith and personal self-fulfilment suffused Casanova's pleasure-principle in living, delineating a path from cradle-side folk medicine to Enlightenment metaphysics.'[13]

Casanova first refers to his use of cabbala in his memoirs when recounting his relationship with Bragadin who himself flirted with the occult. When he saved Bragadin's life the senator was quick to pronounce that the young man's medical expertise must have a supernatural source. Casanova confessed that he did indeed possess cabbalist skills. He claimed that he had acquired them from an old hermit and that, in fact, his oracle had predicted his meeting with the senator. From that point onwards Bragadin and his two close friends were in his thrall. Casanova regularly exploited his reputation as an occultist for his own ends, either as a harmless party trick to amuse, entertain and seduce, as an entry into elite social circles, or as a way of fleecing the gullible rich.

On the wilder shores of these belief systems, the heady mix of promises of access to the secrets of the universe, of magical powers, of discourse with spirits, of untold riches and even of immortality was catnip to certain aristocrats, particularly when combined with grand theatrics. Such were the Duchess de Chartres, the Countess du Rumain and the Marquise d'Urfé. All were of the highest rank. As mentioned above, Chartres was a cousin of Louis XV. She was a libertine, the same age as Casanova, and had close connections with freemasonry and an interest in the occult. The marquise also suffered from a disfiguring skin complaint. When she caught wind of Casanova's arrival in Paris in 1750, along with rumours that he was a healer in possession of secret knowledge, she contacted him. The pair struck up a friendship, with Casanova demonstrating to her his cabbalistic skills. He even devised a regime that cured her skin ailment, which he ascribed to the supernatural intelligence with whom he was in contact. On his return to Paris in 1757, using nothing more than showmanship and gibberish, Casanova successfully treated the nephew of Marquise d'Urfé for a bout of sciatica. For aristocratic devotees of all things mysterious, such as the marquise, Casanova's various extraordinary successes made perfect sense; they were in the presence of an exceptionally skilled occultist. He quickly gained d'Urfé's confidence and over the next seven years proceeded to defraud her of something in the order of a million francs according to her nephew.

At this time, Casanova befriended the Countess du Rumain, for whom he frequently consulted his oracle. The two became lovers and the countess provided him with funds now and then. She also used her position on his behalf. When Casanova came to the aid of a Venetian woman who was facing a dire situation on account of an unwanted pregnancy, Rumain both found a place of sanctuary to enable her to have her child in secret, and also intervened with the police commissioner, Monsieur de Sartine, during a court case in which Casanova was accused of kidnapping the woman.

While these points of contact and social networks go a long way to explain how Casanova was able to keep company with so many illustrious people, we should not neglect the impact of the man himself. James Rives Childs speculates: 'It is perhaps not too much to say that he was one of the most notable conversationalists of Europe.'[14] He was a charismatic individual who strove self-consciously to impress others.

Chapter 4

The Gambler, the Duellist and the Gentleman

'I loved gambling … morning and evening I played at the Ridotto
and lost.'
'I craved a duel.'

Giacomo Casanova, History of My Life

Gambling and duelling were widespread throughout Europe, and although they were practiced by commoners and nobility alike, they were of particular importance to the latter. For the aristocracy they embodied two key values: the rejection of money as a way of reckoning social worth; and honour. Both activities featured prominently in Casanova's life.

For Venetian noblemen as well as European aristocrats generally, willing submission to the vagaries of chance, in both gambling and duelling, became entwined with character and identity. It became a test of a man's honour, his honesty, and his self-control, in the face of catastrophic loss. Parallels were drawn with war and codes of chivalry, notably by the controversial sixteenth-century writer Pietro Aretino, a writer with whose works Casanova was familiar. Referring to Aretino's *The Talking Cards* (1543) Jonathan Walker notes: 'a man could gain reputation as much by playing cards as by taking part in battle; card players might resemble duellists as well as soldiers; the vicissitudes of the gambler's life and fortune were similar to those of the soldier's.'[1] A nobleman's studied indifference to the outcome of a wager would demonstrate his independence from material possessions. Likewise, his ability to remain composed in the face of death by sword or pistol rather than tolerate an insult would mark his superiority of character to that of commoners. What mattered was blood, not money. The more heavily one lost at cards, and lost with equanimity, the more one's reputation was enhanced. 'Debts of honour' that were incurred when a gambler played on trust rather than with ready funds, needed to be paid promptly if an individual's reputation was not to be tainted. On the other hand, their reputation would be strengthened if they were generous towards their debtors. While losses incurred through the honest application of the rules of the game would be treated stoically, it was not the case if they were incurred through cheating. A nobleman's honour might impel him to challenge the perpetrator to a duel. That said, there was a relatively relaxed attitude towards cheating. It was treated more as a hazard than a crime, and it was up to the players to have their wits sufficiently about them not to be duped.

The gambler

Casanova's initiation into gambling had taken place around the age of 12 or 13 when he was a young scholar in Padua. To help to understand gambling's place in his life we need to survey the context. Gambling in the Italian peninsular went back at least to ancient Rome and probably further. But from the early seventeenth century, Venice was to become one of the centres of a gambling craze that was to consume much of Europe for the best part of two centuries, embracing all ranks of society. There were a number of contributing factors. Until the fifteenth century, gambling, predominantly using cards and dice, was largely a social affair between peers conducted on the basis of equal odds. This dynamic changed with the introduction of mercantile gambling, whereby gambling could be run as a business for profit. There would typically be some sort of statistical imbalance favouring the house or bank, enabling them to harvest, say, 10 per cent of the monies wagered. Players could now gamble purely for the excitement of the game rather than as a means of socialising, and the larger the stakes, the greater that excitement would be. Bank games such as basset and faro became popular, where several players would compete against the bank rather than each other. This made interactions more impersonal and less likely to generate accusations, insults, threats and violence. Because the focus now was on the thrill of the bet, games became simpler and shorter. It was the destination that mattered, not the journey. Chance was prioritised over skill.

Moral and religious sensitivities, as well as concerns for the maintenance of good social order, were outweighed by political, pragmatic and financial considerations, essentially endorsing the practice. Professional gamblers proliferated as it became a legitimate way to obtain an income. The emergence of capitalism, expansion of financial services and increased circulation of money, allowed gamblers to exploit different sources of wealth more easily in order to support their habit. Having once lost money at cards, Casanova borrowed a diamond to raise a loan from a pawn broker in Treviso who charged 5 per cent.

The consequences of this gambling mania for many were disastrous, especially amongst the nobility. The assets and reputation of a family carefully husbanded for generations could be wiped out overnight. Gambling dens, legal and illegal, sprung up everywhere, with all the various evils that accompanied them: cheating, duelling, heavy-handed debt collection, drunkenness, prostitution and so on. Another concern was social mixing, perceived as a threat to the Republic's hierarchal structure. 'Nowhere was the social mix greater than in the city's gambling halls,' observes James Johnson. 'Here agents of the Inquisitors, expert in penetrating the mask, regularly identified a wide assortment of types: patricians and noble ladies, merchants, Jews, foreign diplomats, vagabonds, prostitutes.'[2]

Lotteries also became immensely popular. The principle of lotteries, rewards linked to some form of random draw, had been around for millennia, but from the sixteenth century the game was revolutionised. Mercantile profit-making was at the root once again: gamblers paying for the chance to win; organisers and backers obtaining a return. Urbanisation was the key to success in this case, allowing large numbers of players to take part for a small, individual sum.

It was in Venice where the shift to mercantile gambling took place. It had become one of the Republic's main forms of entertainment by the time of Casanova's birth, particularly for foreign visitors. Gambling itself was long established there. The Republic was built upon risk-taking, leading it to become one of the world's greatest maritime commercial empires. Venetians even bet on the outcome of elections. Election to office in the Serenissima was a tortuously complicated procedure which combined the element of chance (nominators of candidates for office were drawn by lot) and judgement (the track-record of the candidates themselves). Gambling was illegal but tolerated, especially during Carnival. It carried on everywhere. Less affluent citizens made use of inns, bridges, street corners and squares, while the nobility and the better off preferred locations that were more private, where gambling could be combined with other entertainments. Typical of these locations was a *ridotto*, housed within the residence of an aristocrat. A later development similar to a *ridotto* was the smaller *casino* (small house), which was more akin to a club and could be rented out for social gatherings. As gambling became more widespread these *ridotti* and *casini* multiplied throughout the city. Their character varied enormously. Some were highly respectable meeting places for intellectual debate. Others were more sordid. Alongside gambling were reports of rape, prostitution, fraud, violence and sexual depravity. There were prosecutions but because of the status of those who owned and frequented them, the law was not pursued with any degree of vigour. By the beginning of the seventeenth century, *ridotti* and *casini* had become places where mercantile games flourished. It is clear that by this time nobles were not simply permitting gambling but exploiting it as a business.

Casanova has left us an account of a particularly elegant casino that he rented for several months from 1753 to 1754, and which had once belonged to the English ambassador Lord Holderness:

This casino was composed of five rooms, the furnishings of which were of exquisite taste. There was nothing that was not done in favour of love, good food, and every kind of pleasure. Meals were served through a blind window set into the wall, occupied by a revolving dumb-waiter which entirely filled it. The masters and servants could not see each other. This room was adorned with mirrors, chandeliers, and a superb trumeau over a white marble fireplace, lined with small Chinese porcelain tiles all painted, and made interesting by romantic couples in a state of nature who by their voluptuous attitudes fired the imagination. Small armchairs matched the sofas which were on the right and on the left. Another room was octagonal, all lined with mirrors, paved, and ceilinged in the same way: all these opposing mirrors rendered the same objects from a thousand different points of view.[3]

The initial reaction of the government was to attempt to regulate or outlaw. Limits were placed on the size of bets and the supply of credit. In 1522 Venice was gripped by lottery mania. The authorities set up their own lotteries in response and suppressed the rest, with the proceeds channelled towards worthy causes. There was a hope that state-organised gambling might divert people from less desirable forms. Such hope was in vain. Government involvement if anything seemed to intensify people's desire to gamble, with restrictions only leading to an increase in crime, such as illegal usury. The growing scourge of illicit gambling and the failure of the authorities to curb it led the Great Council in 1638 to allow the establishment of a public *ridotto* (to become known simply as the Ridotto). Permission was granted for it to be hosted in the San Moisé palazzo of the patrician Dandolo family for the duration of Carnival. So began Europe's first state-sanctioned gambling house. Other *ridotti* later came to be licensed by the state.

The Ridotto was strictly regulated. The gambling itself was run by the *Barnabotti,* who were the bankers. They were a category of impecunious nobles whose upkeep otherwise fell upon the state. Profits were split between the *Barnabotti* and the government, although the *Barnabotti* themselves were sometimes funded by other wealthy individuals who would take a cut from the Barnabot's share. The Ridotto may have been open to the public but the high minimum stakes and dress code meant that in reality only the more affluent could participate in the gambling itself. Part of the dress code was a requirement that everyone wore masks except the bankers. There was also an expectation that neither the players nor the bankers displayed emotion over the outcomes of the bets, no matter how dramatic those outcomes might be. For the luckless gambler a retreat was available in the form of a darkened room dubbed the Chamber of Sighs. Until 1774 the Ridotto was a central fixture in the pleasure-seeking lives of the denizens of Venice and its numerous foreign visitors, by which time the toll being taken upon the Venetian nobility had become so great that the government moved to put an end to it. This did little to reduce demand, and gambling continued on merrily in illegal *ridotti* and *casini*.

Gambling always raised sensitive issues for cultures that had for so many centuries been rooted in Christianity. Impatient with the operations of blind chance, many succumbed to the temptation to divine the future or to influence outcomes through supernatural means. Astrology could be used to predict the result of elections, and magic to manipulate the turn of a card or the fall of the dice. But attempts to interfere with destiny trespassed upon the domain of God. Venetian authorities themselves made a careful distinction between gambling, which was regarded as immoral but not blasphemous, and conjuring with occult forces, which was both. There are reports of playing cards being baptised, dreams interpreted, and the soul of Judas interrogated, all in the service of winning a bet. Sixteenth-century polymath Girolamo Cadano's work on games and probability combined mathematical insights with conjecture about the supernatural. Like Socrates two millennia before him, and Casanova two centuries later, Cadano refers to the influence upon himself of a 'genius', a sort of guardian angel that was able to spy into the workings of fortune. Cadano suggested a gambling strategy based on 'geomancy', an ancient form of divination rather like reading tea leaves except the patterns are generated by tossing soils or rocks on the ground.

Casanova's memoirs make clear that gambling was a major part of his life, and includes numerous accounts. When he was 18, travelling through Chioggia, he lost all his money playing faro, pawned most of his clothes for thirty sequins, and lost that as well. Two years later, he lost all his money at Corfu. But on his return the same year, Lady Luck smiled, so much so that he became a local celebrity. He made his first modest fortune in 1750 as a consequence of buying a quarter share in the bank of a Barnabot at the Ridotto, and in 1753 he borrowed money at 5 per cent for a month to share the bank with a gambler called Antonio Croce. Their lucrative venture was brought to an abrupt halt when it was raided by the authorities. In 1760 he pocketed substantial winnings from cards in Aix-en-Savoie. But in Stuttgart in the same year, there was an attempt to swindle him out of 4,000 louis (almost 100,000 livres). This was an eye-watering sum. It was the equivalent of the average annual wage of 200 Parisians. Rather than pay, he fled. In 1761 in Naples, he lost 2,000 ducati (20,000 livres) in three hours. From the mid-1760s his more flamboyant card-playing days were behind him, although during a couple of spells in Rome, in 1770 and 1771, Casanova claims to have won a large sum of money by deducing winning lottery ticket numbers through the use of cabbala.

An informant's report for the Venetian Inquisition dated 22 March 1755, observes that Casanova 'is a capable gambler who is able, in town, to con the nobility of money through his numerous acquaintances [among them],'[4] a point that the same spy repeats in another report four months later. This raises the question of Casanova's morality. Was he a cheat and a confidence trickster or did he act more in accordance with the ideals described by Aretino in *The Talking Cards*? The evidence would seem to support the latter. For a start, Casanova had a poor opinion of professional gamblers, despite at one time considering becoming one (an eight-day losing streak dissuaded him). The reason for his disdain was because they so frequently resorted to fraud. It irked him when people assumed that he himself was a 'Greek' (slang for a card sharp), and he makes a clear distinction between cheating and expertise: 'Such [losing] is the destiny of every man inclined to games of chance unless he knows how to seduce Fortune by playing with a real advantage based on calculation or skill. A wise player can do both without being labelled a cheat.'[5] Consequently, Casanova familiarised himself with concepts of probability to improve his chances of winning and was a keen student of cards, writing a history on the subject. His attitude seems to have closely chimed with Aretino's depiction of the ideal noble gambler and was consistent with Casanova's notions of honour and chivalry. As a young man on Corfu, he teamed up with a professional called Maroli, Casanova's easy manner making him popular with the punters, smiling when he was losing, and looking unhappy when he was winning. He was deeply hurt by any accusations of avarice, as occurred on Corfu by a woman with whom he was very much smitten. Similarly, given such notions of honour, it does not come as altogether a surprise that his first duel was triggered when he was 21 by an attempt to cheat him at cards.

For Venetian nobles, gambling was part of a broader culture of conspicuous consumption. It was esteemed for being the behaviour of someone who was able to rise above the grubby concerns of those whose identity was inextricably tied to their capital. They demonstrated their contempt for money through their ruinous gambling habits. Whenever Casanova had money, he spent it with abandon. He scorned the thought of amassing wealth in the fashion of affluent commoners. In 1757 the Paris lottery and his dealings on the Amsterdam financial markets had made him immensely wealthy. Yet by 1759 he was running out of funds and resorting to fleece the Marquise d'Urfé to sustain his lifestyle.

All that said, there was a grey area that Casanova was willing to inhabit. He may not have stooped to cheating, although this is disputed, but he was prepared to team up with someone else who was a 'corrector of bad luck' or, on occasions when he discovered cheating taking place, to keep silent in return for a share of the profits. There were also times when he would deliberately lose, for example in the pursuit of a woman (according to him, it was a strategy that never failed). At a deeper level his passion for gambling does appear to reflect his affinity for the operations of chance in life more generally. And alongside chance, the moment: that place of almost frozen time when events coincide.

Ultimately, Casanova's relationship with gambling seems to have been a somewhat tortured one. In his early 20s he did manage to stop gambling for a while, to the relief of his friends. But it spoke to him too directly. Its excitement and immediacy, its rituals, its codes of honour, the demands it placed upon resilience and quick wits, its entanglement with speculations about mathematics, fate and the supernatural were all too beguiling. For all his talents Casanova probably lost more often than he won; in the long run this was inevitable, unless the player only held the bank or they were a skilled 'corrector of fortune'.

The duellist

One of the striking features of European society prior to the twentieth century was its long tradition of duels of honour. This tradition arose in its modern form during the sixteenth and seventeenth centuries, evolving from an earlier medieval world of tournaments, jousting, feuds, trial by combat and chivalry. Protagonists initially possessed a rapier, dagger, shield and helmet. The dagger, shield and helmet were then abandoned over time, and the rapier was replaced by lighter swords such as the smallsword. In the eighteenth century such a sword was a must-have accessory worn daily by anybody who professed to be a gentleman. Casanova refers to wearing one on several occasions. From the second half of the eighteenth century the pistol became increasingly popular. Duelling was a special interest of the aristocracy for much of its history although others of lower status, such as Casanova, did take part. It was prevalent in the military amongst all ranks. Duels took place between men who were largely of a similar social class. A nobleman's reputation could be ruined if he refused a challenge from someone of equal standing but he could do so with impunity if the challenger was an inferior or deemed not to be a true gentleman.

The duel of honour took root in Italy in the sixteenth century on the back of the development of courtesy theory, discussed below, spreading to France and then to the rest of Europe. It acquired impetus in 1526 when Francis I (1515–1547) challenged Charles V (1519–1556) to a duel, even though nothing came of it. Under Henry IV (1589–1610) it is estimated that 10,000 Frenchmen were killed in duels. Research into rates of mortality and injury in London has found that a fifth of participants in sword duels were killed and a quarter wounded. For many young men, taking part in a duel was a rite of passage.

The nature, popularity and persistence of duelling varied from nation to nation. Into the eighteenth century, Sweden was quickly falling out of love with the duel of honour, and in southern Europe it was not as fashionable as it had been. Further north in Prussia and Poland, it remained something of a passion. In Russia, duelling was a custom that was imported from the west and was relatively infrequent until later in the eighteenth century. Here, it was not to reach its peak until the early nineteenth century. As regards Russia, Irina Reyfman remarks: 'the duel became a working mechanism for resolving all kinds of conflicts, both serious and trivial – from quarrels over official business, to confrontations caused by social inequality within the nobility, to clashes brought about by sexual rivalry, cheating at cards, an awkward word, a joke, a scowl, a frown.'[6] Although in France it was no longer quite the scourge it had been in the previous century, the duel of honour remained prevalent for much of the 1700s. From the 1760s onwards, the English and Irish preferred pistols, whereas elsewhere, such as in Italy, the sword remained dominant.

One particularly influential text that helped to shape the culture underpinning the honour duel was Baldassare Castiglione's *The Courtier* (1528) which dealt with matters of honour and courtly etiquette. Castiglione was an Italian diplomat and soldier of minor nobility whose early sixteenth-century work was to be the model for many other commentaries on conduct and manners. *The Courtier* portrays a gentleman as someone who is possessed not only of military prowess but also a classical education and an appreciation of the arts. He carries his accomplishments with grace and an apparent indifference, concealing the hard work required to achieve them. He appears natural, unaffected and self-controlled. He eschews arrogance and behaves with a humility that belies his status. He takes an active role in public service. Significantly, he will not tolerate any slight against himself (otherwise he will forever carry the shame of it). Although Castiglione focused little on the subject of the duel of honour itself, it is not difficult to recognise here the seeds of behaviour that were to become so characteristic of it: that counterintuitive mix of formal politeness, insouciance and lethal violence. Initially published in Venice in 1528, *The Courtier* was quickly translated into various languages, spreading this ideal of a Renaissance gentleman throughout Europe. In due course, duelling was to become a highly ritualised affair, its protocols underpinned by *codes duello*. Duelling manuals and courtesy books proliferated. The grounds for, and conduct of, an honourable duel were enumerated in meticulous detail.

In the eighteenth century the concept of courtesy morphed into gallantry, embedding within it ideals of chivalry and respect towards women.

That such a tradition of formalised violence could become entrenched for so long is puzzling to the modern mind. How could countless numbers of men, mostly from the highest echelons of society, educated men, men of wealth and authority, place themselves in mortal danger over matters that were often, to our eyes, exceptionally minor or even laughable? On one occasion a Monsieur de Valencay challenged his friend, a notorious duellist called de Bouteville, because he had fought a duel without inviting him to be his second. On another a Count de Bussy was embroiled in a duel because his uncle, whom he hardly ever saw, was rumoured to have accused a man of being a drunkard. Byron killed his cousin in a duel over a dispute about who had the most game on their estates.

But matters of honour were no laughing matter. Your reputation, particularly amongst the aristocracy, the gentry and affluent commoners, was of huge importance. Crucially, the truth or falsity of any deemed insult was not particularly relevant. You may well be cheating at cards but for your reputation to be injured by being publicly accused of cheating at cards was intolerable. It was a matter of manners and politeness. One of the most serious insults was to be accused of lying as it was a direct attack upon a man's gentlemanly status (an accusation which even today is prohibited amongst the honourable members of the House of Commons).

To allow yourself to be treated with disrespect was to jeopardise your standing in the eyes of others. Life chances might suddenly become more scarce: invitations to important social events; political alliances; favourable marriages for your children; government appointments; financial and business deals. They were all of a piece. The primary aim of a duellist was not to kill his opponent but to restore his honour in the clearest way possible – that is, by demonstrating courage in the face of death. Not to do so would be to risk social death, with all the devastating economic and political consequences that could flow from it, both for you and for your family. It was a stark choice. Whether you won or lost the duel was a secondary consideration. It was the taking part that mattered. Consistent with that notion, value was increasingly placed not so much on a man's fighting skills and desire to overcome his opponent but on his remaining steadfast.

But if it was honour that was at stake, rather than winning or losing, then that raised questions of fairness. There was little point to a contest if one of the participants possessed a decisive advantage over the other, for instance in terms of their ability or size and reach. What courage did it take for a skilled swordsman to fight a beginner in the knowledge that he was almost certain to win? It was largely for this reason that detailed codes were drawn up prescribing the organisation and conduct of a duel. It was also important to be able to verify that a proper duel had been fought. Given that honour and reputation were such valuable commodities, there was an incentive for combat to be faked. The conditions for the conclusion of a duel would be agreed upon in advance. If swords were used the affair could be ended upon the drawing of first blood combined with an apology. This first blood was often from the armed hand, which effectively removed the benefit of a longer reach. That said, although a duel could be concluded if the first blood option was chosen, it was generally frowned upon as being unmanly. Duellists could choose to fight to the death if they so wished. Other restrictions on what was and was not allowed during combat further reduced the advantages of the more skilful swordsman. He was not allowed to continue his attack upon an opponent who had been disarmed. He could not switch his sword from one hand to the other, an option that was more likely to favour someone who was better trained. The adoption of the pistol was another way of ensuring that combatants fought on a level playing field, even though, theoretically, it was a more lethal weapon. Unlike the time and training it took to produce a swordsman, a good eye and a steady hand were all that was needed to make a capable adversary with a pistol. Duelling pistols came in pairs that were identical to ensure nobody had an advantage.

The ideal result of a duel was reconciliation, with the honour of both men restored, perhaps followed up with an apology or a mutual recognition of honesty and integrity. It would be even better, of course, if such an outcome could be achieved without the duel taking place at all. When a challenge was issued it was not unusual for friends, acquaintances, superiors, and even the courts, to get involved in an attempt to arbitrate. Delicate negotiations might be undertaken to find ways of saving face. It became an expectation that the seconds – friends of the duellists tasked with managing the affair – would attempt to stop the duel from going ahead or at least find ways of minimising injury. It was not unknown for them to load pistols with gunpowder but no ball. In the community more widely, passers-by might intervene to try and thwart a contest. Once again, duelling codes created opportunities to resolve a dispute. It might be that there was an injunction against a duel taking place prior to the morning after a challenge had been issued, providing a cooling-off period during which wiser counsels might prevail. This was another advantage of pistols over swords. Whereas a gentleman could be expected to be wearing his sword when he was out and about, pistols were not usually so available. The delay it took to fetch them could allow tempers to subside.

Duels ostensibly promoted a form of justice, albeit one that existed outside the normal jurisdiction of the law. The notion that one-to-one combat was a legitimate way of determining a person's innocence or guilt harked back to medieval trials by ordeal and a Christian belief in providence: if a man was innocent then God would intervene to save him. It was further legitimised by the social status of noblemen. In the past, noblemen had been a source of legal authority in their own right. It is perhaps no coincidence that duels of honour emerged at a time when the old feudal system was breaking down and with it the nobility's ancient rights and privilege (a word derived from 'private law'). In addition, the increasing use of artillery in warfare was reducing the opportunities for a gentleman to distinguish himself on the field of battle in single combat, making private duels a handy substitute for any nobleman who wanted to prove his bravery and martial prowess (even if that might not be in the spirit of the precepts of courtesy). There were practical considerations as well which made the pursuit of a grievance outside the law appealing: going through the courts was a notoriously tortuous, costly and unpredictable business. In flouting the law on the grounds of honour, duelling could also be regarded as an expression of the moral superiority of the aristocracy and an assertion of its independence. Parallels can be drawn here with gambling. Likewise through duelling, the nobility demonstrated that even the prospect of death would not deter them from following a life according to what they nostalgically perceived to be the ancient virtues of their forefathers. What more ostentatious way could there be to display your aristocratic credentials and your loyalty to the ideals of your class than to risk your fortune on the turn of a card or your life for some trivial offence?

There had long been critics of private duelling, one notable example being the English politician and philosopher, Francis Bacon (1561–1626), who in the early seventeenth century was actively campaigning against it in his capacity as the attorney general, complaining along with others that duellists possessed a false understanding of concepts such as honour, valour and injury. Bacon was supported by men such as Walter Raleigh (1552–1618), who argued that trivial insults should be ignored. James I (1603–1625) issued a proclamation in 1614 'against private challenges and combats.' Louis XIII (1610–1643) outlawed duelling in France in 1626, and further edicts were put in place in an attempt to wipe it out by his successor Louis XIV (1643–1715). Frederick William (1640–1688), the Great Elector of Brandenburg-Prussia, criminalised duelling in 1652, and again this was followed up by further measures from his successors, including Frederick II. The Church added its weight to the opposition. It had been decreed that duellists and their seconds were to be excommunicated and deprived of Christian burial as early as 1563. But the penalties for duelling, ranging from fines, imprisonment and execution, were rarely implemented, at least against the nobility. This was hardly surprising given the power that these men and their families wielded and their importance to the military. For commoners the law was applied more rigorously.

Over the course of the eighteenth century, attitudes towards violence became less tolerant, although this change was not uniform across Europe. Duelling codes and conventions sought to reduce the chances of serious injury, especially with regards to pistols. Technical advances such as rifling were prohibited, limiting their accuracy. Sights were disapproved of. Distance regulations lessened the chance of a successful hit. A misfire could be accepted as a shot, which, given that for the large majority of duels only one or two shots were allowed, cut down the opportunities to do damage. Duellists might be expected to fire upon a visual signal which reduced the time they had to take aim (it was regarded as unsporting to consciously aim the pistol or to practise beforehand). An injury 'sufficient to agitate the nerves' could put an end to a duel. Unsurprisingly, the same research that found that approximately half the participants in London who had been involved in sword duels had been either killed or significantly injured, also discovered that over 70 per cent of pistol duellists were left entirely unscathed. There was also a change in attitude towards swordsmanship. It came to be regarded as more like a sport; an activity which promoted general physical and mental well-being and part of the education of a gentleman. New methods of fencing focussed on defence rather than attack. Duels were consequently more likely to end when an opponent was disarmed or at the drawing of first blood.

The relationship between concepts of honour, reputation and physical courage that were once so tightly bound together with duelling began to unravel. What constituted honour and dishonour was more and more contested. True honour was not to be found in superficial courtesies but in adherence to sincerely-held Christian virtues, and was primarily a matter for one's own conscience. It was not a quality you had to prove through staging some kind of spectacle, whatever its rituals and niceties. As has already been noted, passive bravery, more in keeping with a Christian ethos rather than a soldierly one, became increasingly respected. In urban environments such as London, there was a growing expectation that gentlemanly conduct should be governed by moderation, self-control and goodwill; anger was a vice to be avoided. Influential and widely-read commentators, such as Rousseau, argued in favour of magnanimity. Judged by these standards, duels were self-indulgent and unsociable. As the century wore on, reports on them in the press became increasingly critical. A pistol duel was preferred if there had to be one, as it demanded both courage and emotional control; you had to stand and wait while your opponent fired and could not return fire until allowed to do so.

The reputational benefits of duelling were undermined as attitudes in society hardened against it. If your conception of honour was based upon public respect and that respect was no longer forthcoming, then what was the point of it? Improvements in the mechanisms of law and order may also have taken their toll. Honour cultures, whether in the southern states of nineteenth-century USA or amongst modern inner-city gangs, have tended to thrive in communities where centralised authority is weak, and where individuals have been thrown back upon their own resources. Instead, courts became used more often to settle issues that previously could have provoked a duel – such as adultery – and policing was becoming more effective, especially in large urban centres. All that said, while there were signs towards the end of the eighteenth century that the tide was turning against duelling, it was still common in many parts of Europe, particularly amongst the military.

Beyond the noble ideals, the reality of duelling could be a lot messier and more sordid. Inevitably some men ignored accepted conventions in order to obtain an advantage over their opponent or cynically engineered challenges in the pursuit of personal gain. No doubt there would have been occasions when the outcome of a duel was such a foregone conclusion that it was little more than socially sanctioned murder.

In Casanova's memoirs there are various references to duels, many of them involving himself directly. Describing a duel in 1762 between a Swiss officer called Schmit and a French officer called d'Aché, he observes: 'The honest man who bears a weapon must always be ready to use it to avenge an insult that wounds his honour, or to provide satisfaction for an injury he may have given. I know it's a prejudice which, and perhaps rightly, is called 'barbaric', but there are social prejudices from which a man of honour cannot escape.'[7] Utterly composed, Schmit allowed d'Aché to fire twice before offering a reply: '[Schmit] fired his first shot into the air, then, aiming at d'Aché with his second pistol, he struck him in the middle of his forehead and stretched him out dead. Putting his pistols back in his pocket, Schmit set off alone at once, as if he were continuing his walk.'[8] Clearly, Schmit was a perfect gentleman.

There are many extraordinary aspects to Casanova's life but when we consider the duelling culture of the time perhaps the most extraordinary of all was that he managed to live to write about them. He records fighting at least nine duels over a twenty-five-year period, as well as one sword fight which perhaps might not strictly be described as a duel. He appears to have won all of them and generally escaped unscathed. The exception was his one pistol duel against Count Branicki, which almost led to his hand being amputated.

But it may well be that Casanova fought more than nine. It is possible that he omitted duels that took place during the wilder years of his early 20s.

Curiously, he fought his first and his last duel against the same man, Count Medini, the first in Padua in 1746 or 1747, and the second in Sorrento in 1770. On both occasions gambling was the cause. Medini was to end his days as a debtor in a London prison. The year following his duel in Padua, Casanova fought another gambler in Milan, the self-styled Count Celi. He was prostituting a young dancer called Marina whom Casanova had met several years previously. Celi, who was also Marina's lover, was using her as part of a scheme to defraud the unwary. When Casanova intervened to prevent Celi's mistreatment of Marina, 'by putting the point of my sword to his throat', Celi challenged him to a duel.[9] This particular duel ended up as a foursome when Casanova's opponent brought along some help and a Frenchmen stepped in to take the Venetian's side (it was not uncommon for seconds to fight each other). The Frenchman turned out to be Antonio Balletti who we have already met (the son of Sylvia Balletti) and the two quickly became close friends. On Casanova's first visit to Paris he was confronted by a Chevalier de Talvis after, according to de Talvis, Casanova insulted a respectable lady. On his second visit, indiscrete comments about a debt owed to him lead to a reluctant duel with his good friend La Tour d'Auvergne. In The Hague, Casanova fought a burgomaster's son whom he had upset by placing winning bets against him during a session of billiards and, on another visit to Paris, he ran a man through with his sword who had stolen his ring. This man was Giuseppe Santis, a professional gambler and adventurer. Casanova had another dispute over a ring, this time with a fraudster in Spa. But his most noteworthy duel took place in Warsaw in 1766 against a Polish General called Count Branicki. It was so famous that it made the newspapers in London. Casanova published two versions of the encounter, *The Duel*, in 1780, and as part of his memoirs.

Having spent the best part of a year in Russia, in 1765 Casanova made his way to Poland well-stocked with letters of recommendation, arriving in Warsaw in the October where he was warmly received by prominent Polish families along with the king himself. Resident in Warsaw at this time were two Italian dancers, Anna Binetti, an old friend of Casanova's, and La Catai. The two dancers were bitter rivals and Polish society had divided in support of one or the other. Casanova's friends had rallied to La Catai so Casanova felt honour-bound to do the same, vexing Binetti. It was from this rancour that the duel arose.

Count Branicki was a friend of the king and had distinguished himself as a soldier during the Seven Years War. Branicki is described by Casanova as a man who could 'kill without discourtesy.'[10] He was also Binetti's lover. In

March 1766 Casanova attended the theatre where he briefly visited Binetti in her box and then that of another dancer, La Casacci, in hers, with Branicki following. The count engineered a confrontation and called Casanova a coward, to which the Venetian responded by issuing a written challenge to a duel. As duels would normally take place only between men deemed to be of equivalent status, Branicki's acceptance was a matter of great moment for Casanova.

Preparations quickly got underway, the two men meeting face-to-face to agree how the duel would be organised. The Venetian was a very capable swordsman and was expecting this to be a sword fight. But he was a novice when it came to duelling with pistols. Branicki, on the other hand, was an expert shot and wanted a pistol duel despite, apparently, having given his opponent the right to choose his weapon. Casanova assured him that he was not a fencing master, consistent with the idea that to be honourable one duellist should not have a decisive advantage over the other. But Branicki continued to insist and Casanova relented, which raises the question as to why Casanova would put himself at such a clear disadvantage when, with no stain on his honour, he was within his rights to choose swords. In his appeal to his opponent, Branicki had flattered him by referring to his gentlemanly character, and perhaps this and the count's high rank was too much for Casanova to resist. After all, he had been anxious throughout his life to be accepted in aristocratic circles.

The next day, Branicki arrived with his entourage and they headed off to where the duel was to take place, engaging in some small talk en route. Despite Casanova's request, Branicki arranged for the duel to be conducted inside Poland, making it illegal. When offered the choice of pistols, Casanova took the first pistol to come to hand without checking either, again demonstrating himself to be an honourable man by not attempting to gain an advantage: 'Branicki, taking the other, says that he guarantees on his honour that the weapon I have in my hand is perfect. I reply that I am going to test it on his head. At this terrible answer he turns pale, he throws his sword to one of his pages and shows me his bared chest.'[11]

Both men were wounded – Casanova in the hand, and Branicki in the abdomen. Branicki's injury was so serious that everyone assumed he was going to die. Three of his officers drew their sabres to cut Casanova down but were restrained by Branicki. Convinced his wound was fatal and concerned that his rival was going to hang, he gave Casanova his purse and told him to leave. Hitching a lift on a peasant's horse and sleigh, Casanova made his way to Warsaw and took refuge in a monastery where various nobleman friends rushed to his aid. There were rumours that Branicki had died, spurring some of his men to go hunting for revenge.

Branicki survived. The ball had only grazed his intestines. He had not eaten the night before and believed that this had saved his life. As for Casanova, it turned out that his threat to shoot Branicki in the head had caused the general to take up a more defensive position and thereby hampered his aim. There was a good chance that Branicki would have otherwise killed him. Honour restored, the two men were to remain on friendly terms. Discussing events with each other afterwards, Casanova claimed that it was the first time that he had ever used a pistol in a duel and that his declared intention to target Branicki's head had merely been a ruse to unsettle him. The injury to Casanova's hand was to take eighteen months to heal.

Throughout Casanova's memoirs duels are in the air. There are references to duellists fleeing kingdoms to escape the authorities and soldiers being demoted on account of taking part in one. There was an awareness that quarrels had the potential to escalate quickly and draw a challenge or, at least, for one to be a carefully considered option. Unsurprisingly, duels were a frequent topic of conversation. The practice was so prevalent that when Casanova had to bandage his hand after hurting it in a fall, everyone assumed his injury had been on account of a duel. And while the participants of duels may have been overwhelmingly men (there were a couple of instances of female duellists) that does not mean women were passive by-standers. Women were actively involved in both restraining and, as we have seen, encouraging contests.

Not all challenges, of course, were carried out. On one occasion, Casanova simultaneously challenged three officers by letter to duels to the death to take place over a three-day period, but the men failed to turn up. These were the men who had attempted to swindle him out of 4,000 louis. Following upon the Branicki duel, Casanova received five challenges by people unknown to him, which he ignored. There is also a suggestion that a proportion of challenges were little more than bluff and bravado, such as the time he ended up brawling with Count Torriano, whom he came across beating a woman with whom Casanova was having an affair. Torriano offered a challenge but then backed out of it. Casanova comments bitingly: 'it [Torriano's shifty behaviour] seemed to me to suggest that it would come to nothing, and that this duel would go up in smoke like so many others when one of the two heroes is cowardly.'[12]

In a poignant footnote, later in life Casanova was himself to suffer an accusation of cowardice. Living in Venice but in much reduced circumstances, he was secretary to a Genoese diplomat. In his secretarial role, he was involved in a row at the home of Carlo Grimani with a man called Carletti who publicly insulted him. Although opinion was split as to who was in the right, Casanova's failure to defend his honour was deemed craven. He found himself derided and ostracised. He was in his late fifties at the time. The humiliation must have been unbearable for such a proud man who throughout his life had been willing to risk death to defend his reputation. Casanova's anger led him to pen a bitter satire, representing Carletti as a dog, and Carlo Grimani – a member of an illustrious patrician family – as illegitimate. It was a terrible misjudgement. Amidst the furore Casanova was forced to leave Venice for the last time.

Chapter 5

The Political Landscape

'It is a fancy common to all nations; each one believes itself the first. They are all right.'

Giacomo Casanova, *History of My Life*

Casanova was immersed in Europe's political life, mainly as a close-up observer but on occasion as a participant. He seems to have spied for the French government after fleeing to Paris in 1757. Residing in Trieste in 1773 while friends lobbied for him to be allowed to return to Venice, Casanova worked to support Venice's trading interests and was involved in trying to resolve a dispute between the Venetian Inquisition and a community of unhappy Armenian monks. He had a junior but nonetheless significant role in diplomatic negotiations to avert a war between Venice and the Dutch Republic in 1784. He met the most important rulers, ministers, diplomats and ecclesiastics of his time. He wrote a political history, *History of the Troubles of Poland* (1774), and in 1769 a refutation of Amelot de la Houssaye's critical *History of the Government of Venice* (1676). As an inveterate traveller he had to contend with the religious and political complexion of the continent. Its shifting boundaries, diplomatic tensions and wars, with all their intended and unintended consequences, were likely at some point to intrude. He used the distraction of a night-time skirmish between Austrian and Spanish troops in Marino in 1744, during the War of the Austrian Succession (1740–48), to make a move on the wife of a travelling companion with whom he was lodged. The same Austrian-Spanish hostilities lead to him being separated from his lover Bellino the following year at Pesaro, putting an end to their affair. Travelling to Cologne in 1760, five army deserters fired their muskets at him in an attempt to waylay his carriage.

The nation and the state

The diversity of self-governing entities and the relationships between them was dizzyingly complex. Cantons, circles, city states, confederations, duchies, empires, Imperial Villages, kingdoms, leagues, Papal States, prince-bishoprics, principalities and republics, with their equally variegated rulers, jostled amongst one another for survival and advantage. Few of these conform to our idea of what now constitutes a nation; kingdoms and republics perhaps but as for the rest, not so much. Today Europe is far more uniform, dominated as it is by the nation-state. Yet Casanova regularly refers to the English, Spanish, Swiss, Italians, Germans, Russians and so on, often describing them according to their national character even where such nation-states did not exist as in cases such as Italy and Germany. At this point it is worth pausing to explore the concepts of nation, nationalism, sovereignty and state.

Prior to the late seventeenth century a national community was not assumed to have a strong political dimension. Their territorial relationship was not always clearly defined and may have been historical (as was the case with Jews). When Casanova refers to Italians, he is talking about people who share a common history and culture. But when we think of nations today, we tend to think of political entities with clear territorial boundaries – that is, nation-states. Legitimate political authority is deemed to reside in those governed within that territorial boundary, especially in democratic societies. It is not, say, in the person of a monarch for whom that territory was an inherited possession and who may, indeed, live in a different country altogether. This was case for the kingdom of Hungary, whose sovereigns included the Austrian Habsburg, Empress Maria Theresa, who ruled from Vienna. Whereas cultural nationalism was long established, particularly in the form of national stereotypes, notions of social contracts and popular sovereignty only began to take hold in Europe at the end of the seventeenth century, notably in England (Great Britain from 1707), and through the eighteenth century.

The trickiest problem facing any state was the peaceful transfer of power. It was the moment when the polity was at its most vulnerable to threats from without and within. There were broadly two solutions: hereditary and elective. Popes, Holy Roman Emperors, Venetian Doges and Polish monarchs were elected. The electors could be comprised of aristocrats, high ranking ecclesiastics, institutions (such as monasteries), or some combination of the three. Primogeniture hereditary systems were more typically the rule although the Ottomans preferred agnatic seniority (the eldest male rather than the eldest son). In Russia this primogeniture system broke down in 1722 when Peter I (Peter the Great, 1682–1721) decreed that it was up to the present Tsar to decide upon their successor. Peter died three years later without himself having made an appointment. His successor was then installed by senior government advisors who drew on the support of the army. This was to be Peter's widow Catherine, originally a Lithuanian peasant and scullery maid. It established a pattern of succession mired in intrigue and palace revolution that persisted into the second half of the century until the reign of Catherine II.

Such hereditary systems meant that most of Europe was governed by networks of families according to rules of inheritance that did not respect state boundaries. As a consequence, the interests of the people in the territories ruled, and the dynastic interests of their ruling families, were not always aligned. Where there was a conflict between the concerns of France and the concerns of the Bourbons, Louis XIV (1643–1715) would likely favour the Bourbons. The claim 'L'état c'est moi' [the state is me] ascribed to Louis may be apocryphal but it described the position of an absolute monarch pretty well. It allowed Louis to justify the sacrifice of substantial quantities of French blood and treasure in pursuit of personal and dynastic ends that were of little benefit to the people of France.

It was during this period that the idea of a nation became politicised and increasingly understood in terms of a unified, ethno-territorial state. The creation of this politico-cultural nationalism was to produce one of the most potent social forces in the shaping of European society. Its most dramatic manifestation was the French Revolution, where doctrines of popular sovereignty had gained traction through the work of Rousseau and publications such as *What is the Third Estate?* (1789) by Abbé Sieyès. But the absence of democratic mechanisms by which means the will of the population could be interpreted raised problems. Without them it was left to individuals and affiliated groups to decide for themselves, with all the potential for disagreement and conflict that entailed.

The emergence of nationalism meant that populations came to expect the interests of the nation – as they began to conceive it – to take precedence over those of the ruler. In Anglican England this contributed to the overthrow of the Catholic, pro-France, and would-be absolute monarch James II (1685–1688) to be replaced by the Protestants William (1689–1702) and Mary (1689–1694) as joint monarchs who recognised that sovereignty rested with Parliament. As loyalties began to shift away from the person of the leader, there was a growing recognition on the part of governing elites that they had at least to give the appearance of respecting the outlook of the people. Frederick II of Prussia was careful to stress that he was a servant of the state who used his immense power to work on its behalf rather than arbitrarily for his own narrow self-interest. Habsburg Joseph II (1780–1790), reinvented his court theatre as a German national theatre, and Frederick William II of Prussia (1786–1797) likewise turned the 'French Comedy House' in Berlin into a national theatre. Those who refused to acknowledge this phenomenon of nationalism, such as Louis XVI (1774–1792), were playing with fire.

In the same period, the doctrine of the divine right of kings was used to assert that monarchical authority was a gift from God, that such authority was absolute, and that a sovereign was accountable to no-one but God. The archetypal example was Louis XIV. Debates were had about what to do with tyrants and whether monarchs were granted power on the basis that they were meant to use it to serve the people they governed. But, by and large, the rightful sources of political authority were recognised to be individual rulers and institutions representing elite groups. The realities of the exercise of power were, of course, far less clear cut, as the English Civil War and its aftermath demonstrated.

Ironically, as rulers of the seventeenth and eighteenth century looked to secure their hold on government, they reinforced those very notions of the nation and national identity that were to undermine their claims of self-sufficient legitimacy. The vehicle for this consolidation of power was the state, that in theory, by this time, was understood to be a territory with its own constitutional form in which there existed a single source of law and legitimate force. This source of authority was independent of external bodies such as the Church. Its prime functions were law-making and enforcement, taxation, and the administration of public services. In practise, this theoretical conception was only partially realised. Countries tended to be a patchwork of competing authorities, bureaucratic systems, and deeply entrenched local traditions that enjoyed significant independence from the crown. In France there were *parlements* (courts of appeal), the local jurisdictions of the nobility, foreign enclaves, autonomous provinces, town councils and even private tax collectors. There was also, of course, the Catholic Church which, under the authority of the pope, possessed its own wide-ranging administrative, legal and financial powers.

There were strong incentives for rulers to attempt to realise this state model or, at least, move closer to it. It would weaken potential threats to their authority internally, and make it easier for rulers to exploit their country's resources in order to compete more effectively on the international stage. To this end, Louis XIV drew upon the doctrine of the divine right of kings to override local prerogatives and integrate more closely France's different regions and institutions. The king chose not to convene the Estates General, undermined the autonomy of *parlements*, and established a network of provincial officials and assistants to execute the king's will. With varying degrees of success, similar attempts at reform and centralisation could be found across Europe, notably Prussia under the Hohenzollerns, the Habsburg Monarchy under Empress Maria Theresa and her son Joseph, and Spain, Naples and Sicily under the Bourbon Charles Sebastian (1759–1788).

Central Europe

Casanova visited pretty much every European state and territory of significance with the exception of Hungary and Scandinavia: an astonishing feat. Comparing a map of eighteenth-century Europe with one of today, the most conspicuous difference is the broad swathe of territory running down through the continent diagonally north-west to south-east, approximately from Belgium, the Netherlands and Germany to Italy, Greece, Bulgaria and Romania. This huge region was dominated by three political entities: the German-speaking lands of the Holy Roman Empire to the north and moving into the centre; below it to the south-east, dynastic Habsburg domains that were held separately from the Empire (in addition to the Austrian Netherlands); and the Ottoman Empire in the south, occupying the Balkans. The 1,000-year-old Holy Roman Empire and the 500-year-old overlapping Habsburg Monarchy were made up of numerous sovereign states, ranging from territories the size of a village to the size of England. These conglomerations had arisen as a consequence of centuries of war, treaties, marriage alliances and inheritance. The Holy Roman Empire alone contained over 300 states, the most important of which included Austria, Bavaria, Bohemia, Brandenburg-Prussia, Hanover and Saxony. For well over 300 years, including the bulk of the eighteenth century, its emperor was a Habsburg.

The direct authority of the Holy Roman Emperor outside his own lands was weak, partly due to the established autonomy of the states he governed, and partly because the position of emperor was elective, which allowed opportunities for states and institutions to wrangle concessions in return for their vote. But the emperor's role was more than ceremonial. If any rulers within the Empire attempted to abuse their position with regards to their own citizens or the interests of their neighbours, the aggrieved parties could appeal to the emperor who would recruit support from the rest of the Empire to put them back in their place. In this way, the stability and order of the region could be policed. Such was its composition that no one state had the power to resist the combined will of the rest. It also gave the emperor an important position of influence to obtain support amongst the Imperial states for his own interests, as in the case of the War of the Polish Succession (1733–1738). Despite its ramshackle appearance, the fact that this arrangement endured for so long was testimony to its effectiveness. It took the ambitions of Frederick II, the impatience of Joseph II, and the intervention of Napoleon, to finally bring it to an end.

The Habsburg dynasty was established in the eleventh century. The greatest extent of its territorial reach occurred in the sixteenth century under Charles

V (1519–1556). Its domains included Spain, Flanders, Sardinia, much of Italy and parts of France, in addition to its possessions in central Europe. It also claimed vast territories in the Americas. After Charles V, the dynasty split into two branches: Austrian and Spanish. In the eighteenth century, succession disputes involving these two branches were to plunge Europe into years of devastating warfare. Charles II of Spain (1661–1700) died childless in 1700, sparking the War of the Spanish Succession (1701–1714). Competing dynastic claims between the French Bourbons and Austrian Habsburgs had combined with fears amongst other nations, notably Britain, that too much power could end up in the hands of one family. The death of Augustus II (1709–1733) led to the War of the Polish Succession, seeing the French and Spanish Bourbons line up in support of Stanislas Leszczyński, (1677–1766), the father-in-law of Louis XV (1715–1774), against the Austrian Habsburgs and the Holy Roman Empire. A couple of years later began the War of the Austrian Succession, in which Bavaria, France and Prussia contested Maria Theresa's right as a daughter to inherit the Habsburg territories from her father, Emperor Charles VI (1711–1740). One and a half million souls are estimated to have perished as a result of these three conflicts alone, out of a European population in 1750 of around 140 million (more than 1 per cent).

The Ottoman Turks began their conquest of the Balkans in the fourteenth century, and by the end of the fifteenth century it was complete. They then moved into central Europe, reaching as far as Vienna. Following defeat by the Habsburg Monarchy at the Battle of Zenta in 1697, the Ottoman Turks were pushed back south out of Hungary and Transylvania. For much of the eighteenth century the Ottoman economy was growing, as was that of most of Europe. Tax-farming reforms had led to a loosening of centralised power and a rise in the influence of provincial notables in a mutually beneficial relationship with the state. Up to the middle of the century its military was able to hold its own but by the 1760s it had fallen behind its European rivals in matters of training, organisation and technology, as the devastating Ottoman-Russian War (1768–1774) was to demonstrate. As with 1697, this was to be another decisive turning point for the Ottomans in Europe, destabilising as it did their control over the Balkans and resulting in a dramatic regional shift of power in Russia's favour. By the end of the eighteenth century, central authority from Constantinople had significantly collapsed with military officers, known as captains, in control of what were essentially their own private armies.

The west

It was the English-dominated British Isles that witnessed the greatest transformation of a state's fortunes. In the middle of the seventeenth century, tormented by civil war and political instability, England was a second-rank power. By the beginning of the nineteenth century the United Kingdom of Great Britain and Ireland, as it became in 1801, was the most successful nation in Europe.

Casanova lived in London from 1763 to 1764, travelling there to unite Teresa Imer with her son but also on the lookout for a business opportunity, one that was probably lottery-shaped. London was now very prosperous, after all. One observation and one anecdote recorded by Casanova indicate why.

First the observation. Describing his journey from Dover to London, Casanova celebrates English transportation: 'I admired the beauty of the carriages that are provided by the post to those who travel without having one of their own, the fairness of the prices, the ease of payment, the speed, always at a trot, never a gallop.'[1] Later on he notes, 'nothing's more beautiful than the roads of England.'[2] High praise indeed from such a well-seasoned traveller. From the 1730s onwards, numerous Turnpike Acts and Turnpike Trusts resulted in an extensive network of fast and efficient highways. It took 256 hours to travel from Edinburgh to London in 1700; it took 60 hours by 1800.[3] On the other hand, roads for much of Europe were badly maintained and impassable in poor weather or for larger, heavier vehicles. That is if roads existed at all. Travel was typically uncomfortable, time-consuming and expensive. Internal customs barriers and tolls, absent in Great Britain apart from turnpikes, made matters worse. To be able to move yourself and your goods in a timely manner from A to B at reasonable cost gave you a significant competitive edge. But good roads did not just happen. If it takes a village to raise a child, it takes a well-organised state to produce effective transport infrastructure.

Unlike other countries that enjoyed the benefits of a centralised state, Great Britain's was not an absolute monarchy. But its ruling elite was remarkably small. Since England's Glorious Revolution (1688) and the Bill of Rights (1689), the British sovereign ruled under the authority of Parliament. Although it was a representative body, both of its constituent parts – the House of Lords and the House Commons – were controlled by fewer than 200 peers and their families throughout the eighteenth century. The influence of these landowning mercantile families, and the interests of the landowning class in general, went deep into local government. In Great Britain, there were few other sources of competing authority of any political significance: the 1707 Act of Union, merging the Scottish and English Parliaments, had resolved one potential cause of instability; the Anglican Church was under the control of the state; and the Toleration Act of 1689 allowed freedom of worship to Protestant Nonconformists. Such a concentration of power facilitated legal, administrative, economic and social reforms conducive to business and commerce, which in other countries would have encountered much stronger resistance. For example, a growing population, which both increased demand for foodstuffs while suppressing the cost of labour, was to lead to a revolution in agricultural practice and the accumulation of enormous wealth for big landowners.

Next, the anecdote. Having lost fifteen guineas playing whist at a social gathering in London, Casanova paid off his debt with gold. He was taken aside by one Lady Harrington as he left the table: 'With us, paying with hard cash [gold] is a little impolite, although easily forgiven in a foreigner.'[4] Casanova was expected to pay with banknotes. He discussed the incident later with an Italian friend called Martinelli who explained that British confidence in the value of paper money had been a key ingredient in its growing prosperity. 'By this policy,' Martinelli informs him, 'the English nation has doubled its currency. All the wealth it possesses in hard currency serves it for foreign trade, and it carries on its domestic trade with banknotes representative of the same real wealth.'[5]

Such financial arrangements, and the public's trust in them, gave the British a major advantage over their rivals. A professional bureaucracy enabled efficient assessment and collection of taxes, the reliable income from which could be used to pay for government-borrowing at low interest. Government debt was bought by, amongst others, those wealthy landowners who ran the country and who had oversight of state spending. It was a win-win: the rich received a guaranteed return on their investment in the knowledge that it enabled the government to raise huge sums of money to protect their interests. From the second half of the eighteenth century onwards, the country was able to use this financial muscle to subsidise the wars of its allies and amplify its military power. It was upon these political and financial foundations that Great Britain constructed a global trading and colonial empire cemented by the defeat of France in the Seven Years War, a conflict that was pivotal to the fates not only of France and Britain but of Prussia and Casanova.

The greatest European maritime power in the second half of the seventeenth century was the Dutch Republic which won its independence from the Habsburgs in 1588. The Republic was a technologically-advanced and unusually-urbanised society run by merchant-industrialists. It was also a Protestant state that valued freedom and tolerance. On a trip to Amsterdam in 1758, Casanova was informed by Esther, the teenage daughter of Monsieur DO, of the liberty granted to single women, and he was shortly afterwards amazed to discover that he was allowed to ride in a carriage with her unaccompanied.

Similar to Britain, the Dutch Republic's freedom from the Catholic Church and dynastic entanglements had helped to create an environment that was conducive to commerce. The extent of the Republic's trading and commercial dominance was staggering for a country of around two million. In 1670 it shipped more tonnage than England, France, the Holy Roman Empire, Portugal, Scotland and Spain, put together.[6] In the same year, 2,600 ships sailed under the Dutch Republic's flag. In 1700 the English merchant fleet numbered 1,400. The Dutch East India Company was the richest business enterprise in the world. Superior ships and streamlined shipbuilding techniques; better banking; insurance and financial services; low interest rates; sympathetic governing elites; the exploitation of colonial possessions; control of strategic shipping routes; and the coercion of trading partners to grant its merchants preferential status, all contributed to its remarkable success. In addition, the Dutch Republic enjoyed a diverse range of highly productive industries including agriculture, fishing and textiles.

From the early eighteenth century, rivals began to erode the Dutch Republic's supremacy. The Republic was beginning to stagnate after a period of rapid growth, its size of population remaining unchanged while much of the rest of Europe grew. British and French colonial trade expanded dramatically. The War of the Spanish Succession, and maintaining armed forces, had forced the Republic to incur a costly national debt from which they gained little. Worse, the need to service their debt through high taxation reduced their competitiveness. By contrast, Britain acquired Gibraltar and Minorca, considerably strengthening its presence in the Mediterranean. Countries began to exclude foreign ships from their ports, disproportionately affecting the Republic, while Scandinavian and Hanseatic rivals ate into their trade in the Baltic. As the century wore on, the Dutch Republic began to shift away from manufacturing to finance. It was for reasons of finance that Casanova had visited Amsterdam in 1758, on a secret mission for the French government to raise funds by selling government securities.

At the end of the seventeenth century, the dominant continental power was France although by mid-eighteenth century its relative strength was on the wane. Estimated to be twenty-one million in 1700, it was the most populous country in Europe, only eclipsed in the second half of the century by Russia due to territorial expansion. By comparison, England and Wales had a population of around five to six million. Likewise, on land the French military was usually the most powerful. It could also be particularly brutal. Louis XIV's systematic wasting of the Palatinate incurred long-lasting hatred amongst the Germans and helped to fuel German nationalism. France exerted immense cultural influence across Europe through its political, economic and commercial power, royal patronage of the arts, most notably in the creation of Versailles, and its scientific and intellectual achievements, such as Denis Diderot's *Encyclopedia*. French was the prestige language of the educated classes and Casanova himself wrote most of his works in French. As an aspiring cleric in Rome, it was made clear to him that it was a language he had to know.

France was fundamentally a wealthy country, although its wealth was unevenly distributed. Bad harvests and the costs of war in the final decades of Louis XIV's reign had caused enormous hardship for the majority but under Louis XV and Louis XVI the economy recovered and experienced a boom from the 1750s until the mid-1780s, when France was hit by an agricultural and industrial downturn. Public finances were a mess, typified by short-term fixes to meet the costs of war. One method France used to raise money was the creation and selling of government offices, which became the personal property of the owner to sell or hand down to their heirs. By the 1780s, there were 50,000 of these.[7] Often, the holder was exempt from taxes, compounding the problem of raising revenue in the longer term. Tax collection itself was inefficient. Tax farmers bought the privilege of collecting taxes, paying a lump sum up front to the government and keeping for themselves the difference between what they paid and what they raised. Finances were so precarious that it was increasingly difficult to raise loans, and the interest rates on what could be borrowed were high. By 1787 France had run out of money, triggering the events that culminated in the French Revolution.

The southern neighbour and great rival of France was Spain. The Spanish Empire was still a significant force but had been in decline since its peak over a century earlier, weakened by continuous warfare, internal divisions between the kingdom of Castile and those of Aragon, Catalonia and Valencia, and a series of inadequate monarchs stretching from Philip IV (1621–1665) to the death of Ferdinand VI (1746–1759). In the seventeenth century, Spain lost Holland and Portugal, as well as territories to France, while at the beginning of the eighteenth century the Peace of Utrecht (1713–1715) deprived Spain of Flanders, Gibraltar, Minorca and its Italian possessions. Beyond Europe, the Dutch Republic, English and French were a constant threat to its interests, attacking treasure fleets and capturing land. But in Ferdinand's successor Charles III (1759–1788), Spain finally possessed a ruler who was able to implement the kinds of much-needed reforms that had been pursued by the likes of Frederick II and Maria Theresa.

Economically, Spain was something of a backwater. It was dogged by low agricultural productivity, poor overland transport, and rigid traditions. It was a conservative and oppressively devout Catholic society closely supervised by the Spanish Inquisition, as is clear from Casanova's memoirs. Casanova had arrived in Spain in 1767, planning to take advantage of Charles III's ambitions to modernise the country. He was, in particular, hoping to be made the governor of a new colony that was being planned for the mountainous region of Sierra Morena, to be populated by Swiss immigrants. Unfortunately, 'a monstrous indiscretion' in which he betrayed the confidence of an influential friend, made him unwelcome in Madrid, and his chances of obtaining the governorship vanished.[8]

The Baltic and the east

The Swedish Empire suffered a much steeper and absolute decline. Brilliant military success under the reign of Gustavus Adolphus (1611–1632), particularly during the Thirty Years War (1618–1648), laid the foundations for a Swedish Empire that dominated the Baltic and much of northern Europe until the early eighteenth century. Sweden was a Protestant state, comparatively centralised, and with an efficient bureaucracy. Its politics were dominated by landed nobility although, uniquely in Europe, the peasantry enjoyed representation in the national diet. The strength of Sweden's army rested upon conscription, to which all social ranks were liable. The army numbered 110,000 in 1708 (10 per cent of military-age males) from a population of around one and a half to two million. Its economy was based upon agriculture, and trade in iron and copper.

As the fortunes of war made the Swedish Empire, so they destroyed it. In 1700 began the Great Northern War which was to last over twenty years. An alliance of Denmark, Poland and Russia attacked Sweden with a view to carving up its Baltic territories. Under 17-year-old Charles XII (1697–1718) and with Anglo-Dutch support, the Swedish proved to be more resilient than expected, forcing Denmark and Poland out of the war. Then Charles launched an attack against Russia in 1707 in an attempt to break up the Russian Empire, but a heavy defeat in 1709 to Peter I, at Poltava in present day Ukraine, put an end to any realistic chance of success. Rather than accepting the inevitable, the Swedes struggled on. From 1719 a series of peace treaties ending with the Treaty of Nystad (1721) divided up most of the Swedish Empire amongst Hanover, Brandenburg-Prussia, and Russia, the latter taking the lion's share and becoming the major power in the region.

Poland, or the Polish-Lithuanian Commonwealth, at its largest extent in the early seventeenth century, covered a huge territory east of the Holy Roman Empire, Habsburg Monarchy and Ottoman Empire. It was a major force, more important than Russia, made up of a union between the Kingdom of Poland and the Grand Duchy of Lithuania. Poland was distinguished by a monarchy elected by the nobility. All nobles possessed this right, although in practice, the election was controlled by a small, wealthy oligarchy. The power of the kings themselves was circumscribed. Limits were placed on the size of a standing army that a king could raise. The nobility as a whole was very large, making up a tenth of the population, with most of the rest of the population reduced to serfdom. The combination of an elective monarchy and a serf economy was to be a serious disadvantage. The former encouraged factionalism and foreign interference, and undermined the creation of a stable, centralised state. The latter inhibited the development of commerce and industry. Foreign rivals, notably absolute monarchies, grew wealthier and more able to exploit their country's resources for military ends.

By the eighteenth century the vulnerability of the Polish state was clear. Its independence rested increasingly upon dynastic-based alliances – notably with France – regional balances of power, and calculations of self-interest amongst neighbours who were willing for it to remain independent but weak. By the time of Stanislas II (1764–1795) Poland was essentially a vassal state of Russia and, indeed, the new king was the appointment favoured by Catherine II. Unexpectedly, Stanislas began to implement government reforms to strengthen Poland's administration, finances and military; an unwanted development as far as Russia was concerned. An uprising in 1768 by Russian Orthodox Christians on the issue of religious tolerance gave Catherine a pretext to intervene, setting off a civil war. It resulted in the First Partition of Poland (1772) in which Russia, Prussia and the Habsburg Monarchy shared between themselves almost a third of its territory. The Polish-Lithuanian Commonwealth was then partitioned on two more occasions – 1793 and 1795 – extinguishing the Commonwealth entirely. Over 60 per cent of the lands went to Russia, almost 20 per cent to Prussia, and the remainder to the Habsburg Monarchy.

It was on 10 October 1765, during this decisive period following the election of Stanislas, that Casanova arrived in Warsaw, down on his luck and having failed to find joy in Prussia or Russia, despite meetings with both of their illustrious sovereigns. In Poland he got to know Stanislas well, spending many hours in conversation with him, and even composing two sonnets which were published in a collection of works to celebrate the monarch's birthday. The Venetian was referred to as 'Professor Casanova', and it appears that the king commissioned him to write a history of Poland (which he was to do). Understandably, Casanova was optimistic that he would find employment at the court but in June the following year the renowned Parisian salonnière,

Madame Geoffrin, a good friend of Stanislas, came to visit and poured poison in his ear against Casanova, getting him expelled.

Russia was one of the big winners in the eighteenth century. In the early seventeenth century, there were still doubts amongst some over whether it could even be regarded as part of Europe. This vast country is estimated to have had a population of only seven million in 1650; a third that of France, and about the same as Spain. Fuelled by growing western European demand for commodities, the Russian economy began to expand and modernise. Although it was becoming integrated with Europe through trade, Russia was a marginal land of marginal significance to most Europeans. This was to change entirely.

By the eighteenth century, Russia was governed by an absolute monarch and the Orthodox Christian Church was in the hands of the state. Under the reign of Peter I, Russia's acquisitions along the Baltic and the founding of St Petersburg (1703) turned the country westwards, with a marked increase in trade as a consequence. Peter looked to emulate the west culturally, even in details such as appearance, dress and aristocratic titles. Catherine II similarly promoted an image of herself as an enlightened monarch and patron of the arts with a court that could compare with any in Europe. Like Poland, much of the economy was based upon serfdom, a condition which in Russia became increasingly severe as the century wore on. A noble's wealth was not calculated by ownership of land but ownership of serfs. The nobility itself was entirely subservient to its Tsar or Tsarina; under Peter their position and success had become tied to the service they performed for the state. In the second half of the century, under the reign of Catherine, victories over the Ottoman Turks in the south gave Russia access to the Mediterranean through the Black Sea, while the partitioning of Poland expanded the empire further west. Russia was now a maritime power as well as a land power. By 1800 its population stood at around thirty-seven million, the largest in Europe.

Chapter 6

The Seven Years War: 1756–1763

'The last struggle had exhausted her. I made her do the straight tree and in this position I lifted her up to devour her cabinet of love which I couldn't otherwise reach, wanting her to devour in turn the weapon which wounded her to death without depriving her of her life.'

Giacomo Casanova, *History of My Life*

On 29 May 1753, 28-year-old Casanova returned to Venice having spent three years abroad, quickly falling in love with the young and innocent CC. When he approached her family with a view to marriage her father refused. For all his sophistication, high-society contacts and extravagant life-style, Casanova had few solid prospects. CC's father preferred to wait until his teenage daughter was older and Casanova had established a career. He had CC confined to a convent for four years, to be on the safe side. There she began a romance with 22-year-old MM, a libertine nun of patrician stock. MM became aware of Casanova, who continued to write to CC and would make visits to her church for mass so that she could see him. A passionate affair ensued after MM expressed her interest in Casanova through clandestine messages. MM would escape the convent for an evening, and the pair would meet up at a luxurious casino. Eventually CC joined in.

But there was another party in this mix, a hidden presence who had in all likelihood orchestrated their meeting and who, on the occasion Casanova described above, had watched the two of them make love from a concealed room. This was MM's influential patron, the man who was later also to be Casanova's patron, the recently-appointed French ambassador to Venice, 38-year-old Abbé François-Joachim de Pierre Bernis, destined to become one of the most powerful men in France and, ultimately, a cardinal.

De Bernis was the younger son of a noble family that had fallen on hard times. He was educated at the prestigious Louis-le-Grand college in Paris, before moving on to study for the priesthood at Saint Sulpice (hence abbé, referring to his tonsure and black gown) but who had to leave when he was 19 due to the family's finances. Nonetheless, his noble birth, intelligence, ready wit and affable nature opened doors for him. He acquired some celebrity as a poet, was befriended by Voltaire and was elected to the Académie Française in 1744. The following year, de Bernis joined the entourage of Madame de Pompadour, newly promoted to the position of Louis XV's chief mistress, de Bernis becoming one of her favourites. At this time the War of the Austrian Succession was in full flow.

Establishing himself in court circles as a promising talent, albeit lazy, de Bernis was awarded the position of French Ambassador to Venice on which to cut his teeth, taking up the post in August 1752. His primary aim was to enhance his reputation in Versailles. De Bernis was a pleasure-seeker like Casanova. Contrary to his claim in his memoirs that 'the Venetians were astonished after a time to find me insensible to the charms of women', there is evidence from more than one source to suggest the opposite.[1,2] Given his position, it might not be unreasonable to speculate that his willingness to become Casanova's patron was in part motivated by a desire to ensure the Venetian's discretion.

Prelude to war

The key European figure in both the Seven Years War and the War of the Austrian Succession was Frederick II of Brandenburg-Prussia. In the mid-seventeenth century it was one of the larger entities of the Holy Roman Empire, and under the rule of the Hohenzollern dynasty. Brandenburg-Prussia was larger than the Electorate of Saxony, on the Electorate of Brandenburg's southern border, although less wealthy. Like Saxony, its ruler was one of the Imperial electors. It was a composite of territories spread across northern Europe, ducal East Prussia residing outside the Empire in the north of Poland, and separated from Brandenburg by West Prussia. Starting with Frederick William (the Great Elector, 1640–1688) a series of effective Hohenzollern rulers consolidated its political, military and fiscal position. In 1701, as a reward for supporting the emperor with 8,000 Brandenburg soldiers, Elector Frederick III (1688–1713) was allowed to give himself the royal title of Frederick I, King in Prussia (not 'of' Prussia because West Prussia was a province under the sovereignty of Poland). Elevation to royal status was an important goal for princes of the Holy Roman Empire, for reasons of power, not merely appearance. In the dynastic interplay of the time, the two were intimately connected. When 28-year-old Frederick II inherited the throne in May 1740, his father had bequeathed to him one of Europe's best-trained armies and a healthy war chest, both of which the new king intended to make full use. Frederick's long-term objective was to turn Prussia into the dominant German power.

Frederick himself was motivated by the pursuit of personal glory no matter how terrible the cost, and more recent scholarship has brought into question his brilliance as a military leader. For Franz Szabo, it was more by luck than skill that Prussia was not entirely destroyed by his actions, and much of the military credit that he took for himself should have gone to his generals. Szabo makes this damning assessment: 'Frederick was an opportunist and risk taker dressed in the veneer of an intellectual, but at root he was a heartless killer and a mean-spirited and callous man who was careless of human lives.'[3]

The War of the Austrian Succession was triggered by Frederick's invasion of the rich Habsburg province of Silesia in December 1740. Silesia was of immense economic and strategic importance and was located on the eastern borders of Saxony and Bohemia. Its conquest gave Prussia control of the river Oder and a formidable network of fortresses. It increased Prussia's population by over one million (roughly 50 per cent) and contributed around 40 per cent to the state's income. Previously, in October, Emperor Charles VI had died without a direct male heir but arrangements had long been in place to deal with this eventuality in the form of the Pragmatic Sanction of 1713, enabling his daughter, Maria Theresa, to inherit. Irrespective, Frederick saw it as an opportunity to seize some valuable real estate, supported by France looking to weaken its traditional enemy. The alliance systems in place ensured that the whole of Europe was dragged to war. At the end of eight bloody years, Frederick had hung on to Silesia but had shown himself to be a man who was willing to play fast and loose with international commitments. The war paused because the main protagonists were financially exhausted and feared bankruptcy. But the conflicts between them were unresolved: the Habsburg Monarchy refused to accept the loss of Silesia, and the colonial rivalry between France, Spain and Britain remained hot.

De Bernis left Venice at the end of May 1755, having transformed himself into a skilful diplomat. Bolstered by his close friendship with Pompadour, from September he was entrusted by Louis XV with what was to become known as the Diplomatic Revolution of 1756, the most dramatic change in the structure of European alliances for 300 years. The competing powers in the War of the Austrian Succession understood that the peace treaties of Aix-La-Chapelle that supposedly ended the conflict in 1748 were no more than a truce. Over the previous centuries, sets of alliances had developed, centred on the rivalry between the Habsburgs and the Bourbons. These coalitions maintained an equilibrium that prevented any one state or dynasty acquiring too much power. The Habsburgs were the main threat initially but later it became France under Louis XIV. Sweden, Poland and the Ottomans typically allied with France, while Britain and the Dutch Republic threw their weight behind the Habsburg Monarchy. The latter also engaged Russia to counter threats in the east.

By 1755 the diplomatic ground was shifting. The old coalitions were under strain. Prussia's unreliability was alienating France, and Louis XV disliked Frederick II. Maria Theresa in Vienna was unhappy at the extent to which London was willing to discard its interests in order to negotiate peace, while London was unhappy with Vienna's constant demand for subsidies. France and Britain would have preferred not to go to war but colonial disputes made it increasingly likely. At the same time, the French alliance with Prussia posed a serious threat to the key British interests of Hanover, whose ruler was George II, and to the commercially vital Austrian Netherlands. Britain's objective under the Duke of Newcastle, therefore, was to maintain the peace in central Europe in order to be able to concentrate on France. But Newcastle failed to recognise the extent to which Frederick had changed the dynamics of European politics. In St Petersburg, Prussia was marked as a serious danger to Russian interests, while Maria Theresa's chancellor, Wenzel Anton von Kaunitz, had successfully urged the Empress to prioritise the interests of the Monarchy's core states of Austria, Bohemia and Hungary over less defensible territories such as those in Italy and the Netherlands. This reorganised priority of interests made Prussia its main enemy rather than France, and their primary aim the recovery of Silesia.

Having obtained the backing of Maria Theresa, Kaunitz attempted to bring about a reconciliation with France. As Anglo-French colonial hostilities escalated, de Bernis describes how divisions in court became intense over what action to take towards Britain's erstwhile ally: 'All the court, not excepting the women, hotly supported either one side or another.'[4] The public itself was pro-Frederick, especially the *philosophes* (French Enlightenment public intellectuals), seduced as they were by his Enlightenment credentials. It is clear from de Bernis' memoirs that French government was mired to a paralysing degree in factionalism and vainglorious squabbling. But Louis XV was sympathetic towards Kaunitz's position, and agreed to investigate the possibility of reaching an understanding. In 1755 Louis directed de Bernis to enter into secret meetings with the Austrian ambassador instead of his foreign minister, Antoine Louis Rouillé, who inclined towards Prussia. Little progress was made at the beginning, with de Bernis listing reasons why the king should have been sceptical about Kaunitz's overtures.

It was during these discussions that de Bernis discovered that Britain and Prussia were themselves in negotiations, the fruit of which was to be the Convention of Westminster of 16 January 1756: a neutrality pact in which both parties agreed to respect the territories of the other. Britain wanted to avoid being pulled into a European land war, while Frederick wanted to avoid facing a coalition of British, Russian and Habsburg Monarchy forces. The agreement turned out to be a serious error. With war between France and Britain likely, France would be isolated (Sweden and Poland were by now military minnows). The result was the signing of the first Treaty of Versailles on 1 May 1756, a defensive alliance between France and the Habsburg Monarchy. The French were optimistic that this alliance of old enemies would ensure peace on the continent, allowing them to focus on Britain. Less than three weeks later, the French invasion and conquest of Minorca provoked Britain to declare war.

In 1737 Casanova's mother had left Venice for the last time to live and perform in Dresden in the service of the Elector of Saxony. She took with her Casanova's 8-year-old brother, Giovanni, who was eventually to become director of Dresden's Academy of Fine Arts. They were later joined by Casanova's sister, Maria Maddelena, who married a court musician. Casanova himself visited in 1752 for several months, and, while he was there, wrote a parody of Racine's *The Enemy Brothers* which was performed for the king, who apparently thoroughly enjoyed it. Casanova notes, 'I saw at Dresden the most brilliant court in Europe.'[5] Less than four years later the 'ruin of Saxony' was to begin.

The result of Frederick II's misjudgement meant that he was facing the combined might of France, Russia, the Habsburg Monarchy and much of the Holy Roman Empire with only the support of Britain, a predominantly maritime power, and Hanover. The odds were not good but not as overwhelming as might appear on paper. Prussia was geared for war. The eighteenth-century political philosopher Montesquieu wryly observed that it was not a country with an army but an army with a country. 80 per cent of the government's revenues went to the military in some way or other. Typically, European states aimed for a soldier-to-civilian ratio of 1 in a 100. For Prussia it was 1 in 30, rising to 1 in 14 by 1760. Other considerable advantages were internal supply lines, and a united military and political leadership in the person of Frederick himself. By contrast, his opponents were beset by political division, conflicting objectives, personal animosities and senior generals who owed their positions as much to social rank and political favouritism as to merit. A despairing de Bernis was later to write: 'the same intrigues and the same personal aims thwarted all the operations of our armies.'[7] Other enduring problems were long, vulnerable supply lines and the inability to hold on to territorial gains over winter due to logistical constraints. The Russians in particular lost large numbers of men to illness before they even reached the theatre of operations.

One way Frederick enhanced his resources was to pillage mercilessly the lands that he conquered and was unlikely to hold in the long term, notably Saxony.

His generals would resort to hostage taking and destroy, or threaten to destroy, civilian areas in order to extort money and supplies. Men would be dragooned into his armies, and young women shipped off to assist in the repopulation of Pomerania. When Frederick discovered in Saxony the dies to mint Polish coins, he debased the currency so badly that the economy of Poland, a neutral country, was wrecked. Even by the standards of the day, contemporaries were shocked by the harm and damage that Frederick was prepared to inflict. It should be pointed out that the Electorate of Saxony, whose king had been the elected king of Poland since 1697, had been Brandenburg-Prussia's primary enemy until it was replaced by the Habsburg Monarchy following the War of the Austrian Succession. Poland was huge, and Saxony, small by comparison, was economically advanced. Skilfully exploited, the combination offered the possibility of Saxony becoming the dominant regional power. Importantly, the two states were separated by Silesia, so Frederick's capture of it, as long as he could keep possession of his conquest, had the added benefit of preventing the three territories being united into a single bloc.

1756 and 1757

Recognising that his enemies would strike soon, Frederick judged that his best chance of success was to act first. On 29 August 1756, he invaded the Electorate of Saxony. Not only would its conquest add to Frederick's own resources, including control of the river Elbe, but it would also reduce those of his opponents and deny them a base from which to launch their own campaigns. He wanted to knock out the Habsburg Monarchy, his most dangerous foe, as quickly as possible. Saxony itself was quickly overrun, and for the next three years Dresden was held captive. In September Frederick moved into Bohemia and Moravia. He had a habit of underestimating the abilities of his opponents and, under the wonderfully-named Irish Field Marshall Maximilian Ulysses von Browne, the Habsburgs proved to be far more effective than he had expected, forcing him back into Saxony for the winter. Frederick's strategy had not only failed militarily but also diplomatically, helping to unite the coalition and making any attempts to detach the Russians futile.

As a result of the invasion, the Saxon court relocated to Poland. Zanetta was pensioned off and fled to Bohemia, remaining in Prague for the rest of the war before returning. Because of the war, her pension seems not to have been paid, and at some point Casanova began sending her money. The long-term impact upon Saxony was devastating. Out of a population of two million, it is estimated that up to 100,000, or 5 per cent, were killed. Its economy and finances were destroyed, taking decades to recover. And its significance as a regional power was permanently damaged. Of Prussia's entire spending on the war, a third was paid for by Saxony.

Meanwhile, Zanetta's eldest son had been locked up in Venice since 1755, a couple of months after the departure of de Bernis. On 1 November 1756, Casanova escaped and headed off to Paris, reaching the French capital just over two months later where he made a bee-line to visit MM's old protector and, for the last eighteen months, Louis' Foreign Minister in all but name. Not until 29 June 1757 did de Bernis become Louis' official Foreign Minister, after the Count de Stainville (the future Duke de Choiseul) had managed to contrive the resignation of the ageing Rouillé. It appeared that Rouillé had been left in place because his wife was so attached to the court. You can hear de Bernis' despair: 'One sees by this on what ridiculous considerations the fate of great affairs does sometimes depend. For two years it had been necessary to displace M. Rouillé, and yet from fear of vexing his wife, they preferred to compromise the interests of the greatest powers of Europe!'[8]

De Bernis welcomed Casanova with open arms and, indeed, he seemed to have been expecting him. Things were going well. Russia was on the verge of joining the alliance between France and the Habsburg Monarchy, and formally did so on 11 January 1757, a week after Casanova's arrival. But there had been a recent scare. There had been an attempt to assassinate the king on the day Casanova arrived. Fearing that he was close to death, Louis summoned his confessor and begged for absolution of his sins. In many minds, one of those sins was Madame de Pompadour. Suddenly her position, and that of de Bernis, promoted only days before to the King's Council, appeared under threat, and with it the whole diplomatic revolution of which she was such an avid supporter. Fortunately, the king recovered his senses and the danger passed. Two prominent anti-Habsburg ministers who had moved against Madame de Pompadour were dismissed.

As well as giving his fugitive friend 100 louis, de Bernis set about introducing Casanova to the most important figures at court, advising him to come up with some sort of plan that would raise money for the government. These figures included Pompadour herself, who remembered Casanova from his first visit to Paris, the Duke de Boulogne (Controller-General of Finances), the soon-to-be Duke de Choiseul (one of Pompadour's favourites, Ambassador to the Vatican and, shortly afterwards, to the Austrian Court), and financier Paris-Duverney (Administrator-General of Provisions). As it happened, the latter was in the process of trying to find money to support the Military School, which was established by himself and Pompadour to educate the sons of poor noble families. The political and fiscal pressures on the government caused by the war, highlighted by the tensions between the crown and the *parlement* of

Paris, led Duverney to seek out alternative ways of obtaining the millions of livres he needed.

Described by de Bernis as a financial expert, Casanova claimed that he had a plan which could raise such a sum. In fact, there was no plan and he understood little about finance, although he was an able mathematician. Believing he knew what the Venetian had in mind, Duverney invited him to a meeting of genuine experts, amongst whom Casanova decided to maintain a mysterious silence, at least initially. Duverney's hunch was that Casanova wanted to establish a lottery, a proposal which was being pushed at the time by a Monsieur de Calzabigi but which had met with resistance. Presented with Calzabigi's proposal, Casanova declared that his plan was the same but, unlike Calzabigi, he would be able to demonstrate that it would work. Here Casanova was on much firmer ground, having a strong grasp of probability, gambling psychology and the workings of lotteries. Upon later further examination, including by his friend the celebrated mathematician, Jean le Rond d'Alembert, he was able to convince the government, and the project went ahead with Casanova and Calzabigi as directors.

Casanova's discussions with officials shed an interesting light on the short-term mentality of the French state that so bedevilled its finances, and was to contribute to its ultimate overthrow. Their preference was to sell the lottery off for a fixed sum for others to organise and profit from, just as they did with taxation and many thousands of offices of state. Casanova insisted that to be successful it had to be backed directly by the crown. When quizzed about the danger of the government making a major loss on the first drawing, Casanova astounded his audience by admitting that not only was this possible but it would be extremely beneficial to the lottery's long-term success. This was a different, more modern, way of thinking, one which was sensitive to the perspective of the consumer. Indeed, the whole operation allowed far greater freedom and choice to purchasers than had ever been the case beforehand.

Royal authorisation was obtained on 14 October 1757, offices were opened on 15 February 1758, and the first drawing took place on 18 April 1758. It was France's first national lottery and a huge success – the biggest in Europe up to that point – triggering a lottery mania. The government may have been strapped for cash but the economy was prosperous and people had money to spend.

Sometime in April 1757, de Bernis enquired whether Casanova would be interested in carrying out secret missions. Casanova was agreeable to the idea, as long as he was paid. The money from the lottery was yet to roll in. Although he claims to have been a complete novice in this line, it may not have been the first time that he had worked for de Bernis. De Bernis had employed a network of informers as Venetian ambassador and it was feasible that Casanova was one of them. Casanova had been well-connected, after all.

An assignment duly turned up. Casanova was to visit Dunkirk, get to know the commanding officers of ten or twelve warships anchored there, and provide a detailed report on their state of readiness: supplies, munitions, crews, discipline, administration, and so on. It may be that France had got wind of British intentions to attack the French coast. At this time, the new Pitt-Newcastle administration was planning to strike French ports as a military diversion to support Frederick after his heavy defeat at Kolín in central Bohemia in 1757. On 8 September 1757, a fleet left Portsmouth to capture Rochefort. It was to be a million-pound fiasco.

In August 1757 Casanova set off. He understood that he would receive no support if anything went wrong. He quickly made the acquaintance of the army and navy officers in the town, posing as a Venetian expert on European navies. Within three days he had become good friends with all the captains, and they happily conducted him on tours of their ships. It was child's play to a man of Casanova's charm and boldness. It took him just a fortnight to gather all the information he needed. His report was well received and he was paid 500 Louis (12,000 livres). It has been estimated that the average annual wage in Paris in 1760 was around 450 livres.[9]

Casanova himself was scathing about the whole affair and the willingness of ministers to waste resources on an enterprise that any young officer would have done for simply the opportunity to impress. Referring to the practices of government departments and their officials, he writes 'Money which cost them nothing they lavished on their favourites and on those they liked. They were despots, the people were trampled upon, the state in debt, and the finances in such poor shape that the inevitable bankruptcy would have overthrown it. A revolution was necessary.'[10] There is an indication here of the inefficiency of French government, riddled as it was with cliques, favouritism and court politics. Louis XV maintained his own network of informers and agents, referred to as the King's Secret, which he would use to spy upon his court or conduct secret negotiations with foreign powers, sometimes contradicting the official policy being pursued by his ministers. Confusion, distrust and mismanagement were the inevitable result. It was all very costly. Whereas the Habsburg Monarchy and Prussia spent roughly 300 livres per soldier a year, France was spending 500 livres, two-thirds more.

1757 started off promisingly for the Franco-Habsburg-Russian alliance. Sweden came on side in March. It was not militarily significant but including a Reformed, confessional state would help to counter Frederick from portraying himself as a Protestant champion. Swedish operations in the north were little more than a sideshow throughout the war. On 1 May the second Treaty of Versailles was signed, committing France to an offensive alliance, not merely a defensive one as had been the case previously. Frederick was not sure how he should approach the new campaign but was persuaded by those closest to him that he needed to go on the offensive. On 18 April he launched an invasion of Bohemia, forcing the Habsburgs back towards Prague but once again encountering more resistance than expected. The attempt to take Prague failed, and on 18 June came the hammer blow of Kolín, a major defeat for which Frederick's poor generalship was responsible, forcing him to withdraw back to Saxony. Fortunately for him, the timid command of Charles of Lorraine meant that the Habsburgs failed to take full advantage of the disaster.

In the west, Frederick had to contend with the threat of the French. Their colonial war against the British had been going well and now in March 1757 the French began operations in Westphalia and Hanover. To combat this threat, the British provided the Army of Observation lead by the Duke of Cumberland, one of the sons of George II (1727–1760). Nonetheless, France made good progress and by the middle of August had taken control of Hanover under the Count d'Estrées, and then the Duke de Richelieu. In the same month the Imperial forces of the Holy Roman Empire and the French auxiliary army under Prince de Soubise, another Pompadour favourite, began to converge on Saxony. And in the east the Russians were on the move. Their advance was slow but when they did engage with the enemy they were dogged and effective, as they proved at the end of August when they defeated Prussian forces at Gross-Jägersdorf in East Prussia.

It was looking grim for Frederick, but in September the tide began to turn. Empress Elizabeth of Russia (1741–1762) suffered a stroke. Amidst fears that she might die, and with the political uncertainty that entailed, Russian forces drew back from East Prussia. It was a dire mistake. As well as letting the enemy off the hook, illness and inadequate provisions during the retreat resulted in large numbers of casualties. A lack of supplies eventually forced them to continue to withdraw so that by November they had returned to where they had begun in May. At the same time, Richelieu was running out of steam. His army was exhausted, there were supply problems and he was being obstructed by a diversionary force under the command of a brilliant rising talent, Duke Ferdinand of Brunswick, Frederick's brother-in-law. Then there was the battle of Rossbach in Saxony. On 5 November, Frederick defeated Franco-Imperial forces twice his size, the latter suffering 90 per cent of the casualties. The numbers engaged were not huge but it was still a striking victory. Frederick became a hero amongst Protestant German states as well as in Britain, the tangible benefits of which were an increased British subsidy and the replacement of Cumberland by Brunswick as commander of the Army of Observation. On 5 December, Frederick scored another major success. This was over the Habsburg-Imperial forces at Leuthen. By the end of 1757, nothing had been decided but Frederick was still in the game.

1758 and 1759

In Versailles, de Bernis was getting cold feet. He saw that the war was going badly and feared it would only get worse. Costs were escalating and royal finances were shot. De Bernis catalogued to Pompadour a long list of the difficulties confronting France, declaring that 'it was madness to continue a ruinous war.'[11] From the beginning of 1758 de Bernis began pushing for an armistice and peace negotiations but Louis XV, Pompadour, Vienna, and St Petersburg were determined to bring Frederick down, and preparations for the next campaign began. In fact, Russian operations had already begun. By the end of January 1758 East Prussia was under Russian control. Richelieu was replaced by Louis Count de Clermont but the Army of Westphalia was in a poor state and the French were forced to withdraw all the way back to the Rhine under pressure from Brunswick.

Frederick was ready to begin his new campaign by mid-April. His objective was to attack the Habsburg Monarchy via Moravia and Bohemia. It started well enough but Frederick's forces got bogged down attempting to take the Moravian town of Olmütz. A Habsburg force under the skilful, if cautious, Leopold von Daun was sent to lift the siege. Outmanoeuvred by Daun, hit by the loss of a major supply convoy attacked at Domstadl, and generally a victim of his own poor planning, on 1 July Frederick had to abandon Olmütz and over the next six weeks was forced to retreat back to Silesia.

The Anglo-Prussian alliance was having more success in the west. British naval forces attacked the French coast in concert with an assault by Brunswick across the Rhine. Benefitting from poor communication and cooperation amongst French officers and their commanders, Brunswick was able to inflict an embarrassing defeat on the larger French army at the Battle of Crefeld on 23 June 1758.

Russian progress under General Fermor was slow due to organisational weaknesses but by 26 July they were close to Frankfurt. Attempts to co-ordinate actions between the Russians and Habsburgs were problematic, however, as Fermor was preoccupied with making sure that his forces could be provisioned. In early August, Frederick moved to confront the Russian threat and at the inconclusive Battle of Zorndorf on 25 August both sides took heavy losses. After the encounter, for various reasons, but one of them being Fermor's suspicion that the Habsburgs were letting the Russians take the brunt of the fighting, Fermor adopted a more defensive mentality, much to the frustration of St Petersburg and Vienna. Brunswick continued to obstruct the French, while in Saxony, Frederick's calamitous judgement led to a significant reverse at Hochkirch at the hands of Daun. The war ebbed and flowed. The 1758 campaign finished without a breakthrough, although Frederick's capacity to take offensive action in the future had been much diminished.

De Bernis continued to press the case for peace when there was an opportunity to do so, both at home and abroad. Each setback, such as defeat at Crefeld and the major colonial loss of Louisbourg on 26 July, only strengthened his conviction. De Bernis' relationship with Pompadour, who was still fully behind the war, suffered as a result. Key members of the royal family were also opposed to peace negotiations, including the king's favourite daughter, Elizabeth, Duchess of Parma. De Bernis' position as Foreign Minister was becoming untenable. On 8 October, less than a week after he received the cardinal's hat from Clement XIII, he resigned, to be replaced by the Duke de Choiseul. De Bernis remained for the moment as a member of the Council of State, where he attempted to reform government administration, in particular the chaos of departmental finances.

It was around this time that Casanova presented to de Bernis a plan to raise funds through brokers in Amsterdam, and to ease some of France's financial burden. The idea was to exchange French government securities for those of another country whose credit worthiness was better and would be more readily accepted on the French money markets. With the support of de Bernis and Choiseul, Casanova was given the go ahead to exchange 20 million livres, as long as any loss, which they would inevitably have to make, was kept to a minimum. This was not a small sum. In June, de Bernis had claimed that the government did not have two million livres to send a French army to campaign in Bohemia.

Casanova left Paris on 14 October 1758, returning in early January, his mission accomplished. He had succeeded gloriously, so much so that he seems to have single-handedly resurrected the Parisian bond market. Casanova's own stock rose considerably. There are suggestions that he may have been offered French nationality. While he was in Amsterdam, he engaged in some personal financial dealings on behalf of Madame d'Urfé (because the Paris Exchange had no money) whose gratitude earned him 12,000 livres. In addition, he received a colossal windfall from a Dutch banker for information Casanova divined from his oracle, and which, fortuitously, happened to be correct, making the banker a profit of 3,000,000 florins. When the Controller-General Boulogne learned that Casanova held bills of exchange worth 600,000 livres (10 per cent of the banker's profit), he declined to give him his brokerage fee.

A few weeks after Casanova's return to Paris, de Bernis encouraged him to visit the Controller-General, who had been asking after him. He no doubt wanted to see if there were any more financial rabbits that the celebrated Venetian could pull out of his hat. This would be entirely plausible given the desperate state of French finances. It seems that Casanova had been snubbing Boulogne because of the latter's refusal to pay him his fee. As it happened, the Venetian did possess another rabbit. Casanova suggested a law in which the first year's income from an inherited estate that had not passed from father to son would be taken by the crown. The same law would apply to gifts. Boulogne was happy with the proposal and assured him that his fortune was made. Unfortunately, Boulogne was replaced a week later by Étienne de Silhouette. Casanova claims that his plan was put into action two years later but that he was not paid a penny for it.

On 13 December, de Bernis was dismissed from the Council of State and was sent into exile, as was customary for those who lost the king's favour. In de Bernis' case this was to his abbey of Vic-sur-Aisne. His time by Louis' side seems to have been a trial, beset as he was by rivalries, crushing workload, ill-health, the obstructive practices of Rouillé, and the loss of his close friendship with Pompadour. De Bernis observes ruefully, 'I have always had more difficulty in negotiating with my own court than with foreign courts.'[12] He claims that he was never ambitious but motivated solely by duty to his king and service to his country, describing his promotion to Foreign Minister as a 'fatal obligation'.[13]

The aim of de Bernis' replacement, Choiseul, was to achieve a decisive victory over the British in the 1759 campaign. To this end, in the Third Treaty of Versailles, he scaled back France's obligations to the Habsburg Monarchy, although it was still committed to providing an army of 100,000 men. All participants were struggling with the costs of the war, and even the deep pockets of the British, upon which Frederick increasingly relied, were under strain. The financial position of the French was becoming critical. Choiseul introduced economising measures, there were new taxes, and only nine months in post, the disappointing Silhouette was replaced. In the end, money was found for Choiseul's audacious new plan. The colonial war was going badly and French commerce, in particular, was suffering. Choiseul decided a more direct approach was needed. France would invade Britain. Soubise, whom Casanova had met at Pompadour's private apartments in Versailles, was to take command of the operation.

Under the Marquis de Contades and the Duke de Broglie, the French campaign on the continent began well with a rare victory over Brunswick on 13 April, at Bergen near Frankfurt. The French continued to move north into Westphalia as the Anglo-Hanoverian army withdrew. Versailles was optimistic that 1759 might mark the end of the continental war. But on 1 August at Minden, Brunswick lured Contades from a near impregnable position and inflicted a heavy defeat, forcing the French to retreat. By 7 September they were back almost all the way to Frankfurt. French hopes of a breakthrough were in shreds and the inevitable in-fighting began. Contades was replaced by Broglie but his attempts in November to go on the offensive got no-where. Worse still, in the same month, Admiral Hawke defeated Count de Conflan's Brest fleet at Quiberon Bay. On top of the defeat of the French Mediterranean fleet at the Battle of Lagos in the previous August, any realistic prospect of invading Britain was over.

Further east, Frederick's self-inflicted losses were leaving Prussia facing disaster, only salvaged by Brunswick's successes against France, his brother Prince Henry and the on-going distrust in the field between Russia and the Habsburg Monarchy. The respective courts of St Petersburg and Vienna had agreed upon an operational plan for the new season, with the focus on Saxony and Silesia. Fermor was replaced by General Saltykov. Frederick, for his part, resorted to disruption tactics such as raiding supply depots, cutting supply lines and bribing enemy commanders. He tried unsuccessfully to involve the Ottomans to distract the Habsburgs in the south. In July, Frederick pressurised his generals to attack the Russians, and Lieutenant-General Wedell did just that, going down to a heavy defeat against a much larger Russian army at Paltzig, situated in present day Poland. Then on 12 August 1759, the king's own poor command resulted in an even more grievous loss at the hands of Russo-Habsburg forces at Kunersdorf. But yet again, to the dismay of St Petersburg and Vienna, their armies were unable to cooperate to press home their advantage. Saltykov withdrew to winter quarters while Frederick and Prince Henry were able to do enough to occupy the Habsburgs and avert an advance on Berlin. The season ended with another serious military blunder by Frederick, despite warnings from his officers and direct protest from his brother, which led to defeat at the Battle of Maxen on 19 November, the consequence of which was that the Habsburgs were able to entrench themselves in Saxony.

1760 and 1761

In September 1759 Casanova had embarked on another trip to Amsterdam to raise funds on behalf of the French government. It was at his suggestion but unsurprisingly it received the backing of Choiseul. Casanova's fortunes had been on the slide. He had lost a large amount of money in setting up his silk-fabric business and had become mired in financial and legal disputes. His plan was to restore his financial well-being but this time his intention was to invest money in an annuity sufficient to support himself and his anticipated future wife, Manon. It was not to be. France was too high a risk. There was no chance that he could pull off his previous success.

Instead of returning to Paris, in February 1760 Casanova made his way east and was provided with a passport via the French ambassador to The Hague, Monsieur d'Affry. Casanova does not explain why he wanted to make this journey but it would be sensible to conclude, particularly in the light of his relationship with de Bernis, that Casanova was a French spy. He found no difficulty in befriending the rich and powerful and was, on the whole, a welcome figure in court circles. He would be a handy additional channel of information that Versailles could use in helping them to pitch negotiations and shape foreign policy initiatives. From 1760, for instance, peace was rising up the agenda of the contending powers and it would have been valuable to know how strong the appetite was for an end to the war amongst Imperial states and principalities. For several years, Choiseul provided Casanova with passports and letters of introduction, even when he was expelled from Paris in 1767. In Soleure, Casanova warned his housekeeper not to read or even touch his papers because they contained secrets that he was not authorised to reveal. A complaint from Count von Kettler made in March 1760 was passed to Choiseul reporting that the count 'suspects him to be a most dangerous spy, capable of the greatest crimes.'[14] Kettler was an Austrian Military Attaché to the French with whose mistress Casanova had been having an affair. Choiseul chose not to take any action. All things considered, it would be much more of a surprise if the Venetian were not a spy.

Towards the end of 1760 in Florence, Casanova renewed an old acquaintance whom he had first met in Rome during his youth. Abbé de Gama was in the service of the Portuguese government. He proposed to Casanova that he become a member of the delegation representing Portugal's interests at the peace congress at Augsburg, which was organised to resolve the war and was due to take place in May the following year. Casanova agreed.

1759 had been chastening for France. Choiseul began searching for a way to end the conflict but was faced with some uncomfortable realities. He was not negotiating from a position of strength. The war was going well for the British so they were unlikely to agree to terms acceptable to France. Frederick was willing but would not countenance the loss of any territory. Indeed, he still hoped to make some gains. St Petersburg wanted to score a complete victory over Frederick. The Habsburg Monarchy could not tolerate a Prussia that emerged unscathed and with its long-term expansionist ambitions undimmed. From the perspective of Maria Theresa and Kaunitz, it would merely postpone a final reckoning. St Petersburg and Vienna prepared for war once more.

As the new campaign got underway, Frederick struggled to resist the inroads being made by Habsburg forces into Silesia. In the summer of 1760 he was dealt successive blows. There was the loss of Landeshut on 23 June and the fall of Glatz on 21 July. The siege of Dresden, in July – the city having been liberated in 1759 – achieved nothing except condemnation throughout Europe at the atrocities committed there by his forces. In August the Russians advanced into Silesia from the east. A must-win victory over the Habsburgs at Liegnitz on 15 August gave Frederick something of a respite. Then once again he found himself being outmanoeuvred by the Austrian commander, Daun. As usual, Frederick's enemies found themselves frustrated by the timidity of the Russian command in the field, although in October they did manage briefly to conquer Berlin. The efforts by the French had some success but nothing decisive. Drastic reductions to the navy's budget, tax-increases, cut-backs in foreign subsidies, and more loans, had enabled them put together a substantial force of some 150,000. A successful campaign had been needed to give the French a stronger hand in any subsequent peace negotiations. Unfortunately, the British had been equally willing to pour in large sums of money to support Brunswick.

Choiseul was becoming desperate for peace, and his relationship with Vienna was fractious. He went so far as to declare that France would not fight another campaign. Kaunitz offered to consider possible options and suggested establishing a peace congress. In light of the failure to make headway militarily, the Habsburg Monarchy, which itself was facing economic ruin, doubted that it would be able recover Silesia. Events across the channel were shifting the attitudes of the British in a similar direction. George II died in October 1760 and his successor, George III, was more sympathetic to calls to end the war. His loyalties, after all, were attached more strongly to Britain than Hanover, the birthplace of his father and grandfather. The British had also achieved one of their key goals of the colonial war with the surrender of Montreal in September 1760 (almost exactly one year after the fall of Quebec) and the conquest of Canada. All told, their ongoing and expensive support for Frederick was difficult to justify. An agreement in principle was reached amongst the belligerents to attend the aforementioned proposed congress at Augsburg but in the meantime the war was to continue.

By dint of another gargantuan effort, France was able to field two major armies for the 1761 campaign, under Broglie and Soubise. As before, Choiseul was looking for gains in Europe to strengthen his hand in negotiations with the British. His priority was to protect French interests in the Atlantic slave trade, the Caribbean sugar islands and the North Atlantic fisheries. The French withstood an early assault by Brunswick but were themselves unable to make the decisive breakthrough Choiseul required, despite their superiority on paper. Attempts at Anglo-French peace talks over the summer broke down in the face of the hard line being taken by the British, notably William Pitt, leading to the cancellation of Augsburg and, on 15 August, the formalisation of an anti-British, Franco-Spanish alliance. Spain had an extensive list of New World grievances centred on British privateers and smugglers, along with the failure of the British to recognise Spanish fishing rights off Newfoundland. Neither did Charles III, who was installed on the Spanish throne in 1759, have any love for the British.

For Frederick, the 1761 campaign opened with a programme of organised looting, and as the year progressed, it was looking as though he would be able to cling on once again. Russia and the Habsburg Monarchy had both resorted to issuing bonds along the lines of the British in order to pursue the war but despite a huge advantage in manpower, they were making little progress. Then towards the end of the year Frederick's defences unravelled. In October the fortress of Schweidniz in Silesia fell to Habsburg-Russian forces. This was a major strategic headache. It would allow the Habsburgs to winter in Silesia and they would have access to resources now denied to Frederick. In Saxony, although there were no decisive engagements, by December the Habsburgs had also been able to take control of the south-west, with the same resource implications that were brought about by the fall of Schweidniz. On 16 December the loss of Kolberg on the Baltic allowed the Russians to winter in Prussia instead of having to withdraw to the Vistula. With no intervention by the Ottomans on the cards, and British attitudes towards Frederick cooling, the outlook was bleak.

The end of the war

Anticipating defeat, Frederick agreed to begin peace negotiations to salvage whatever he could. Then everything changed. On 5 January 1762 Empress Elizabeth of Russia died to be succeeded by Peter III (1762), a man who idolised Frederick. The new emperor offered his 'master' peace on incredibly generous terms. He was prepared to return all of Russia's conquests and proposed an alliance that would guarantee Silesia and Glatz if Frederick would support his claim to the Duchy of Schleswig. The peace treaty was signed on 5 May, and the alliance in June. Russia's reversal of policy meant that any offensive action by the Habsburgs was no longer feasible. Vienna began contemplating peace. Talks were also back on the table between the French and the British. None of this prevented the start of the latest campaign, this time with a reinvigorated Frederick, but Russian support was short-lived. On 9 July Peter was deposed, replaced by his wife, Catherine II, who revoked the alliance with Frederick, while standing by the peace treaty.

The accession to the throne by Catherine II, who was hostile towards the French, added urgency to Choiseul's search for peace. The Franco-Spanish coalition was achieving little in the colonial war and British military success continued. An attempt to invade Portugal, an important economic partner for Britain, proved equally fruitless, and Brunswick continued to frustrate the French. The territorial and commercial trade-offs were well advanced by September, and by November 1762 an agreement was reached, culminating in the Treaty of Paris on 10 February 1763. Parallel negotiations were undertaken between Versailles and Vienna as the two disentangled their own treaty obligations, leading to the Convention of Fontainebleau on 2 November. At the end of December 1762, formal peace talks began between Prussia and the Habsburg Monarchy, Kaunitz concerned to avert imminent bankruptcy and put an end to Frederick's intensified plundering. It was for this latter reason that Frederick chose to stretch out negotiations for another seven weeks. Finally, the Treaty of Hubertusburg that ended the war was signed on 15 February.

The Seven Years War is estimated to have resulted in over one million deaths. Apart from the death toll, there were three primary outcomes: the establishment of Britain's commercial, colonial and maritime pre-eminence; the confirmation of Prussia as a major European power; and a shift eastward in the political gravity of the continent with the ascent of Russia. For Casanova, the war made him rich, at least temporarily, and once he had squandered his wealth, Europe's reconstruction motivated him to travel in search of career opportunities. He remained good friends with de Bernis who helped him out when his glory days were behind him. The two were to meet up when he visited Rome, where the cardinal had become France's ambassador.

Chapter 7

Religious Life

'However it acts, Providence is at work, and in spite of everything else those who worship it can only be good souls, even if guilty of transgressions.'
Giacomo Casanova, *History of My Life*

Religion is prominent in Casanova's memoirs. Its rituals, routines and moral exhortations were the warp and weft of ordinary life: baptism, communion, confession, cults, exorcism, festivals, holy days, last rites, marriage, mass, penance, pilgrimage, prayer, processionals, sermons. It was not a surprise that the family of a well-educated young man of precarious means would direct him to a career in the Church; it was respectable and offered solid prospects. But the highest offices were reserved for men of noble pedigree, as much political appointments as religious – men such as de Bernis, who became a cardinal and was awarded the archbishopric of Albi for his services as a diplomat and minister.

The wealth of the Catholic Church was immense and the lion's share of its profits were diverted into the pockets of aristocratic clergymen, many of whom rarely set foot in the dioceses they governed. The Archbishop of Paris received over 500,000 livres annually (a priest might earn 300 livres a year).[1] Unlike people, the Church did not die. Bequests of land and other assets accumulated generation upon generation, century upon century. The Church owned one-tenth of the arable land of France and not only did it collect rents and taxes from its own property but it also benefitted from tithes on all other cultivated land, sometimes as high as 7 per cent.[2,3]

It was, of course, the priests on the ground who were the face of the Church for the vast majority of the population. It was they who administered the sacraments, kept the parish records, dealt with civil authorities, organised charity for the needy and oversaw the schoolmaster and the midwife. Priests would often have been amongst the few literate members of the community and thereby an important link to the wider world. Despite frequently being little better off than their parishioners, they were figures of some status who would be sought out for help and guidance in matters secular as well as spiritual. They were amongst those who were the most sympathetic to the plight of ordinary people, spending their lives amongst them and witnessing at first hand the challenges that they faced.

In France, influential Enlightenment figures such as Baron d'Holbach and Denis Diderot launched withering anticlerical attacks against the Church and its agents. 'It's raining bombs on the house of the Lord,' Diderot wrote after visiting a group of like-minded *philosophes*.[4] But their accusations were probably unfair to the majority of the clergy and not typical of Enlightenment opinion elsewhere in Europe. Although there were undoubtedly abuses, most clergy took their responsibilities seriously. Casanova's own attitude to the institution of the Church was generally critical. He decried its oppressive morality and vows of celibacy. He particularly disapproved of monasticism. Casanova saw it as a movement which was mired in ignorance and hypocrisy. Here is his description of the monk Brother Stefano, who in August 1743 accompanied Casanova for four weeks during his journey from Ancona to Rome:

> a man of thirty, with red hair, of a very strong constitution, a true peasant, who had become a monk only to live without tiring his body. ... His coat was veritably a mule's load. It had twelve pockets, all full, as well as a large back pocket ... which alone contained double what all the others could contain. Bread, wine, meat – cooked fresh and salted – chicken, eggs, cheese, ham, sausages: there was enough to feed us for a fortnight. ... He was a fool who had the brains of Harlequin and assumed that those who listened to him were even more foolish. But in his stupidity, he was shrewd. His religion was singular. Not wanting to be a bigot, he was scandalous: to make the company laugh he talked revolting trash.[5]

And at the other end of the ecclesiastical hierarchy, here is Casanova's description of dinner at a monastery with an abbot who seems to be quite a gourmet: 'His Rhine wine was exquisite. A salmon trout was served, he smiled, he told me in Ciceronian Latin that there would be pride in not wanting to eat it because it was fish, and he justified his sophism very well.'[6]

Cultural and economic power translated into political power. The Roman Catholic Church under the leadership of the papacy had increased its influence across Europe from the eleventh century, asserting judicial and investiture authority over ecclesiastical affairs that had once belonged to lay rulers. Ownership of the Papal States made the pope a temporal sovereign in his own right. For five more centuries it retained its religious monopoly of power across most of Europe, only sharing it in the east and south-east with the Orthodox Catholic Church and the Ottomans. This was to change in the early sixteenth century when the religious and political challenge that the

Protestant Reformation posed to Roman Catholic Europe was to be a potent ingredient in a series of vicious conflicts. They culminated in the Thirty Years War, taking place mainly in the territories of the Holy Roman Empire and the Habsburg Monarchy, and varyingly estimated to have left between four and eight million dead. The Peace of Westphalia that ended the war in 1648 also circumscribed papal authority. The signatories recognised that Calvinism and Lutheranism were religions alongside Catholicism, and European rulers could decide which would be the state religion. All Christian countries in Europe were confessional states (that is, they officially subscribed to a particular religion). The Balkans and Europe to the east were largely Orthodox. The Dutch Republic, Switzerland, Great Britain, parts of Ireland, most territories bordering the Baltic, and much of the Holy Roman Empire were Protestant. The rest of Europe was Catholic although within these Catholic confessional states were significant pockets of Calvinist influence, such as in France.

The shift of power from the papacy back to secular rulers was a trend which was to continue into the eighteenth century as sovereigns sought to reform and centralise the institutions of state, minimise competing sources of authority, and assert greater control over the clergy. One notable casualty were the Jesuits. The Society of Jesus was founded in the middle of the sixteenth century and was under the direct command of the pope. It was a formidable weapon in the fight back against Protestantism and reforming those abuses in the Church which had triggered the Protestant revolt. The Jesuits were educators and missionaries, establishing schools and religious training colleges across Europe. De Bernis, Choiseul and Voltaire all studied under them at Louis-le Grand in Paris along with key revolutionary figures such as Desmoulins, Dumouriez and Robespierre. Jesuits became influential advisors to sovereigns and political leaders. Father Pérusseau was confessor to Louis XV. But their proximity to power and fealty to the pope lead to hostility and suspicion. Rumours of Jesuit conspiracies abounded. In the 1750s and 60s they were expelled from France, Portugal and Spain. By 1773, antagonism towards the Jesuits had become such that Pope Clement XIV was impelled to suppress them altogether. Ironically, it was one of their old alumni, Cardinal de Bernis, French Ambassador to Rome at the time, who was partly instrumental in their downfall.

Accompanying this political challenge was the assault of the Enlightenment. It questioned core tenets of Catholic theology such as the belief in miracles and divine intervention as well as the veracity of the Bible. But despite these political and intellectual blows, it would be wrong to draw the conclusion that either Catholicism or the Christian religions as a whole were in decline. The cultural hold of Christianity upon the vast majority of the population was strong. There is perhaps evidence of growing scepticism in certain quarters, such as in Paris around the time of the revolution, but like the ferocious anticlericalism of the *philosophes*, this was not widespread. Even amongst those who were predisposed to Enlightenment values, few were prepared to reject religion outright. Rather they sought to accommodate both perspectives.

Casanova is a case in point. Reason taught him that an immaterial soul could not combine with a material body but at the same time he acknowledged that there were limits to human understanding. Consequently, he could declare that he believed in an immaterial God. Despite his dislike of 'fanatics' (that is, those who were excessively pious) Casanova himself became one under the influence of an ex-Jesuit priest called La Haye during a low point in his life. On another occasion he was within a whisker of entering a monastery, giving up all his possessions and becoming a monk. The Venetian was typical of most people of most times. With greater or lesser scrupulousness, people charted a course that attempted to reconcile their own personal needs, impulses and moral code along with what was demanded of them by their family, neighbours, the government, their faith and their social position. Except for fanatics, compromise between the spiritual and the worldly was the norm. The rhetoric of a Rousseau or a Voltaire was going to make little difference to the Christian religious outlook of the majority unless forced upon them by the vicissitudes of political circumstance.

In reality, dissatisfaction with the established Churches led not to a rejection of God or Christianity but to the emergence of new trends, movements and forms of devotion. The roles and presence of women became increasingly important. Non-cloistered, religious orders were established that enabled women to undertake charitable, educational or missionary work. Religious voluntary associations flourished, comprised of lay worshippers, often organised according to a particular trade, who would employ their own chaplain to perform services. The associations might provide, amongst other things, funeral services for their members and support for relatives of the deceased. Particularly significant was the emergence within both Catholic and Protestant Europe of more austere spiritual movements that emphasised personal faith and responsibility such as Catholic Jansenism, Anglican Methodism and Lutheran Pietism.

Influenced by English Puritanism, Pietism originated in the German Protestant states of the late seventeenth century. It took root at the new University of Halle in Brandenburg-Prussia under the leadership of professor and pastor August Hermann Francke (1663–1727). Pietism prioritised holiness and the inner light of spiritual experience over empty theological formalism. Believers would meet in small groups for prayer and Bible study, drawing on the Bible and using the example of Christ to aid their own moral renewal. They were characterised by a strong work ethic, sense of duty and proselytising impulse, establishing schools and workhouses for the poor and actively promoting the Word of God in the workplace and the neighbourhood. Pietism was very much a social movement. Of course, to Casanova's mind such people were fanatics by definition.

Pastor to Glaucha in Halle, Francke was a gifted organiser. Supported by a sympathetic monarch in the form of Frederick William (the Great Elector) and winning over patrons, with minimal resources Francke set about establishing a complex of largely educationally-focussed institutions which became vehicles for philanthropy, the promotion of Pietist beliefs and the transmission of useful knowledge and skills. These institutions included a school for the poor; an orphanage; a fee-paying elementary school; a boarding school for sons of the nobility; a grammar school; teacher training colleges; a publishing house; bookshop and a Bible institute that produced large numbers of Bibles at relatively low cost. By the time he died, Franke was famous across Europe and overseas. His various foundations housed 2,200 children and 167 teachers. The movement spread across German-speaking states, Switzerland and the Baltic. Its advocacy of universal primary education, grounded in discipline and spirituality, influenced educational reform even amongst Catholic leaders, notably Empress Maria Theresa.

Pietism had a direct impact upon the English religious reformer, John Wesley (1703–1791), an Anglican priest who became the founder of Methodism. Wesley was an evangelist with an interest in mysticism and a fervent desire to live a devout Christian life. On a journey to America, contact with Moravian Pietists left him deeply impressed. When Wesley returned to England he spent time discussing the nature of faith with a Pietist missionary called Peter Böhler and later attended a Moravian service in Aldersgate Street, London, where he underwent something of a spiritual awakening. Shortly afterwards, Wesley visited Moravia to study. On his return he founded his own religious society in 1739, separate from the Pietists and within the Church of England, touring the country to preach and reaching out in particular to the poor. Wesley's message was that anyone could receive God's grace through faith and directly experience God's presence. Following the model of the Pietists, he organised worshippers into small groups to study the Bible, pray, and discuss their beliefs. They were led by lay preachers instead of Anglican priests. In 1767 there were around 20,000 followers in England but this was to climb rapidly. In 1791 Methodism split from the established Church and became an independent religion. By 1830 there were almost a quarter of a million official members and many more that were informally connected.[7]

The appeal of Methodism needs to be understood in the context of an Anglican Church that had become rather sterile and detached from the spiritual needs of ordinary people. The Church of England emphasised toleration, self-restraint and rationality rather than emotional engagement. Amongst more affluent and educated Anglicans there was a growing scepticism in the literal truth of the Bible, and a willingness to embrace deism with its conception of a more distant, non-interventionist God. Growing populations in urban centres outside London meant there were not enough churches or priests where they were needed, while ambitious clerics who looked to enhance their careers remained close to the capital to curry royal patronage. The problem of parishes with absentee priests was rife.

A similar phenomenon was taking place in France, based upon the work of an early seventeenth-century Dutch Catholic bishop, Cornelius Jansen (1585–1638), an opponent of the Jesuits, whose ideas became popularised after his death. Jansenism emphasised man's sinful nature. Drawing on the theology of Saint Augustine, one of the Church Fathers of late antiquity, Jansenism argued, amongst other things, for the importance of God's grace in obtaining salvation over that of free will, as human freedom would circumscribe God's authority. Such a doctrine undermined the importance of the clergy as intermediaries between the believer and God, as, on this view, the clergy could not provide absolution. Jansenism was a belief which the Jesuits regarded as heretical given the similarities to Calvinism. Jesuits, by contrast, put greater faith in the possibility of people obtaining salvation through the exercise of free will and the commission of good works. This theological conflict was to become a political one and was to dog the French state and Catholic Church for generations.

As with Methodism and Pietism, for Jansenism the relationship between the Almighty and the individual was a personal one. Central was the love of God and the notion that redemption could only be achieved through perfect contrition (that is, repentance motivated by an understanding that sin is offensive to God, and no other ulterior motive). In 1692 French theologian and Jansenist, Pasquier Quesnel, published commentaries on the Bible entitled *New Testament in French with Thoughts on Morality*. It was a major and controversial work which stressed the importance of faith and devotion. Jansenism's uncompromising attitude towards grace reflected a similarly rigorous moral outlook which attracted those who felt that the Catholic Church had become too lax. Jansenists were suspicious of earthly pleasures, such as the theatre, which they believed led to corruption and was a distraction from genuine communion with God. Jansenists were particularly critical of the worldliness of the Jesuits.

A major feature of the Catholic religious landscape were monasteries. Surprising though it may seem, during the period of the High Enlightenment, there was a surge in monastery building. Well over 25,000 of them housed more than 350,000 religious at their peak by the middle of the eighteenth century. In Spain and Italy, nearly 1 per cent of the population was a monk or a nun (2 per cent of adults) and they comprised the majority of the Catholic clergy. Monasteries varied greatly in size. Some might house just a handful of monastics but others were huge and owned large tracts of land making them a significant component of many local economies. It is estimated that they owned around 5 per cent of the agricultural land in France and about 10 per cent of all land in Catholic Europe.[8] St Sergius-Trinity near Moscow owned over 100,000 serfs.[9] Derek Beales writes: 'They possessed farms and forests, which they sometimes managed themselves and sometimes leased out; they developed suburbs; they made and sold beer, wine and liqueurs; they acted virtually as banks; in fact they were involved in commercial and industrial enterprise of almost every kind.'[10] Monasteries were as much an urban phenomenon as rural. Lisbon possessed around 50, Paris over 150, and Naples almost 200. The heads of monasteries were important political figures, both locally and at the level of the state. Several eighteenth-century popes came from monastic orders, and the influence of the Jesuits has already been mentioned. The second half of the century saw the power and extent of monasteries decline substantially, in part triggered by the dissolution of the Jesuits. Reforms by Joseph II more than halved the number of monks and nuns in the Habsburg Monarchy. The upheaval of the French Revolution and revolutionary wars led to the dissolution of almost all monasteries in France, as well as many others across Europe, although there was a revival in the nineteenth century following the final defeat of Napoleon in 1815.

Members of monastic orders, of course, frequently came in for criticism. On discovering that the paradise of Eldorado contains no monks, Voltaire's Candide exclaims, 'What! You have no monks instructing and disputing, and governing and intriguing, and having everyone burned alive who is not of their opinion?'[11] They were depicted as parasites who lived off the industry of others. Tales of greed and debauchery were commonplace. And there was some truth to all this. Casanova, after all, had affairs with nuns, and while very few monastics lived a life of luxury, most were insulated from the grinding poverty and insecurity that was typical for much of the population. For many, the motivation to enter a monastery was to satisfy a profound devotional urge to serve God. For some, such as Stefano, it was based upon a worldly calculation of material self-interest. Others looked to take advantage of occupational and educational opportunities that might otherwise be unavailable to them, especially women. For substantial numbers of both men and women it was a matter of coercion by their parents or guardians in order to preserve the family patrimony. Those entering a monastic order had to renounce all claims to their inheritance. It eliminated the need to provide expensive dowries for daughters of the well-to-do. Evidence based upon appeals against the forced placing of a young person into a monastery suggests it was a problem that affected males at least as much as females.[12]

Despite the caricatures that opponents liked to paint, monasteries and monastic orders did provide important social functions. Their initial expansion indicates that they were responding to the genuine spiritual needs of the community, including, but not exclusively, of those who became its members. In times of particular distress, for example during epidemics, people would look to the religious to intercede with God and try to placate his wrath.

Monasteries had long been centres of learning, education and cultural transmission. Until the invention of printing, over many centuries books had to be copied by hand and this took place mainly in monasteries. Inevitably, this led to the formation of large and important libraries, with all the implications for teaching and scholarship that entailed. It was what tempted Casanova to become a monk. Monastics educated the children of the poor, as well as cared for the sick, elderly and those with disabilities. Monks served as parish priests. Monasteries distributed alms and would offer relief if the harvest was poor. They would act as boarding schools for young women – called *educande* in Venice – such as Casanova's teenage lover, CC, to ensure that their reputations were not compromised prior to marriage. The monasteries also provided hospitality and accommodation to travellers, especially pilgrims. During his escape from Venice to Paris, Casanova dined at a Capuchin monastery.

One of the disturbing features of Christianity since the fourth century had been the rise of religious intolerance, both towards pagans and fellow Christians. Persecution of religious groups, for example Jews, had existed previously but the grounds for that persecution had been political. If the members of this or that sect or cult obeyed the law, the Romans generally left them to get on with things. They would intervene if they perceived a threat to civil order. In Christendom, on the other hand, it was often theological dogma that was the cause of oppression, conflict and chilling cruelty. But by the eighteenth century, there was a growing recognition of the need to accept religious difference, motivated by war weariness, the Enlightenment quest for freedom of thought and conscience, and a Europe which was now established as multi-confessional.

Perhaps the greatest champion of toleration was Voltaire. Indeed, until Voltaire, the word carried negative connotations suggesting, as it did, indifference to God's truth and an abdication of religious duty. It was Voltaire who transformed the conception of toleration as a vice into that of a virtue. For much of his long life, he drew attention to the viciousness, inhumanity and social harms of religious bigotry. True religion, for Voltaire, should have been a source of peace. After an extended stay across the channel, in 1734 he published *Philosophical Letters* recounting his observations of English society. Although Voltaire is critical of certain aspects of organised religion, he praises the country's liberties and compares favourably the co-existence of religious groups in Anglican England to the more repressive practices of the French. 'An Englishman,' he notes, 'as a free man, goes to heaven by whatever route he likes.'[13] Interestingly, matters were pretty much the same over a generation later when Casanova visited. Enquiring how many sects there were in England, Casanova was informed, 'No one can know for certain, since almost every Sunday a new one is born, and another perishes.'[14] Great Britain was by now well on the way to becoming the strongest and most economically successful power in Europe, supporting Voltaire's contention that religious toleration and prosperity went hand-in-hand. It is worth pointing out that he was not advocating for members of different religious groups to possess equal rights. This was clearly not the case in Great Britain for Catholics and Nonconformists.

Voltaire's most celebrated admirer was Frederick II. Since his teens, Frederick had been a devotee of the great man. The two corresponded for over 40 years, and Voltaire took refuge in Prussia from 1750 to 1753. Frederick was a vociferous reader with a sharp mind. He was a believer in progress based upon reason and knowledge. He was, in short, a man of the Enlightenment. He was disdainful of organised religion and did little to hide the fact. Prussia was a Lutheran state and, like everywhere else in Europe, its citizens were largely devout. However, such was Frederick's authority that he was able to practise a degree of toleration unusual in Europe, and that elsewhere would have provoked considerable unrest amongst ordinary people.

For Frederick, toleration was born of a happy marriage of principal and political self-interest. If through their skill and labour, people could contribute to the economy of Prussia, and in so doing help to supply the resources Frederick needed for his war machine, then what kind of Christian they were was irrelevant. In his *Memoirs of the House of Brandenburg* (1751), he notes, 'False zeal is a tyrant that depopulates provinces; toleration is a tender mother that makes them flourish.'[15] Frederick had fully learned the lesson of Louis XIV's expulsion of the Huguenots in 1685, which resulted in the loss of 400,000 of France's most economically dynamic citizens to the benefit of Great Britain, the Dutch Republic and Brandenburg-Prussia itself. His sympathy and the sympathy of his father for the Pietist movement should be seen in this light. Pietism was central to the Prussian ethos of duty and obedience that did much to underpin military efficiency and success. The movement's focus on hard work made its followers productive subjects. And by promoting education in society as a whole, Pietism promoted Prussia's economic and social well-being. A striking demonstration of Frederick's religious impartiality was his authorisation of the building of a Catholic church in the centre of Berlin, something that would have been impossible in London. He made a point of welcoming refugees and intellectuals suffering persecution, such as Rousseau, Christian Wolff, Julien Offray de La Mettrie and, in 1773, after the dissolution of the Society of Jesus, ex-Jesuits. In an echo of the Romans, as long as the Prussian constitution and laws were respected, people were free to worship and express their religious opinions as they liked.

By contrast, for most of the century Frederick's Habsburg rivals pursued a policy of purging Protestantism from their domains, and Empress Maria Theresa, a devout Catholic herself, continued to do so. For Maria, it was a matter of saving souls. Not until the accession of her son Joseph, who was heavily influenced by Enlightenment ideals, was there a shift of position. Soon after Joseph became the sole ruler of the Habsburg Monarchy he introduced the Toleration Patent of 1781, and the following year an Edict of Toleration for Jews, part of a radical programme of social and institutional reforms. Although the Patent prohibited public worship, it allowed the main non-Roman Catholic faiths to worship in private and gave them recognition under the civil law to practise trades and professions, and to buy property.

Religious conservatism amongst the general population meant that toleration could be taken only so far before risking a backlash. Religious reform was often resisted. In Britain, attempts to allow the naturalisation of Jews caused rioting. An attempt to reduce official discrimination against Catholics led to the Gordon Riots in London and nearby towns. One week of violent protest resulted in ten times more property damage than occurred in Paris throughout the Revolution.[16] Joseph II's attempts to prune back what he believed were superstitious religious practices were met with staunch opposition from the peasantry. An attempt at Mainz in 1778 to replace Latin with vernacular hymn books lead to eruptions of violence. Matters got so out of hand that it took 300 troops to restore order. When the French revolutionary armies sought to impose religious reforms on countries they had invaded, people clung even more tenaciously to their faiths and it only increased their resistance against the aggressors. Within France itself during the revolution, the dismantling of Catholicism did much to inflame division and counter-revolution especially in the Vendée region in the west.

One group that was particularly affected by discrimination were Jews. All faiths in Europe were liable to violence and persecution but the vast majority of believers had, at the very least, the theoretical option of being able to reside in a confessional state of their own persuasion. Not having a state of their own made Jews particularly vulnerable. Antisemitism was widespread throughout Europe and had deep roots. It is estimated that in the late Middle Ages a million Jews were expelled from western Europe, resettling in the east. These were Ashkenazi Jews, subject to numerous regulations. They were often segregated from society, required permission to travel, prohibited from owning land, allowed to practise only certain occupations and were burdened with extra taxes. Ashkenazi Jews lived on sufferance, subject at any moment to communal violence or the whim of a ruler on whose protection they relied. In central Europe and the west lived a much smaller but more prosperous group of Jews, Sephardic Jews, who were more educated and cosmopolitan. These tended to be more integrated into society and located in important commercial centres, such as Amsterdam, Frankfurt, London and Venice.

But this broad outline hides a more diverse pattern of relationships, one which blurs the sharpness of the east-west divide. Jews were a very heterogenous group. Ashkenazi Jews in Poland-Lithuania (the home of 80 per cent of all Jews in the eighteenth century) were to some degree integrated into society and, simultaneously, were separate. This was because they not only lacked legal rights but because they had a strong sense of their own identity and chosenness – a belief that they were God's chosen people. Jews were allowed freedom to worship in Prussia but, like his idol Voltaire, Frederick II was antisemitic. He used quotas to try to limit the number of Jews and placed them into different categories with different sets of rights. In 1791 Jews were accorded full legal rights in France in the wake of the revolution. In Livorno in Tuscany, as well as for other 'port Jews' elsewhere, the economic usefulness of Jewish merchants earned them privileged status. In a major Jewish community in Altona (part of Danish ruled Holstein-Glückstadt), Christian and Jewish maidservants were treated the same. The Jewish experience was enormously varied.

Casanova's memoirs record around forty encounters with, and references to, Jews. Widespread antipathy is evident. For Jews to go out during Christian festivals was to risk being abused or attacked. When Casanova was visited by the Jew Moses and his daughter Leah in Turin on a Maundy Thursday, he advised them to stay with him in order to avoid the risks of being seen in public. On a visit to the Hague, French Envoy and later Ambassador, Monsieur d'Affry, warned Casanova not to do business with the Jews, as they were not to be trusted. When Casanova stayed with a Jewish family and requested that their daughter share his meal with him, the daughter assumed it was because he suspected that, being Jews, they wanted to poison him.

The Jews whom Casanova met were largely financiers or tradesmen of various descriptions. They included bankers; money lenders; pawn brokers; a clothier; a confectioner; a costumier; a customs official; an embroiderer; a furniture dealer; a horse dealer; an impresario; and a painter of portrait miniatures. He twice fell in love with a Jewess, both called Leah, the second of which affairs can be counted amongst his most intense. While imprisoned under the Leads, Casanova shared a cell with a Jewish money lender whom he particularly disliked. On separate occasions, he beat up two Jewish men and had his servant beat up another either for breaking their word to him or insulting his honour.

Casanova, as on so many things, was knowledgeable about Jewish history and beliefs, and knew at least some Hebrew. During his student days he wrote a thesis on whether Jews should be allowed to build new synagogues, and he was, of course, a skilful practitioner of the cabbala. One Christmas Eve, Casanova chose to dine with the family of a Jewish Dutch banker called Boas to celebrate the Feast of the Maccabees, rather than the birth of Christ with a Christian family. Nonetheless, if he was not as antisemitic as Voltaire or Frederick, for much of his life Casanova did share many of the prejudices that were widespread at the time. Like the nobility, his dislike of those whose priority was to accumulate wealth rather than spend it would have inclined him to be unsympathetic.

In his late 40s these negative assumptions seemed to change after Casanova's encounter with the family of a Jewish money lender called Mordecai. Casanova was travelling to Ancona when he received a request to allow a Jew to accompany him. His initial reaction was dismissive: 'I don't want anyone, let alone a Jew.'[17] As is often the case with Casanova his intrinsic humanity gets the better of him and he changes his mind. The following morning, Mordecai asked him directly why he did not like Jews. The Venetian was similarly direct: 'Because... out of religious duty you are our enemies. You think you have an obligation to deceive us. You don't look upon us as your brothers. You push your usury to excess when, in need of money, we borrow it from you. In brief, you hate us.'[18] After some more debate and time in each other's company, Mordecai invites Casanova to lodge with his family to which Casanova agrees. He records: 'While waiting for the maid to arrange everything the valet has brought down, I take pleasure in going to the synagogue with Mordecai, who, having become my host, seemed to me like another man, having seen his family, and his house, where I found everything very clean.'[19] Casanova was travelling on to Trieste, and Mordecai provided him with a warm letter of recommendation to another

Jew called Moses Levi, who proved to be exceptionally welcoming. He had an equally good letter of recommendation for Baron Pittoni, the Chief of Police, and Casanova could not but help contrast the responses he received: 'What a difference between the cold reception of Baron Pittoni's and that of the Jew Levi!'[20]

Chapter 8

The Public Sphere

'The true man of letters must be the friend of all who love letters.'
Giacomo Casanova, *History of My Life*

Origins

One of the features of ancient city states such as the Athens of Pericles or the Roman Republic, was the involvement of the citizen body in their governance. They were not democratic in a modern sense but there were mechanisms such as popular assemblies which allowed substantial numbers to have a voice in how they were governed. Through such means, government acquired legitimacy and a degree of transparency. If we contrast this with the relationship between the ruler and ruled that dominated much of Europe in the early seventeenth century, the role of subjects was more passive. The processes of decision-making took place out of sight of all but a select few. Monarchs sought to establish their legitimacy as a thing in and of itself, closed off from the rest of society.

From this emerged what has been described by the influential cultural scholar, Jürgen Habermas, as 'representative publicness', in which a ruler 'presented himself as an embodiment of some sort of "higher" power.'[1] This authority was displayed through forms of language, conduct, dress, ceremony, ornament, architecture and other cultural trappings. It was largely through the court and Church that products of scholarship and high culture were patronised and regulated: music, painting, poetry, philosophy, history, theatre. There did not exist other significant independent social spaces in which it was possible to explore human experience, to critique power or to scrutinise how society was organised and managed. Even when theatres were not directly attached to the court, they were places of 'representative publicness' where the high born presented themselves as separate from the people.

From the mid-seventeenth century we witness examples of society opening up. This was accelerated in the eighteenth century as the impact of new economic and financial forces helped to expand political and cultural activity outside the court and the Church into what has become known as the public sphere. The global exploitation of commercial markets led to greater demands for capital and for increasing military and political involvement to safeguard investments. In addition, European rulers were engaged in costly wars on the continent. To supply the necessary resources meant going beyond traditional taxation and borrowing arrangements. It required better systems of tax collection to ensure a reliable source of income which, in turn, required professional bureaucracies. On top of this was the impulse amongst monarchs to centralise power more generally. The character of government consequently became less aristocratic and territorial. Much control over matters such as finance, administration, employment practices, the law and the military were previously embodied in rights held locally by nobles, the Church, town corporations, trade guilds or people who owned offices purchased from the crown. The resulting more depersonalised state apparatus constituted a public authority, with the public defined as those citizens who were subject to the power of state officials. It also signalled the emergence of the state as an entity separate from the person of the ruler, and the notion of the law as separate from the authority of the ruler. These changes facilitated the development of the public sphere and its institutions, such as the press and voluntary associations, which evolved independently from the state and the Church. In short, the public sphere grew out of the relationships between private individuals, whose number and importance increased as economies expanded, in part stimulated by overseas trade.

Signs that the political and cultural monopoly of the court was breaking down could be seen earliest in England. Conflict between the crown and Parliament in the 1640s led to a flood of pamphlets debating political and religious questions. In 1644 John Milton published *Areopagitica: A Speech of Mr John Milton for the Liberty of Unlicensed Printing, To the Parliament of England*, in which he argued the case for open discussion without censors. In the 1650s, the first specialist coffee houses were established in Oxford, becoming known as 'penny universities', initially frequented by the educated and prosperous. In the 1670s and '80s coffee houses mushroomed across London. The penny admission price would allow access to books, poetry, pamphlets, bulletins, journals, moral weeklies and newspapers such as *The Bee, The Daily Courant, The Spectator* or *The Tatler*. Some coffee houses acted as community libraries with texts collected and maintained for subscribing members. Patronised by men of different social ranks, coffee houses were vibrant centres of business, gossip, news and literary and political debate where criticism of the court and Parliament could flourish. Coffee houses also took hold in Paris. In 1689 near the Comédie Française was founded the famous Café de Procope, a venue for such luminaries as Beaumarchais, Condorcet, Crébillon, Diderot, Fontenelle, Rousseau and Voltaire. While not as numerous as in London and Paris, by the end of the century the coffee house was a well-established Viennese institution that offered a range of entertainments including garden concerts.

Newspapers and periodicals were to be an essential ingredient of the public sphere. Their origins were tied to the growth of international trade and the importance of intelligence to merchants about distant events. Traders' newsletters had been around since the late Middle Ages; the more accurate a merchant's knowledge, the better they would be able to assess risk and calculate profitability. This intelligence was conveyed initially by means of private letters, with merchants developing the first regular mail routes. Trading centres became hubs of news traffic which was commodified through journals that printed news reports and letters.

The first decade of the seventeenth century saw newspapers proper materialise. In 1609 Johann Carolus of Strasbourg bought a printing workshop to speed up the production of his previously handwritten news reports, so giving birth to the *Relation* – generally recognised as the first modern European newspaper. But Carolus had to make sure only to include material that would be approved by the authorities. Newspapers were carefully regulated and typically only allowed to report on foreign affairs. Much of Europe from the late seventeenth century was to be governed by absolute monarchs sensitive to political criticism, while additionally in southern Europe, in Spain, Portugal and the city-states of Italy, the Catholic Inquisition remained a powerful engine of repression. An exception was England. The onset of civil war from 1642, the disintegration of royal authority and the gravity of national political events created the opening for a more liberated press. The coming to power of Cromwell saw a reimposition of controls but a more permissive legal environment resumed in the aftermath of the Glorious Revolution of 1688 and the expiration in 1695 of the Licensing Act. Governments in much of the rest of Europe were to remain more restrictive until well into the nineteenth century. Towards the end of the seventeenth century, the content of periodicals moved on from information to include instructional pieces and, more contentiously, subjects which went beyond the factual to the reasoned and judgemental, such as book reviews, learned articles, essays on manners and morals, literary criticism and so on.

State authorities made early use of periodicals while at the same time regulating and censoring non-state publications. Authorities found them useful for various purposes, such as informing the population about court events, foreign affairs, matters relating to trade or disseminating official decrees. *The London Gazette* was the newspaper of the English crown. It was founded in 1665 during the Great Plague of London, and it was originally called *The Oxford Gazette* (to where the court of Charles II had temporarily relocated). The first London issue, issue 24 (5 February 1665) gives accounts of disputes between foreign powers; a peace agreement; the business of the Court of Claims; wrecked ships; the reappearance of convoy vessels which had gone missing; a naval engagement; the arrival of a foreign dignitary; concerns of the pope; and the burial of a Mr Anthony Parsons of Durham who during his life had been a non-conformist but, we are assured, 'dyed a true Son of the Church of England.'[2] *The London Gazette* was itself modelled on the French *Gazette* established in 1631 under the patronage of Louis XIII's Chief Minister, Cardinal Richelieu.

The audience for these publications was primarily the educated classes: administrative officials, judges, lawyers, doctors, scholars, priests and military officers. Along with wealthy merchants, financiers and manufacturers, this group was to take up a prominent position in the public sphere. State journals were a tacit recognition of the significance of this emerging source of social and economic power. But the court and the public were not detached from each other. Many members of the nobility, as well as a few of the most successful commoners, moved between both worlds while, outside the court, there were venues where people of a wide variety of ranks could mingle: coffee houses, masonic lodges, academies of literature and natural philosophy, theatres, salons, spas and pleasure gardens. As the boundaries between prosperous commoners and the nobility became less stark, one of the consequences was to polarise society between the haves and the have-nots, the latter comprising the mass of the population. The development of the public sphere touched most of Europe. Even a state as economically undeveloped and as politically despotic as Russia flirted with the idea, although ultimately the experiment failed. Peter I and Catherine II attempted to kick-start a public cultural and intellectual life. They used subsidies to support Russian writers, printers and periodicals. They established foreign-style institutions such as academies and universities, and imported foreign writers, artists, performers, natural philosophers and engineers. Diderot, whose library Catherine bought, was one of these.

From this new public space there developed the notion of 'public opinion'. The term was being used in Great Britain and France from the early eighteenth century, pointing to an informal, legitimising authority beyond what was constitutionally enshrined in the body or office of the monarch and the institutions of state. It was an expression of the concerns of citizens on issues of cultural and national interest, with an expectation in the latter case that the government should take those concerns into account in its policy-making. Although it was an inclusive term, in reality it was understood to reflect the views of independent, educated and propertied members of society. In keeping with Enlightenment principles, these were, after all, the people best positioned to inform themselves about important matters, to engage in reasoned debate, and to reach objective conclusions that demanded respect. For some, like the French physiocrats (economists who believed that agriculture was the source of wealth), ideal government would be based upon an absolute monarch who was guided by such opinion. Thinkers, journalists, political activists and critics often located themselves in relation to public opinion, either as self-appointed representatives speaking on its behalf or as its educators, particularly on topics such as morality, manners and cultural taste. Later in the century it became entwined with ideas of popular sovereignty, most notably during the French Revolution. Of course, there were no mechanisms by which public opinion could be plausibly measured. And it was vanishingly unlikely that there existed out there in society a single, unifying point of view. 'Public opinion' was rather something to be claimed and asserted. Nonetheless, for all its fuzziness, by the late 1780s, public opinion was acknowledged across Europe as a force that had to be reckoned with.

Politics

Political organisation and debate within the public sphere were most advanced in Great Britain. Many millions of pamphlets had promoted intense and widespread political discussion during the constitutional turmoil of the seventeenth century. The weakening of censorship and regulation at the end of the century allowed publishing to flourish. Political activism was fuelled by a parliamentary system of government with rival parties and regular elections. Competing interests drew on journals, periodicals and newspapers to push their cause. Whigs and Tories formed political clubs that would meet at coffee houses and taverns to plot their campaigns. The unusually partisan nature of British politics made it tricky for the government to prevent information from reaching and being critiqued by the outside world although there were some tools at the government's disposal that allowed it to exert a degree of control. The government subsidised sympathetic journalists and newspapers. It prohibited the publication in newspapers of unofficial parliamentary reports, and a ban was imposed on taking notes in Parliament. Laws were available to prosecute texts deemed to be seditious, licentious or blasphemous. In 1712 the government introduced a Stamp Act, placing a tax on publishers with the effect of making life difficult for newspapers aimed at a less wealthy and broader popular readership. Publications that were supported by the government were exempt.

At elections, constituents expected to be fêted with food and drink; to have the opportunity to attend hustings and rallies; to be able to examine candidates in

Beggars

Poverty was an ever present threat to most. It is estimated that at times as much as 10 per cent of Europe's population was indigent.

The dance of death: death and the beggar, etching by D. Chodowiecki, 1791, after himself. (*Public Domain: The Wellcome Collection*)

Beggar family, ca. 1735–37 by Jean-Baptiste Marie Pierre. (*Public Domain: The Metropolitan Museum of Art*)

A group of beggars, 1798–1813, by Jean Duplessi-Bertaux. (*Public Domain: The Wellcome Collection*)

A blind beggar, 1757, coloured mezzotint by C.W.E Dietrich. (*Public Domain: The Wellcome Collection*)

Blood Letting

The ancient and widespread practise of bloodletting was based upon humoral theory, one of the aims of which was to manage the movement of blood around the body in order to restore a healthy balance.

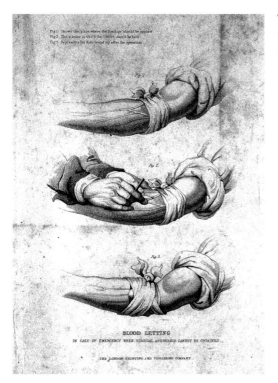

Three diagrams illustrating how to bleed an arm, stipple engraving. CC BY 4.0. (*The Wellcome Collection*)

Artificial leeches. CC BY 4.0. (*The Wellcome Collection*)

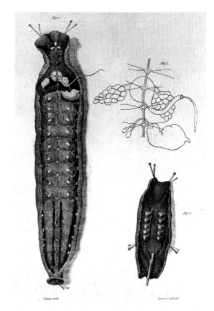

From *A treatise on the medicinal leech*, 1816, by James Rawlins Johnson. CC BY 4.0. (*The Wellcome Collection*)

Casanova

Casanova's portrait by his brother Francesco, a
renowned painter of battle scenes, c. 1750–1755.
(*Public Domain: Wikimedia Commons*)

Casanova portrait, 1760, Francesco Narici. (*Public Domain: Wikimedia Commons*)

Medallion portrait of Casanova, 1788, engraving by Johann Berka, used as frontispiece for *Icosameron*. (*Public Domain: Wikimedia Commons*)

Manuscript page from *History of My Life* (*Histoire de Ma Vie*), Vol. X, Chap. II, p.1. (*Public Domain: Wikimedia Commons*)

Duelling

Casanova records fighting at least nine duels and appears to have won all of them.

Position pour le Garde de Tierce, et la Coup de quarte sur les Armes, 1700-1769, James Gwin. (*Public Domain: The Yale Center for British Art*)

False Courage, 1788, Thomas Rowlandson. (*Public Domain: The Metropolitan Museum of Art*)

Gambling

Gambling was a craze throughout Europe. Casanova was a gambler himself and the co-director of a lottery established to support Paris's Military School, to become the most successful lottery in history to that point.

The Reading of the Lottery Winners, 1746, by Anne Claude Philippe, comte de Caylus. (*Public Domain: The Metropolitan Museum of Art*)

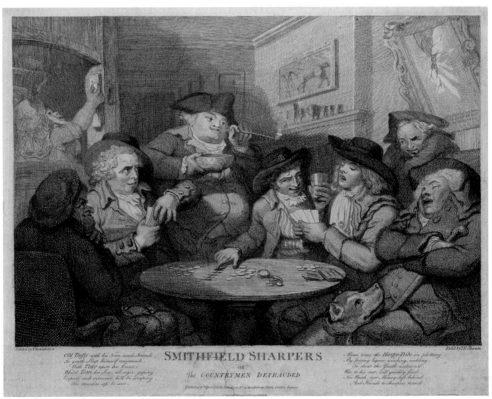

Smithfield Sharpers, or the Countryman Defrauded, 1787, John Keyse Sherwin British after Thomas Rowlandson. (*Public Domain: The Metropolitan Museum of Art*)

Promiscuity

Casanova comments on 'the general dissoluteness of the times' and records how on his first meeting with the famous French singer Marie Le Fel he discovered that her three children had been fathered by three different high status men.

The Garter, 1724, Jean François de Troy. (*Public Domain: The Metropolitan Museum of Art*)

Marie Fel, 1757, by Maurice Quentin de la Tour. (*Public Domain: Wikimedia Commons*)

The rake carouses in a tavern full of prostitutes, 1735, engraving by Thomas Bowles. (*Public Domain: The Wellcome Collection*)

Religion

Portuguese Synagogue in Amsterdam, 1737, Balthasar Bernaerts, after Louis Fabritius Dubourg. (*Public Domain: The Metropolitan Museum of Art*) Simultaneously a testament to the historical persecution of Jews in Europe and the relative tolerance of Amsterdam.

The Unfortunate Calas Family, c. 1765, Jean-Baptiste Delafosse, after Louis de Carrogis. (*Public Domain: The National Gallery of Art*) The Calas scandal ignited one of Voltaire's most famous campaigns against religious intolerance.

Interior of St Peter's, Rome, c. 1754, Giovanni Paolo Pannini. (*Public Domain: The National Gallery of Art*)
A striking representation of the ancient wealth, prestige and power of the Catholic Church.

Superstition

Formal religious institutions existed alongside, and often overlapped with, a range of other widespread supernatural traditions.

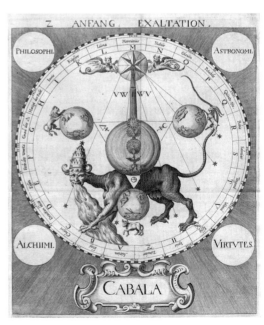

From *Cabala, Speculum Artis Et Naturae In Alchymia*, 1654, Stephan Michelspacher. (*Public Domain Mark 1.0. The Public Domain Review*)

Credulity, Superstition, and Fanaticism,
1762, by William Hogarth. (*Public
Domain: The Metropolitan Museum of Art*)

Mary Squires the fortune teller foretells
the future to Sir John Hill, etching, 1753.
(*Public Domain: The Wellcome Museum*)

Theatre

The theatre was one of the key institutions of the public sphere. It was popular and often rowdy. From 1730 to 1780 there were thirty-six riots or instances of serious disorder in London theatres.

The Pit Door, 1784, after Robert Dighton the Elder. (*Public Domain: The Metropolitan Museum of Art*)

Mezzetin and Harlequin Use the Picture Frame to Catch Pantaloon and Pierrot, c. 1729. (*Public Domain: The National Gallery of Art*)

The Seven Years War

The Seven Years War was one of the central events of the eighteenth century and shaped Europe's destiny for generations to come. It also made Casanova rich (at least temporarily).

Portrait of Frederick II by Anton Graff. (*Public Domain: Wikimedia Commons*) The chief protagonist of the Seven Years War.

Dresden from the Banks of the Elbe River, 1782, Adrian Zingg. (*Public Domain: The National Gallery of Art*)

The Fortress of Kingston, 1756–1758, Bernardo Belloto. (*Public Domain: The National Gallery of Art*)
Hilltop stronghold near Dresden

Venice
A seductive blend of ancient and modern, both Casanova's Venice and Venice today.

Shop Window. (© *Kevin Butters*)

Al Vaporetto. (© *Kevin Butters*)

Doorway. (© *Kevin Butters*)

Two Gondoliers. (© *Kevin Butters*)

Cellist. (© *Kevin Butters*)

Outside Florians Cafe. (© *Kevin Butters*)

the flesh; to shake hands and exchange pleasantries. The candidates themselves would advertise in the press and distribute printed material, further extending the reach of political life. Colonial and European wars heightened popular interest in political events. They also had major commercial implications. Military intervention might benefit certain businesses, while raising the money to pay for it in the form of excise taxes might penalise others. There was a strong incentive for businesses to try to influence decisions by pleading their case before parliamentary committees, ministers, officials, Members of Parliament and the general population. Access to power inspired the formation of trade organisations to finance and coordinate lobbying. Lobbyists pushed the government to justify their decisions and to release official information into the public sphere for scrutiny, while at the same time providing their own competing sources of information. Lobby groups were part of a countrywide campaign in 1733 that forced the government to back down from an excise scheme to reduce the burden of taxation from land owners by raising taxes on tobacco and wine.

The 1733 Excise Crisis illustrated another feature of expanding British political consciousness: the development of extra-parliamentary campaigning. Parliamentary parties, trade bodies, religious groups, local government, voluntary associations, and so on could coalesce to support a particular cause. As well as the extensive use of newspapers and other print media, collective petitioning of Parliament, which had become a regular part of English culture since the Glorious Revolution of 1688, was also a way that people could voice their opinions on political or religious matters. As a right of all subjects, petitioning could extend direct political engagement to those who would otherwise be excluded. Its participatory nature meant that petition drives spurred other activities such as meetings and demonstrations with the aim of maximising the number of signatures. Petitioning took place on a huge scale by the end of the eighteenth and into the nineteenth century. By 1792 abolitionists had flooded Parliament with hundreds of anti-slave-trade petitions and hundreds of thousands of signatures.

One of the most dramatic examples of extra-parliamentary politicking was the John Wilkes affair. Amongst other things, Wilkes was a journalist, a Member of Parliament, a political radical, a hedonist, a rogue, and, by a strange quirk of fate, the lover of La Charpillon, the courtesan Casanova's infatuation for whom had driven him to the brink of suicide. It was the time of the Seven Years War. In 1760 George III had ascended the throne, and along with him came Lord Bute, the king's favourite, who was given a place in the cabinet before being promoted to Prime Minister in 1762. Bute was treated with suspicion and resentment by other ministers, and was disliked by the general public, particularly after the resignation of William Pitt who had turned the war in Britain's favour. Pitt had fallen out with George III who was looking to pursue a more conciliatory foreign policy. 'The favourite', according to Horace Walpole, 'was unknown, ungracious, and a Scot: His connection with the Princess, an object of scandal.'[3] The scandal in question, that Bute was having an affair with the Dowager Princess of Wales, George III's mother, was probably untrue.

It was into this febrile environment of war, party politics, internal government tensions and disputes over the conduct of foreign affairs that Wilkes launched *The North Briton* in 1762. Wilkes, whose aim was to restore Pitt, lambasted the Prime Minister and his native Scotland with gusto, and played on the rumours of his supposed affair with George III's mother. Wilkes's continuous vilification of Bute and his ministers did much to intensify the public's animosity towards the king's favourite. In addition to Bute, Wilkes took aim at excise taxes and government corruption in general. Walpole notes: 'the *North Briton* proceeded with an acrimony, a spirit, and a licentiousness unheard of before even in this country.'[4] In the notorious issue No. 45 of 23 April 1763, Wilkes rounds on the 'ignominious peace', 'dictated', according to him, by 'the King of Prussia', and describes Bute, 'the Scot', as an 'insolent, incapable, despotic minister'.[5] He even goes so far as to impugn the honesty of George III himself: 'Every friend of his country must lament that a prince of so many great and amiable qualities, whom England truly reveres, can be brought to give the sanction of his sacred name to the most odious measures, and to the most unjustifiable, public declarations, from a throne ever renowned for truth, honour, and unsullied virtue.'[6] Throughout, in typical Wilkes fashion, he makes appeals to 'the English nation', 'the discerning and impartial public', 'the liberties of Whigs and Englishmen', 'the whole body of Englishmen', 'the voice of the people', 'the public', and 'a brave and insulted people'. Significantly, Wilkes declares that the monarch is 'responsible to his people.'[7]

The government's response was to issue a general warrant for Wilkes' arrest, and anyone else who was involved in the publication on the grounds of 'seditious libel', a vaguely defined crime that involved criticising the government. Controversially, the warrant did not name a specific individual, giving enormous discretion to those who wielded it. A public outcry ensued. Wilkes was sent to the Tower of London but after a week was set free on the basis of his parliamentary privilege and went on the attack, accusing the government of threatening the liberty of the individual and of the press. The government tried to nullify Wilkes by expelling him from Parliament in order to remove his parliamentary immunity. To do so, he was charged on two counts of libel but fled to Paris before he could be prosecuted, remaining there for the next four years. In January 1764 Wilkes was duly convicted in his absence and declared an outlaw.

Wilkes' unsparing assaults on the government, his acerbic pen, his open defiance and his colourful personality had made him hugely popular, in America as well as Britain. Biographer A H Cash writes: 'His image could be found on tobacco papers, halfpenny ballads, porcelain dishes, punchbowls, teapots, prints, and Broadsides.'[8] Fearing a public backlash, the government decided not to arrest Wilkes when he returned to England in 1768, in debt and hoping, forlornly, for a pardon. He now stood for election on an anti-government, public-liberty platform, winning the seat for Middlesex. He waived his parliamentary privilege, handed himself into the authorities and was sentenced to two years in prison, thereby cementing his hero status. Thousands gathered in protest, one outcome of which was the Massacre of St George's Fields, when troops killed and wounded a number of demonstrators, sparking riots across the capital. A struggle then ensued between Parliament and the electorate, the latter repeatedly re-electing Wilkes, and the former repeatedly expelling him, until in April 1769 Wilkes's seat was awarded to the losing candidate. From prison and upon his release he continued to be a thorn in the government's side: in 1774 he became the Lord Mayor of London, and in the same year was elected to Parliament once again, this time retaining his seat.

The ability of Wilkes to draw on and mobilise public opinion led to the development around him of a nationwide movement. As well as demonstrations and merchandise, there were Wilkite clubs, letter writing campaigns, petitions and the continuous outpouring of printed material, including ballads, handbills, pamphlets, political cartoons and, of course, newspapers. In 1769, hundreds of Wilkites met at the London Tavern in Bishopsgate to pay off Wilkes' debts and support him in his fight against the power of the king and his ministers. They established the Society of Gentlemen Supporters of the Bill of Rights. The society was to go on to organise meetings and petitions across the country, campaigning against what it saw as abuses of the royal prerogative and in favour of parliamentary reform. In the short-term, the consequences of Wilkes' crusade resulted in the freedom of the press to report on Parliament and the abandonment of general warrants. In the longer term, the popular agitation he led established a powerful impetus for democratic reform and illustrated the value of extra-parliamentary pressure.

It was 13 June 1763 that Casanova arrived in London, seven weeks after the publication of No. 45 and the beginning of the Wilkes uproar. Casanova's political perspective was that of a foreigner who had lived all his life under governments where personal freedom and rights were far more circumscribed, whether under the patriciate oligopoly of the Republic of Venice or the absolute monarchy of Old Regime France. What strikes Casanova is the lack of deference to rank amongst the lower orders, to the court in particular: 'A man dressed for court would not dare to walk the streets of London; a porter, a deadbeat, a wretch from the dregs of the people will throw mud at him, laugh in his face, bump into him, all to provoke him into saying something disagreeable in order to start a fight.'[9] He refers to an occasion when there was a riot at the Drury Lane Theatre despite the presence of George III. As far as newspapers and journalists were concerned, Casanova was of the opinion that the press very much abused their freedom.

The degree of open interaction between the rulers and the ruled evident in Britain was rare in the rest of Europe. Whereas in Britain the guiding assumption was that government should be transparent, under absolutist regimes such as France the opposite was the case. Unlike Britain, the French government's financial affairs were kept secret until 1781. While in Britain, the crown, Parliament (consisting of the Lords and the Commons) and, increasingly, public opinion, were recognised as sources of political legitimacy, in France such political legitimacy was officially the sole monopoly of the king, at least until the French Revolution. Only the king could speak on behalf of the entire nation. His role was to preserve the constitutional order that he had inherited, including the privileges of its various components such as the nobility, Church, courts (*parlements*) and guilds. People lived as members of overlapping groups subject to a variety of authorities and asserting a variety of rights. Within this environment the public sphere was more restricted, particularly in matters of politics, and the control and censorship of printed materials. But politics were not absent.

In an age of sincere belief in God, when subjects contested some aspect of their own state's chosen religion there were likely to be political implications. Across different parts of Europe and within different confessions many worshippers felt that their spiritual needs were not being met. They wanted something more personal and devout, whether this was Pietism in Lutheran Prussia, Methodism within Anglican England or Jansenism within Catholic France. In each of these cases, as like-minded people joined together, they freely developed their own codes of behaviour, practices and ways of organising themselves. Not being run by the state, the Church or any recognised constitutional body these religious affiliations were part of the public sphere. Inevitably tensions arose between these groups and those members of the Church who regarded them as a destabilising faction, if not heretical.

Within an absolutist state, the monarch played a central role in how such tensions resolved. Frederick II was more than happy to accommodate Pietism and had sufficient authority to protect it, but for Louis XV, Jansenism was a knottier problem. On the one hand, its puritanical outlook had attracted popular support within France. On the other, it shared sufficient similarities with Calvinism to make many within the Catholic Church uneasy, in particular the influential and more worldly Jesuits. Moves by the papacy in the late seventeenth century to suppress Jansenism led to resistance within France amongst not merely its supporters but also those who objected to papal interference in French religious affairs, notably the monarchy and the French courts. But by the early eighteenth century this political dynamic had shifted. The consolidation of royal power meant that the papacy was regarded as less of a danger than internal religious divisions. Jansenism further alienated itself from the sympathies of the crown by questioning the basis of its religious and secular authority. Jansenism maintained that royal authority was not derived directly from God, as the absolutist doctrine of divine right insisted, but from the people as a body who comprised the Church and the nation. As a result, when Clement XI issued a bull condemning Jansenism it sparked a major and decades-long political struggle between those who supported the bull – they being the Church and the crown – and its opponents, led by the *parlement* of Paris, keen to defend its own jurisdictional authority against papal and royal incursions. Printed accounts and arguments publicising the controversy nationwide allowed the conflict to become part of a broader public debate, eluding the monarchy's attempts at control, and resulting in its own position coming under scrutiny. Of particular concern to Louis XV was the attempt by the *parlements*, echoing Jansenist doctrine, to portray themselves as a representative body which spoke on behalf of the nation, thereby elevating their constitutional significance relative to that of the monarch's.

The Jansenist controversy declined after the 1760s but it had expanded the political space beyond the control of the court, Church and constitutional bodies. This was a space which was to be filled by *philosophes;* clandestine publishing; foreign press; Voltaire's campaigns against injustice; opposition to parlementary reforms; discussion of royal fiscal and administrative reforms; and the activity of local assemblies established in the decade prior to the French Revolution. In addition, the growth of state administration and the court meant that politically sensitive information increasingly leaked into the public arena where it could be debated. Sometimes this was deliberately managed. Court politics were fractious and competing interests supplied information to the outside world to garner support for their own policy preferences and ambitions or in order to damage those of their enemies.

Books

The public sphere embraced more than politics, of course. It engaged with society's entire cultural domain: art, music, theatre and, most important of all, whatever could be written and read. The flourishing of print media went hand-in-hand with improvements in literacy, the one stimulating the other. Increasing affluence, population growth, urbanisation and an expansion of occupational groups such as financiers, manufacturers, merchants, professionals and skilled artisans meant that across Europe the commercial demand for the written word allowed writers to earn a livelihood independent of court patronage. Writers no longer needed to pander so much to the sensibilities and reputational appetites of their aristocratic patrons for whom the work of the writer (or artist or musician) was of less importance than the prestige it brought to their name.

Other trends fed into this expanding market place. Far more was printed in the local vernacular than the scholarly lingua franca of Latin, as had been the case. Reading patterns changed. Previously, households would own a small number of texts, usually religious in character, which they would read and re-read, often as part of communal as well as solitary devotional routines. This continued but people also started to read more, more widely and for their own amusement. The growth of journals carrying book reviews and advertisements spurred demand. Cost was important. If we use subsistence wages as a rough guide, an early eighteenth-century Bible produced by the Canstein Bible Institute of Halle sold for one-twentieth of Luther's first German Bible when it had been published almost two centuries earlier.[10] The expense of reading was mitigated further by second-hand book shops (which might also lend), reading clubs, subscription societies, circulating libraries, public libraries, reading rooms and, of course, coffee houses, allowing access to printed matter at a fraction of their full price.

Large numbers of religious works were published, such as Bibles, sermons, commentaries and polemical essays, the readers motivated by deeply rooted faith as well as contemporary religious movements and controversies. But while there was a growing market for religious texts in absolute terms, this was outstripped by the demand for secular literature. Traditional chapbooks (booklets of poetry, fables, short stories and various miscellaneous content) and almanacs sold in their hundreds of thousands, and there was a flourishing market in drama, erotic literature, geography, history, memoirs, *mémoires judiciaires*, occupational texts, poetry, popular science, school books, self-improvement and travel. From the middle of the eighteenth century, novels became fashionable. Evidence from Leipzig book fair catalogues suggest that by the end of the century the genre of the novel was almost on a par with religious works. The interest in novels, such as Samuel Richardson's *Pamela* (1740), with their exploration of characters' inner lives, took hold first of all in England, where censorship was less restrictive, but quickly became popular in France and elsewhere. Rousseau's *Julie, or, The New Heloise* (1761) was hugely successful, as was Goethe's *The Sorrows of Young Werther* (1774). Novels appealed in particular to genteel female readers, often dealing with themes of virtue, courtship, forbidden love and familial duty, and a number of leading writers themselves were women such as Frances Brooke, Maria Edgeworth, Phoebe Gibbs, Charlotte Lennox and Charlotte Smith. Writing was one of the few respectable careers open to well-educated women, and one which could offer some degree of financial independence.

Inevitably there were those who complained that novels were harmful, along with the 'mania' for reading in general: they were morally corrupting, time-wasting, subversive of the traditional social and political order, and even medically harmful, inducing a wide range of ailments from haemorrhoids to headaches to hypochondria. Casanova observed that there were no novels in the library of the father of his lover, CC, possibly suggesting that in Venice at the time there was a question mark over their respectability. The impact upon women, in this patriarchal age, was a particular cause for alarm, given that women and their concerns were so central to this new genre, as writers, readers and protagonists. Questions were raised over whether so much novel reading might lead women to neglect their domestic duties, to become over-stimulated or to have their heads filled with improper notions. From religious authorities, as with other forms of amusement, there was criticism that they took away time that should have been devoted to God. In reality, most novels were decidedly moralistic, especially those produced by a female author, sensitive as she was to anything in her writing that might harm her reputation.

The debate surrounding novels itself fed into the public sphere, notably through moral weeklies that sought to shape attitudes on morality and politeness. Like the novel, it was a genre that particularly appealed to women. In the vanguard were the London journals *The Tatler* (1709–1711) and its successor incarnation *The Spectator* (1711–12), the latter becoming enormously popular with daily sales in the tens of thousands, leading to numerous similar publications in Britain and abroad such as *Der Patriot* (Hamburg, 1724–26). They were characterised by essays on contemporary literary and social issues, with the aim to instruct while being entertaining. Making their way into *The Spectator* for discussion were such topics as drunkenness, envy, etiquette, fashion, Italian opera, physical defects, superstition, and women's weakness for 'pretty trappings'.[11] What made the moral weekly significant was its secular focus on the private and the social, and its avoidance of politics. It was another example of cultural influence shifting away from the court and the Church. Through moral weeklies, novels, published letters (real or contrived), memoirs and *mémoires judiciaries* (in France, sensationalised legally publishable briefs by lawyers), the ordinary lives of private individuals became a focus of public interest and judgement.

Books and writing were a central part of Casanova's life. He was recognised as being a remarkably knowledgeable man. In a letter from Bernard de Muralt to the renowned scholar Albrecht von Haller, Muralt remarks that Casanova 'appears to have seen and read a prodigious amount.'[12] Throughout *History of My Life* there are numerous references to books and authors, ancient and modern, reputable and disreputable, what he is reading or has read, his visits to bookshops and libraries, books he has bought for lovers and books confiscated from him by the authorities. On his journey from Paris to the Dutch Republic in 1759 Casanova describes settling down to read Claude Helvétius' highly controversial work *On the Mind* (1758), a work which had been condemned by the *parlement* of Paris earlier in the year and burned by the Paris hangman. A collection of volumes on the occult was used as evidence to get him thrown into the Leads. Stopped by customs officials on his entry into Rome, he records: 'I had about thirty of them [books], all enemies of religion or of the virtues it ordains.'[13]During one shopping expedition at Lodi near Milan, he bought for his lover, Clementina, 'over one hundred books, all poets, historians, geographers, physicists, and some novels translated from Spanish or French.'[14] Awaiting the arrival of his lover, MM, at a casino, he remarks on a small library there: 'They [the books] were few but excellent. One found there everything that the wisest philosophers had written against religion, and everything the most voluptuous pens had written on that subject which is unique to love.'[15]

People of letters, salon culture and writers

As already noted, Casanova was motivated in his reading not only by an immense curiosity about the world but also by a desire to impress others and to be recognised as a man of culture and intellect. Appealing against his imprisonment in Madrid in 1768, Casanova describes himself as 'a subject of the Republic of Venice, a man of letters, quite rich.'[16] Voltaire addresses him as a man of letters, and it was the Venetian's custom to seek out other such men on his travels. These people of letters played a key role in the intellectual discourse of the public sphere and the shaping of public opinion. They were governed by a fellowship of interests, norms and expectations rooted in the Enlightenment and that transcended state boundaries and, to some extent, social ones as well.

Antoine Lilti provides a definition which matches Casanova pretty well: 'The man of letters was distinguished by his lack of specialisation, by his capacity for excelling in different literary genres, by his mastery of codes of behaviour elaborated by the urban aristocracy, and by a disinterest in things financial.'[17]

This intellectual culture was a phenomenon in which networks of correspondents across Europe debated and exchanged ideas, hence 'people of letters'. Paris was a particularly important centre, one in which its salons allowed the nobility, affluent commoners and eminent or aspiring writers and artists to socialise. Such largely aristocratic gatherings were reputed to have played a key role in the French Enlightenment. Directed by influential female hosts, they were understood to nurture and disseminate Enlightenment ideas, embracing an egalitarian ethos that encouraged free debate. Recent research, notably by Lilti, has shown that the historical reality was somewhat different: 'the function of salons was to provide an interface between literary life and the amusement of the elites, between the court and the city, and between learned debates and political intrigues.'[18] They were places of entertainment typified by dinners, suppers, readings, dramatics, music, gambling, bright conversation and keeping up with court news. Although salons did have a role in political and diplomatic intrigues, serious debates on philosophy and politics were not usually part of the agenda. Their intrusion would undermine at least two of the key principles of sociability: the avoidance of pedantry and overt disagreement. The management of disagreement and the maintenance of at least the façade of social harmony was an important feature of salon culture, a skill that marked out the most celebrated hosts, such as Madame Geoffrin and Madame du Deffand. For theorists of political philosophy the notion of sociability itself was a subject of debate. It was argued that mankind had come to possess a natural sociability that encouraged fruitful co-existence in society. To be amiable and to please, in this light, was an important virtue, one which salon culture fostered. Here is Voltaire's scathing assessment of salon culture from *Candide*: 'The supper was like most suppers in Paris: silence at first, then a confused babble in which no one can make themselves heard, followed by an exchange of largely insipid witticisms, false news, pointless argument, a little politics and a quantity of slander.'[19]

Salons were private affairs. They took place in private residences in which guests, at least in the first instance, had to be recommended or specifically invited. Salons were an environment in which information was carefully controlled, especially information that was socially and politically sensitive. Their exclusivity meant that they should not be regarded as a component of the public sphere, as important as their mediating role may have been between those groups who were part of the public sphere and the court. It is worth noting that the terms 'salon' and 'salonnière' were not used prior to the French Revolution as descriptors for what we now refer to as salon culture. A salon was simply a room. The retrospective application of these terms can be misleading, suggesting that salons were more homogenous than was the case. They were very diverse. What connected them was the conception of worldliness, or worldly sociability: secular codes of behaviour deemed to be compatible with courtly honour. A commoner could be accepted as a member of high society, or *le monde*, and be invited to salons if they conformed to such codes, tacitly recognising that members of the aristocratic class were their superiors. The forms of politeness and extravagant praise employed by aristocrats and commoners towards each other was not a sign of egalitarianism. For the former to be treated with respect by the latter was their due; for the latter to be treated with respect by the former was an honour. Ultimately it was rank that counted, not brilliance or wealth. The commercial opportunities that existed for writers in Britain were less abundant in France. Unless writers possessed private resources that allowed them to pursue their career independently, patronage was usually required in the form of gifts or the award of a pension or a position. Attending salons gave writers and people of letters the opportunity of obtaining influential champions and social recognition. For the aristocrat and host, writers added interest to the gathering and the prestige of being a benefactor. They were also useful sources of intellectual and cultural expertise. It was the world of the salons that launched the career of Cardinal de Bernis.

So what was Casanova's relationship with Parisian high society? As far as the salons went, the bar for entry was high, particularly for foreigners. Usually only those in the highest echelons of European nobility could gain access. But there were a number of cards the Venetian could play. The salons possessed an insatiable appetite for novelty, and his escape from the Leads had made him a celebrity across Europe. He was a captivating story teller, and everywhere he went he received requests to recount the exploit. There was his remarkable success on the Amsterdam money markets and his reputation as a master of the occult. Most importantly of all, he had as his protectors one of the most powerful men in France, de Bernis, one of the richest women in France, the Marquise d'Urfé, along with the Countess du Rumain, another aristocrat of considerable influence. If those were Casanova's qualifications, how would he measure up against the criteria of worldly sociability? Superlatively, is the answer. His lifestyle, manners and values were very much that of a courtier. He was witty, sensitive to the nuances of civility, adept at flattery, self-deprecating, appropriately deferential, and could write light, gallant verse, a valued skill in *le monde*. Casanova was a master of the arts of seduction, and his sincere aim was always to please.

Evidence from his memoirs suggest that Casanova was indeed embraced by *le monde*. In passing, he mentions that he befriended d'Alembert at Madame Graffigny's – a woman of letters whose salon was among the half dozen or so of those that were most influential. He attended a concert and a supper hosted by La Riche de la Poupliniere, an exceptionally wealthy tax farmer who operated a salon at his chateau at Passy. Casanova did, of course, receive an invitation to the salon of the Marquise d'Urfé who, according to her nephew, had twelve people to dinner every day.

During his involvement with the Paris lottery Casanova writes how he was accepted into the homes of the greatest families. There is also evidence from his soon-to-be-lover, Giustiniana Wynne, who had recently arrived in Paris at that time. In a letter to her lover Andrea Memmo, she writes: 'He has gained admittance, I don't know how, to the best Parisian society.'[20] Casanova even appears to have set up his own salon. To maintain one was an expensive business, and he refers to needing 100,000 francs, or livres, to maintain such a lifestyle. This seems about right. 40,000 livres was around the minimum outlay to run a salon, and Casanova was far more ambitious than that. To put these sums into perspective, fewer than 250 noble families in France enjoyed an annual income greater than 50,000 livres. Lilti notes: 'these estimates situate the Paris salons within a segment of Paris society that predictably consisted of the court aristocracy and the major financiers.'[21] It comes as little surprise that Casanova was unable to sustain such a lifestyle for very long.

A person of letters did not have to be published. Casanova titled himself as such before he produced his major written works later in life. Voltaire's *Encyclopedia* entry, *People of Letters*, declares, 'There are many men of letters who are not authors, and they are probably the happiest…they are judges and the others are judged.'[22] Nonetheless, for Casanova writing in some form or another was a regular and time-consuming activity. For much of his life he kept a detailed account of his experiences. Following his visit to Voltaire he spent an evening and a day writing down their conversations. After the assassination attempt upon him in Barcelona he was placed under arrest and his papers confiscated. Much to the surprise of the police, they discovered that most of his trunk was filled with note-books. Incarcerated there for over a month without explanation, he used his time to work on a book about the government of Venice, and upon his release he spent the three days he was given to leave the city writing some thirty letters to friends and acquaintances.

Casanova traces his writing ambitions to childhood. He caused some astonishment when he was 11 by composing in Latin an ingeniously witty line of verse in response to a question on grammar. He talks about how at around 19 or 20 he was tentatively starting upon a literary career. He discusses writing style on a couple of occasions, notably in a conversation with the poet and tragedian, Crébillon. Casanova frequently refers to poetry he has written. He and his lover, Clementina, wrote love poems together. He composed an ode to recite at a literary academy in Rome upon being accepted as one of its members. In Venice he attacked the plays of the writer, Pietro Chiari, through verse which was circulated around the city and, according to Casanova, made him a powerful enemy of a soon-to-be State Inquisitor. Asked by Voltaire whether he had written many sonnets, he replied: 'Ten to twelve that I like, and two or three thousand that perhaps I haven't even reread.'[23] But in keeping with an authentic man of letters Casanova did not restrict his talents to verse. He explored a variety of media and genres, from satirical pamphlets to histories, to literary criticism, to science fiction, to drama, and to philosophical dialogues. He even began writing a dictionary on cheese.

Casanova's urge to write was shared by many of his educated contemporaries. For reasons discussed earlier, writing and writers flourished. By the end of the century the old writer-patron culture of dependency was very much in decline and regarded as an impediment to authorial integrity. Some writers could earn large sums but this was unusual. Others had private sources of income. They would typically be aristocrats, professionals, civil servants and office holders. Subscription campaigns could be used to support writing projects. This was a half-way house between private patronage and the public market place. A writer or publisher could raise money in the first instance by recruiting subscribers, perhaps hundreds, who would pay for a book in advance of it being written and receive copies upon its completion. The practice was employed effectively by a number of successful authors, such as Alexander Pope and Frances Burney, and was the means by which the prodigious *Encyclopedia* was funded.

Authorship may have been emerging as a profession but for some time there persisted a stigma attached to profiting from this labour or even publishing at all. It was common in the seventeenth century to distribute handwritten copies of your work to a small circle of admirers. Into the first half of the following century, writers would hide their identity and often received little or nothing by means of payment, perhaps being recompensed with a number of free copies of their work. Rousseau, obsessively jealous of his independence and freedom of thought, chose to earn his living from the exacting task of copying music rather than writing: 'I felt that writing for a living would soon have stifled my genius and killed my talent…Nothing vigorous, nothing great, can flow from an entirely venal pen.'[24] Casanova seems to have been similarly wary of writing for monetary gain. He would raise subscriptions to fund printing costs but overall his ventures appear to have left him out of pocket. In 1768 he wrote the libretto for a successful opera performed for the Spanish court: 'I was thought to be above a poet who worked to be paid; I was rewarded with applause. And in truth, I would have been insulted if they had suggested paying me.'[25] It was his reputation which was his main concern.

The theatre

One of the key institutions of the public sphere, and an important locus of sociability, was the theatre. Like the salons, it was closely bound to the court except, unlike them, increasingly it became governed by public opinion and commercialisation instead of the priorities of state and religion. Court, Church and theatre possessed similarities. Choreographed performance and ritual were central to all three. The ability to speak confidently in public, and present oneself before an audience to maximum effect, were important skills for any ruler to possess, ecclesiastic or temporal. Members of the aristocracy, including royals such as Gustav III (1771–1792), Louis XIV and Joseph II, actively participated in theatrical events.

In the sixteenth and seventeenth century, notably in England, France, Spain and the city-states of Italy, court patronage had ensured that the theatre was used as a means of glorifying the sovereign. It did this in two ways: through the direct message of a production's content; and through its lavishness and scale (its 'representative publicness' in other words). Rulers became important figures in the history of the stage. Margaret Greer notes how 'Early modern Spanish drama was born "playing the palace".'[26] Three royal companies were subsidised by Louis XIV, established on the basis of royal monopoly: the Académie Royale de Musique, more commonly known as the Paris Opera (a mixture of opera and ballet); and the Comédie Française and Comédie Italienne. The titles of the latter indicated the languages in which the productions were performed, at least initially; the Comédie Française was a royal theatre, not a national one. Sacred drama was popular in Italy and Spain in the seventeenth century. The cult of martyrs encouraged by the Catholic Church leant itself to sacred tragedies that drew not only on biblical characters but also figures such as Thomas More (1478–1535) and Mary Stuart (1542–1587). The Jesuits were particularly active in using the stage for religious ends.

Further east in the German-speaking lands of the Holy Roman Empire and the Habsburg Monarchy, for much of the century the dominance of the court persisted, underpinned by cultural rivalry amongst the numerous princelings that comprised the region. Popular theatre did exist, often parodying courtly drama, but the lack of large urban centres of the likes of London and Paris, and an absence of a strong German literary tradition, limited commercial demand to the comic and vulgar. But even here a more inclusive theatre-going public was to emerge. The devastation wrought by wars such as the Seven Years War meant that theatres were a luxury rulers found difficult to afford. Many were opened to the public to help them cover the costs. For the same reasons of economy, rulers switched from programmes that employed more prestigious foreign actors and singers to a less expensive German-speaking stage that was more accessible to a broader audience. Particularly active in developing this German stage was Emperor Joseph II who transformed the Vienna court Burgtheater in 1776 into the German National Theatre – a public institution – providing it with subsidies generous enough to enable it to compete with more celebrated European venues.

The transformation of the theatre into an institution of the public sphere that catered for the entire social spectrum expressed itself in a number of ways. In the less authoritarian environment of Britain, theatres were places of protest, nationalism and political ridicule. Gay's hugely successful *The Beggar's Opera* (1728) satirised Italian opera while taking aim at corruption, injustice and poverty. The courtly-themed, neo-classical dramas of playwrights such as Jean Racine were falling out of favour in France by the middle of the eighteenth century. These dramas were replaced by those of writers such as Françoise de Graffigny and Diderot, whose work focussed more on the concerns of commoners. Realism, sentimentality, contemporary settings, and characters drawn from across society featured increasingly. Similar tendencies were found elsewhere such as in the work of Carlo Goldoni in Venice, and of Leandro de Moratín in Spain. Given that censorship in France made political criticism difficult, it was ironic that one of the most politically explosive plays of the century was performed in Paris. Beaumarchais' attack upon aristocratic privilege through *The Marriage of Figaro* caused a furore when it was premiered in 1784, Napoleon later describing it as 'the Revolution in action.' Theatre was employed in German-speaking Europe as a means of developing a sense of national identity in the absence of any other national institutions. For some, the stage was viewed as a means of education and a way of advancing social progress in agreement with Enlightenment principles. In Poland, Stanislas II founded the National Theatre ('national' in that its productions were by Polish authors) as a vehicle to promote Enlightenment ideas. Richard Steele (founder of *The Tatler* and joint founder of *The Spectator*) made use of sentimental drama to impart moral lessons, while Ludvig Holberg in Scandinavia, and Denis Fonvizin in Russia, employed social satire for a similar purpose.

Broadly, then, commercialisation and expansion of the theatre in eighteenth-century Europe entailed a gravitational shift away from the court. Proprietors had to take account of the preferences of their paying customers if they wanted to stay in business. This was the case even for public theatres that enjoyed royal subsidies. If the public did not get what they wanted, they made their feelings known. Rowdy expressions of disapproval or approbation during a performance were commonplace. Soldiers were routinely present to inhibit misbehaviour at the Comédie Française, as they were at other venues in Europe. From 1730 to 1780 there were thirty-six riots or instances of serious disorder in London theatres.[27]

In much of Europe the social status of performers was low, exacerbated by enduring religious hostility, particularly from amongst groups such as Jansenists, Pietists and Methodists. French priests commonly withheld the sacraments and proper Christian burial from actors. For a number of reasons, this changed as the century wore on and the theatre started to acquire respectability. Theatres were becoming large businesses with more specialised roles rather than being family, co-operative affairs. In France, the Comédie Française began to function as something like a national regulating authority and dispute arbitration service. Strong competition across Europe for talented performers saw salaries rise rapidly. There was the construction of more and more architecturally sophisticated, standing playhouses, accompanied by increasing professionalisation and a growing perception of acting as an art rather than a craft. Importantly, writers, actors and impresarios, such as Diderot, Steele and David Garrick, sought to establish the theatre as a tool for the moral improvement of society.

The theatre was central to Casanova's life. His mother and putative father, as we know, were both actors. When his mother performed abroad, he was cared for in his infancy by his grandmother in a poor dwelling close to the Theatre of San Samuele where his parents had plied their trade. Later he played the violin in the pit as a member of the orchestra. It is likely that Casanova's early life would have been populated by actors, artists, dancers, costumers, craftsmen, dramatists, impresarios, musicians, singers, theatre owners, wig-makers and writers. He would have been witness to the entire art and artifice of the stage. Then there was Venice, culturally the most vibrant city in Italy and the tourist capital of Europe, with a theatre in almost every parish, with its Carnival, its never-ending festivals (religious and secular), its balls, its masques, its concerts, its operas, its casinos and its magnificent and sumptuous palazzos. Venice was a world of make-believe, of light and reflection, a city of bridges without roads, a tangle of reality and fantasy. It was a place of relative tolerance and the disarmingly exotic. For Casanova, theatricality was in his blood and the air that he breathed. It was his instinct to entertain and seduce. Casanova did not fear but embraced what was extraordinary or unconventional. On his second trip to Paris, his swindling of the Marquise d'Urfé was pure theatre replete with magic formulas, otherworldly beings and elaborate ceremonies.

The expansion of public theatre in the eighteenth century was part of a trend which saw a more general commercialisation of leisure and culture. In part it was a reflection of growing demand as a result of increasing wealth and population but it was also due to changes in the urban environment, with the provision of street lighting and a sharp decline in outbreaks of the plague, which had previously been endemic in Europe, and had led to restrictions on public entertainments. Sometimes activities which had been extensions of the court were now opening up to the public, as with spas and pleasure gardens. References to such pursuits crop up a number of times in Casanova's memoirs. In the space of less than a dozen pages covering a short slice of his time in London, Casanova describes one of the high society assembly balls organised by his ex-lover, Teresa Imer (Mrs Cornelys), and his visits to the pleasure gardens at Ranelagh and Vauxhall.

Museums, art galleries, public concerts and concert halls, all began to provide cultural experiences to a widening segment of the population that were once the preserve of the ruling elite. By the second half of the century it was the authority not of the court but of the public that was to count in matters of taste and beauty, guided by critics, academics and people of letters.

Casanova inhabited a space that allowed him to move with surprising ease between the worlds of the aristocrat and the commoner. It was a remarkable feat for a man without claim to noble blood and in the absence of an occupation or official position of any distinction. There are a number of reasons he was able to achieve this, as outlined in Chapter 3, but one of them was that he could declare himself to be a man of letters and draw upon the respectability that went along with it. It was not an idle boast but it did depend upon living at a time when the resources needed to cultivate and demonstrate such learning had become more generally available. The expansion of the public sphere meant that intellectual and cultural debate was less restricted by lack of access to the close-knit circles of the nobility or to the libraries of the Church, universities and wealthy noblemen. Casanova strove to be acknowledged in his own right as a man worthy of respect regardless of his family background. He may not have achieved the recognition he desired in his own lifetime but that he should have even entertained such an ambition is a reflection of the extent to which society had opened up beyond the court realm.

Chapter 9

Men and Women

'Sorrow and joy kill more women than men. This shows that women are more sensitive than us but also weaker.'

Giacomo Casanova, *History of My Life*

Casanova's life was about more than his relationships with women but nonetheless they were a central part and form the bulk of his memoirs. He details at length how those relationships unfolded, alongside his intentions, regrets, emotions, rationalisations and psychological insights. But before moving on to describe them, it would be useful to outline something of the experience of men and women in the eighteenth century. This should give us a better insight into the nature of those relationships generally, as well as into the perspective of women in particular.

Gendered beliefs and values

Most women lived under the authority of a male guardian (father, husband, brother, master, patron) who had the power to confine them to their own houses or incarcerate them in madhouses and convents. During their lifetime they would have to adjust to this authority being passed from one man to another, a transfer that no doubt reinforced the sense that they were an object to be owned. It is worth remembering that in eighteenth-century Europe people could, in fact, be owned. The idea of women as property was not an abstract one.

Casanova purchased a girl he named Zaire when he visited Russia. She was a peasant girl he bought from her parents for 100 roubles after checking with his hand that she was still a virgin. Checking a girl's virginity in this way was a practice Casanova records several times in his memoirs (and not only with girls of the lowest status). He notes that Louis XV did the same when meeting O-Morphi for the first time. O-Morphi was a girl Casanova claims he was instrumental in introducing to Louis, and she was the subject of a well-known painting by François Boucher called *Resting Girl* (1752). Having bought Zaire, as well as her becoming his servant, Casanova records that it gave him the right to go to bed with her.

This selling of daughters was not restricted to Russia. Jean-Jacques Rousseau and a friend bought a girl called Anzoletta from her mother in Venice. She was 11 or 12. Their plan was to use her for sex when she matured. For destitute families who were half-starved for most of the time, prostituting their daughters, or even selling them, was not unusual. In England, there existed the custom of wife sales, when a husband would auction his spouse at a market, and in this way publicly dissolve their marriage. While we have to be cautious when teasing apart emotional, sexual and metaphorical meanings in his memoirs, Casanova does at times refer to women in a manner that conveys an impression of physical ownership and rightful entitlement.

Despite the major changes that were taking place in European society, there were dominant continuities in attitudes regarding men and women and their expected roles. Anomalies existed, of course, and some contested the beliefs and practices of the time but there was a pattern of gendered difference that remained broadly unchanged from prior to the eighteenth century and beyond. Men dominated the formal structures and institutions of society and were the final authority in families and households. They were the artisans, bureaucrats, courtiers, managers, politicians, priests, professionals and scholars. The identity of men was more closely tied to their occupation than that of women. Men populated the better paid jobs and this tended to be the case even in sectors dominated by women or where men and women did the same work. Women were perceived to be driven more by their emotions, to be more sensitive and intuitive, and although imaginative and quick-witted, less capable of profound thought. Qualities associated with the female ideal included among other things compassion, chastity, humility, tenderness, devotion and agreeableness. Men, on the other hand, were considered not only physically superior but mentally superior. Defining positive characteristics for men included courage, ambition, determination and gravitas, with male strength contrasted against female fragility. Women's primary functions as wives and mothers shaped what activities were deemed the most appropriate for them in the wider socio-economic world. Attending to the health and well-being of other members of their household legitimised their place in society as domestic servants, textile workers, medical practitioners, nurses, teachers and providers of charity and poor relief. It was also the case that the household responsibilities of women were more varied than was to be the case after the eighteenth century. They might include brewing, spinning and caring for livestock.

The household

Central to interactions between men and women was the household. In its form and function it differed in a number of ways from the modern idea of a residential family unit, as diverse and fluid as the reality of today's families may be. In particular they were places of economic production as well as consumption. It would typically have been established around a married couple, with formal authority residing with the husband. But to be viable both parties would need to contribute through their finances, property, material possessions, skills, tools or labour. Commercial ventures were often funded by a wife's dowry. For this reason, although subordinate, there was an expectation by the wife that her voice would be heard and that she would be treated with respect. She could wield considerable authority in her own right over other adults in the household's day-to-day organisation, especially women.

Over time, the household might accrue children, stepchildren, servants, lodgers, apprentices, tutors, wet nurses, daughters-in-law, unmarried sisters, widowed aunts and widowed mothers. If the wife died, the husband may well remarry and have children by his new wife. Multifarious relationships and alliances existed beyond those of blood kin. As a result, the roles of women were more varied than in the domestic settings as they began to evolve from the late eighteenth century. To contribute to the family economy, women might take in washing or sell produce that they had cultivated. They might engage in proto-industrial activities such as spinning, mediated by capitalist merchants. It was not unusual for the wife to be significantly involved in the running of the household's primary business alongside her husband.

Casanova became a member of the Gozzi household in Padua. He was one of several boarders who were being tutored by a young priest, Dr Gozzi. Other members included the priest's father, who was a shoemaker, his mother, sister and at least one servant. Unfortunately, when the father was not working, he was usually drunk. This was more significant than it might seem at first sight. A household involved mutual obligations and male authority was not unassailable. Survival for many was precarious, and it was vital that households functioned effectively both for the sake of its members and of the community locally. Male heads who were neglectful or incompetent, who could not appropriately train, discipline or manage others, who drank, gambled or were violent to excess, were a headache all round. If the stability of the household was threatened then its members, notably the wife, could appeal to the Church or local authorities to try to bring him to order. Public shaming was another way of trying to get him to mend his ways.

Male guardianship and marriage

Male guardianship was how the world operated and many women valued the support and protection it gave them. There were women who challenged this status quo, who strove in different ways to carve out lives independent of male control but they were a rarity. For the most part they would not have seen their fathers, brothers and husbands as forces of coercion, but loved ones who had their best interests at heart. Individually there were men who would use the power it gave them in ways that were abusive or neglectful but social expectations, personal affection and basic human decency acted as a restraint. That said, some level of violence by husbands against their wives is likely to have been common, even if the extent is difficult to measure. Male guardianship may have given men power over women but it came with responsibilities. The failure to carry out those responsibilities could injure a man's honour, with all the social and economic repercussions that came along with it.

This duty of care is illustrated repeatedly throughout Casanova's memoirs. He was acutely conscious of the need to ensure his lovers' safety, well-being and reputation and often, too, that of women with whom he had little or no romantic involvement. After what seems to have been a somewhat tempestuous relationship with Zaire (she almost killed him by throwing a bottle at him in a jealous rage), when Casanova left Russia, he generously gifted her back to her family in the knowledge that she would then move on to the household of a wealthy 56-year-old architect who was already fond of her and would take care of her. When he seduced the daughter of a prosperous peasant family with promises of marriage, Casanova went to great lengths to find her a suitable husband with good prospects. Likewise, Casanova facilitated the marriage of Mariuccia to a wigmaker by providing her with a dowry. She was the daughter of a poor family with whom he had had a brief affair in Rome.

When he was wealthy and a celebrity in Paris, Casanova put himself at grave risk for the sake of Giustiniana Wynne. He had been infatuated by Wynne in Venice several years earlier but her mother had made sure that it would not go anywhere. Now coming across Giustiniana in Paris, pregnant, facing disgrace and on the verge of suicide, Casanova responded to her appeal for help and, after failed attempts to abort the child, finally arranged for her to be confined in a convent and give birth to the child secretly.

This sense of obligation towards a woman also translated into ensuring that sex was mutually pleasurable. Preferably Casanova would use his ingenuity to turn the act into an occasion, one in which all the senses would be stimulated and which would extend over as long a period of time as he could arrange. He was filled with dread and remorse at the thought that he may in some way have contributed to the unhappiness or harm of any woman of whom he was fond. Casanova would generally never have sex with a woman, however strong the temptation, if he thought there was a danger that he might infect her with the pox (although he once did break this rule when he was young). When writing his memoirs, he took care to anonymise women whose reputation or family's reputation might be harmed by his disclosures. Sometimes Casanova would use initials, at other times false names. But this discretion tended not extend to actresses or other women of low status. No doubt he believed, like his contemporaries, that they had little reputation worth protecting.

Marriage, at the core of the family and the household, was one of society's central institutions. Unwed men and women were treated with suspicion. They were individuals who were thought liable to subvert the proper social order. The future well-being of most women depended upon marriage, holding out the prospect as it did of companionship, sexual fulfilment, respectability, children, and security, particularly in old age. Although there existed the danger of women being robbed and abandoned by their husbands, marriage, at least if she did not marry down, enhanced a woman's status and this was enhanced further if she bore children, especially sons. As mentioned, she acquired authority over others in her household such as servants and daughters-in-law. When Casanova quizzed a woman about why she was marrying a man who was neither handsome nor rich, she explained that it was in order to become the mistress of her own household. A wife's status and prosperity would be intimately tied to that of her husband and his family, for better or worse. The degree to which she played a part in choosing her husband varied, although almost certainly her parents and other relatives would be closely involved in marriage negotiations and supplying a dowry, often the equivalent of a woman taking her inheritance in advance. The wife's property would usually come under the control of her husband. Love was welcome but its absence was not a deal-breaker.

Some women might take matters into their own hands and elope, such as Casanova's mother, but severing the support networks that a family provided along with the social stigma that went along with it, was a risky strategy and more the resort of women of lower status. Indeed, generally men and women from poorer families had greater freedom to choose their spouse, and love-matches were more common. A family's status was less of a concern for the poor: the practical demands of day-to-day survival trumped most other considerations. Anne Shute observes: 'among peasants and others in the lowest orders, marriage was often a casual transaction.'[1] The children of the poor also tended to leave home sooner, weakening parental authority. Women typically married in their mid-20s, men a little older. A girl of 13, or even younger, could be married and Casanova refers to 13-year-old girls as being of marriageable age, but such cases were quite rare. Once married, a woman was expected to be entirely obedient to her husband's will, including acceptance of any punishment that he meted out to her. In a number of countries, husbands were legally liable for the actions of their wives, which justified their rights to discipline them, by force if deemed appropriate. If punishment under such circumstances resulted in death it could be written off as accidental. The same went for parental beatings of children. The husband also had an unconditional right to sex. For a wife to refuse her husband was regarded as a sin.

Marital breakdown was on a par with the modern day, partly the result of one spouse, usually the husband, abandoning the other but mainly the result of much higher levels of mortality. With the exception of Venice, widowers in most of Europe tended to remarry quite quickly. Wives were important in the management of the household, especially if there were young children to care for, and on the whole their ministrations made a man's life more comfortable. She might also bring with her a dowry. 'Because men depended on the unpaid or low-paid labour of women in the home and often at work,' observes Robert Shoemaker, 'they quickly sought to remarry when widowed, and such men were able to find willing partners, largely because their superior wealth and earning power made marriage an attractive prospect for most women.'[2] For widows, the situation was different. Free from male authority, they were treated with suspicion. Yet, at the same time, there was an expectation that widows should not remarry but remain faithful to their dead husband. If they were older and had little in the way of economic resources, widows were at a distinct competitive disadvantage relative to younger women who had never married.

Sex

Attitudes towards sex varied hugely depending upon gender. Chastity and fidelity were valued highly in women, rooted in the concerns for bloodlines, inheritance and property, but were less important for men. Adultery was a crime for which wives as a consequence were liable to be punished more heavily than husbands, particularly if his unfaithfulness was with a slave or unmarried woman, typically a servant. Men, by contrast, were sensitive to being cuckolded or labelled as a cuckold. In England, if a husband murdered his wife's lover this would be regarded as a mitigating circumstance and the murder downgraded to manslaughter. In the words of Lord Chief Justice Holt in 1707, 'adultery is the highest invasion of property.'[3] It seems likely that this stigma of being a cuckolded husband was the cause of Casanova's violent reaction towards the unfortunate inn boy whom he threw down stairs referred to in Chapter 1. Clearly the sexual experience of women was significantly shaped by ideological, legal and social practices which from a modern perspective could only be described as coercive. But like male guardianship these would have been norms that the majority of men and women would have long been socialised to accept as natural. Rape was generally a capital offence but rates of conviction were low, and the rape of a wife by her husband was not recognised as a crime.

For unmarried women, including young girls, there were numerous obstacles preventing them from making accusations. Shame would have been a powerful inhibitor. If the attacker were a member or friend of the family, then the dire penalty to which a successful conviction could lead might deter victims from pressing charges or witnesses from testifying. There was the possibility that an accusation could backfire and the woman herself be punished. In the case of female slaves, they were not allowed to testify against their owners. There was also, as Margaret Hunt points out, 'the lack, especially among very young girls or lower-status women, of any strong sense of a right to bodily integrity.'[4] Even if a woman did take a case to court the chances of success were low. It was generally thought they were unreliable witnesses, willing to lie to cover up the shame of engaging in consensual sex. A woman of lower status was even less likely to be believed if her attacker was of higher status. In addition, class and gender solidarity with the defendant on the part of those presiding over the case was liable to weigh against her.

Children

In the domain of sex and marriage, of course, there was the complication of children. Childbirth could be hazardous. Women dying in childbirth was quite unusual but the toll on the health of many was considerable.[5] Options for birth control were limited, consisting largely of coitus interruptus (although a sin), abstinence, condoms, and old wives' tales, all of which methods Casanova records. One nun whom Casanova helped through her clandestine pregnancy had been surprised to find she was with child as she had only had intercourse with the father once: she had been under the impression that a woman could not conceive unless she had had intercourse at least three times. On the other hand, some men and women were reluctant to tie the knot should their marriage be a childless one. Couples might engage in premarital sex with an understanding that they would marry once they were confident that they could have a family. But there was the rub. What happened when a man backed out of this understanding? The woman could be left facing some grim choices.

Unwed mothers suffered ostracism and worse. They could lose their jobs and homes, be beaten, whipped, fined or sent to workhouses. Many illegitimate children were sent to foundling hospitals, where more than half of babies and children died and the mortality rate could be as high as 95 per cent. Abortion was an option but this itself was risky. Apart from the dangers to the mother's health, it was a serious crime. In France, it was a capital offence. A woman could try to hide the birth; infanticide and abandonment were widespread but, again, could incur severe punishment. In England, the 'murder of bastards' was one of the most common reasons for women being executed. In France, if an unwed woman did not register her pregnancy and the child was stillborn, it was deemed to have been murdered. If a woman was pretty, she might be able to attract a male protector who would take her as his mistress. One option for some women, and one contemplated by Giustiniana Wynne, was suicide.

Unsurprisingly, Casanova sired quite a number of children. His memoirs record him fathering at least nine, one of whom was stillborn, as well as several more who are likely to have been his. One such was Daturi, the 20-year-old Venetian he discovered in London in prison for debt, and who believed that Casanova was his godfather. As in the case of Daturi, sometimes Casanova discovered that he was a father to a child years after the event, which was inevitable given his wandering lifestyle. On discovery shortly afterwards of yet another child previously unknown to him, Casanova writes, 'I laughed at myself at finding children of mine all across Europe.'[6] It is also probable that the daughter of his lover, Rosalie, was his. All, of course, were illegitimate, so how did the mothers deal with this?

Three of Casanova's children were passed off as the offspring of the mother's husband. Leonilda was the daughter of Donna Lucrezia. Donna Lucrezia was married to a lawyer and she was ten years older than Casanova, who was 19 at the time. Giacomina was the daughter of Mariuccia, who married shortly after she had conceived. There is a suggestion that her husband suspected Casanova was the father even during Mariuccia's pregnancy. Casanova had a son by his housekeeper, Madame Dubois, who, like Mariuccia, married after she had conceived. This time the husband was entirely complicit. He promised to bring the boy up as his own son and keep the truth of his paternity a secret. In the latter two cases, secrecy, Casanova's higher status, and his position as a benefactor to the men involved, directly or indirectly, would have significantly obviated the shame of being a cuckold.

Three women were able to shield themselves by acquiring the protection of powerful men. Tonina, a servant girl, became the mistress of one of Casanova's friends, John Murray, a British diplomat resident in Venice. Murray agreed to take care of Tonina during her pregnancy and delivery. Teresa Imer was married and, simultaneously, the mistress to Frederick, Margrave of Brandenburg-Bayreuth. Teresa already had two children. Her child by Casanova, Sophie Wilhelmina Frederica, she named after the Margrave, presumably passing Sophie off as his child. Bellino, whom Casanova met when she was pretending to the world to be a castrato, raised their son, Cesare Filippo, with the support of the Duke of Castropiñano, who provided for Cesare's upbringing. Unusually, she passed him off as her brother.

One young woman, Mimi, a landlady's daughter, sent her baby boy to a foundling hospital. The baby's mother had taken Casanova to court but he refused to accept that he was the father and was able to raise enough doubt to win the case. But Casanova was prepared to pay the expenses of Mimi's confinement. Soon afterwards, Mimi ran away from home to work on the stage and found herself a lover. Casanova appears to have kept on good terms with Mimi but it was not long before her fortunes took a turn for the worse after she fell in love with a violinist who exploited her. The case of Mimi is a rare instance in which Casanova failed to take steps to try to ensure the well-being of an ex-lover or to show any remorse for being the principal cause of her adversity.

CC had been able to conceal her pregnancy and miscarriage in a convent with the help of a sympathetic nun and a go-between paid by Casanova. The most anomalous case was that of the child he had by his own daughter, Leonilda, as the child seems to have been deliberately sought. As already mentioned, Casanova's daughter and her husband, the old Marchese della C, were both keen to have an heir, and Casanova helped to provide one.

Casanova's relationship with his children could be described as intermittent at best. Those he did meet in later life, he did so more by accident than by design. To some extent this would have been due to his own particular circumstances and personality but it was also a symptom of the times. In Sweden, which was collecting population statistics from the mid-eighteenth century, almost half of children died before the age of 15, and typically a woman would lose three to four children. Estimates for the rest of Europe are similar. For poorer families the mortality rate would have been higher. There are today in Sweden just 0.006 child deaths per woman.[7] The rate of loss during the eighteenth century was bound to have had an impact upon parental psychology. Parents were not blasé about the fate of their children, quite the reverse, but without some psychological and emotional distance they were liable to be overwhelmed with grief. No doubt to some extent they would have been hardened by the deaths of siblings, cousins and other loved ones that they would have witnessed in their own childhood.

In addition to deaths by natural causes, there were the hard practicalities of survival. Children, like their parents before them, would have been viewed from an economic as well as an affective standpoint. For destitute families living on the edge of starvation, children might have to be sacrificed or exploited for the well-being of the family as a whole. They might have to resort to infanticide or, as already mentioned, send their children to foundling hospitals, prostitute them or even sell them. Sometimes children would be farmed out to be brought up by others, either temporarily or permanently. When Casanova visited Amsterdam and came across Teresa Imer, she was in some financial difficulty. So he brought her 13-year-old son Giuseppe back to France with him, becoming his guardian for the next four and a half years. For much of that time Giuseppe seems to have been at a boarding school funded by the Marquise d'Urfé. Casanova would have preferred to have taken his 6-year-old daughter Sophie instead but, interestingly, believed that her mother wanted to hang on to Sophie to support her in old age.

Another reason for the emotional distance between parents and children was that, together, the family and the household were regarded as the elemental institution upon which society was founded. Alongside the state and the Church, it was integral to a hierarchically based social order. Within this order, and to maintain its proper functioning, parents bore the responsibility of nourishing and instructing their children, and most importantly, of instilling in them respect for, and obedience to, authority. In this patriarchal society, the embodiment of authority was the father, the ultimate Father being the Almighty. Priests were similarly addressed as Father, as they were representatives of God's divine authority. 'Pope' is derived from the Greek 'pappas' or 'father'. The notion of the absolute power of the sovereign likewise drew strength from this paternal role, the monarch being placed in relation to the state as the parent was in relation to the family. The patriarchal family structure acquired all the more legitimacy for being perceived as natural. Parental roles consequently carried a heavy legal and symbolic importance. It resulted in child-parent relationships that were more formalised in comparison to egalitarian modern European societies where rights have become centred on the individual.

Casanova's own upbringing reflected the times. His parents had little to do with him, and while his memoirs demonstrate respect, there is not much warmth expressed towards them or, in fact, towards any members of his family, with the exception of his grandmother and perhaps his brother Francesco. It may be that the lack of parental interest in Casanova arose because he was not expected to survive childhood. His parents left him in Venice when he was a year old while they travelled to perform on the London stage. He was 8 when his father died at the age of 36, and he himself so weak that he too seemed close to death. His mother took care of him on this occasion but Casanova makes it clear that she was motivated less by affection than by a combination of duty and practical necessity. On his ninth birthday, to see if he would benefit from a change of air, he was packed off to nearby Padua, where he stayed until he was 14, with only the occasional visit home. Casanova's sister, Faustina Maddalena, died at the age of 3 or 4 when he was around 11. Casanova's mother continued to pursue her stage career to support her family. She travelled as far afield as St Petersburg, and then, when Casanova was 12, to Dresden, where she was to live for most of the rest of her life. When Casanova was 17, his grandmother died.

Non-marital relationships

It was assumed that Casanova's mother, being an actress, took lovers, notably Giuseppe Imer, a successful actor, impresario and the father of Teresa Imer. The prettier, more successful and accomplished an actress, the more she could expect to attract higher status men. This was something of a paradox. As we know, actors, dancers and other such performers were amongst the most stigmatised groups in society, regularly decried by the Church. Casanova claims that his grandfather died of a broken heart when his daughter ran away with a dancer-turned-actor. Yet here they are, women with illegitimate children, married and unmarried, fêted by society, and mistresses to wealthy and powerful men. The complexity of relationships between men and women is not done justice by a model rooted exclusively in respectability and marriage.

Two love affairs by the Marquis Jean-Francois de Saint-Lambert, a poet and a soldier, illustrate this complexity. The affairs also happen to touch upon two central Enlightenment figures who had a significant influence upon Casanova. These are Voltaire and Jean-Jacques Rousseau. Lambert's first affair was in the late 1740s with the Marquise Émilie du Châtelet who was almost ten years Lambert's senior. At that time, Châtelet was married to the Marquis du Châtelet with whom she had three children. Moreover, she was in an established relationship with Voltaire, who had been living and working with her for the best part of fifteen years in an arrangement with which her husband had been perfectly happy. In 1749 Châtelet died aged 42, giving birth to Lambert's daughter. Lambert's second affair began three years later with 22-year-old Countess Sophie d'Houdetot, thirteen years Lambert's junior, who was married to Count d'Houdetot. As with the Marquis du Châtelet, Sophie's husband seems to have been understanding about the relationship, which was to last until Lambert's death in 1803. But in 1757 Sophie became involved in an intense, apparently platonic, romance with Rousseau, eighteen years her senior, himself in a long-established concubinal relationship with Marie-Thérèse Levasseur who had borne him five children. The romance lasted several months until it was ended by Sophie.

Mistresses, cicisbei, courtesans, gigolos, prostitutes, pimps, concubinage and plain old lovers were a conspicuous feature of society. But we must be cautious when using these terms. In part, this is because some are ill-defined and were used interchangeably, such as mistress and courtesan. More importantly, the terms might give a false impression of sharper distinctions than was the case in practice. Labels are useful for outlining broad characteristics but may not be so useful in describing an actual relationship. One category can morph into another or be composed of disparate elements from several categories. Let's take the example of a woman who becomes a housekeeper for a married man. Occasionally he might pay her for sex. Would we describe the housekeeper as a prostitute and her master her client? If the married man spends more time with her and gives her gifts, has she become his mistress? If the wife dies and the housekeeper moves in with him on a permanent basis (perhaps they have children) would we now describe them as concubines? Real life is messy.

There were a number of considerations which underpinned these different types of relationships. To what extent were they purely sexual? Were they sexual at all? Did one partner have exclusive or shared sexual access to the other? To what degree did they include other social, companionate and affective aspects? Did the partners cohabit? How much control did one partner have over the other? How official or unofficial were the arrangements? Were formal contracts in place? What were the remunerative expectations, if any (cash, non-monetary gifts, pensions, titles, property)?

Prostitution was overwhelmingly a commercial arrangement focussed on the act of sex, with men paying for time-limited, shared access. It was widespread within society and often casual. For poor women and orphan girls, prostitution was a matter of brute survival to fend off starvation and homelessness. For women who were otherwise pursuing respectable trades, it was a way to supplement their income, get them out of a short-term financial bind, or obtain a service of some sort. Casanova records that as a young man he obtained sex from a woman in return for him writing a petition on behalf of her husband. For other women, particularly those who lived and worked in brothels and taverns, it was a full-time occupation and could be quite lucrative for a few.

One particular occupational group associated with prostitution were former servants. These tended to be poor women without a husband for whatever reason. For orphan girls or girls from families which were destitute, domestic service at least offered a roof over their heads. In societies where women were closely monitored, this gave male household members an unusual degree of opportunity. Sexual exploitation of such vulnerable women, particularly young women, was inevitable.

Prostitution was regulated in some parts of Europe, such as Amsterdam, although generally it was illegal. But illegal or not, it was accepted as a necessary evil. What were the authorities to do? Deny substantial numbers of their citizenry their only source of income? Then what? See women and their children starve to death? Face the possibility of civil unrest? Find money from public or other charitable funds to support them? These were unpalatable options. There were practical problems as well. The numbers were too large for the court, police and prison services of the time to handle. There were occasional crackdowns if violations of the law were too blatant or women were obviously diseased but for the most part the practice was just a fact of everyday life. Pimps were as likely to be women as men. It might be a mother prostituting her daughter. It might be a prostitute whose charms had been ravaged by poverty, drink, disease and age, so that she could no longer attract any men and managed a couple of girls or younger women to get by. It might be a successful courtesan who had established a brothel for high status clientele.

A very different kind of prostitute was the courtesan. These women were the reserve of elite men, and sex was only part of the service they provided. Successful courtesans were not only beautiful but also adept hostesses who were well-educated and accomplished. They offered much more, or exclusive, access to their clients. Courtesans were more independent, shifting the usual gendered power dynamics: suitors were expected to spend considerable time, effort and resources in order to prove their worth and win them over. The women's transgressive nature, flouting the norms of chastity, submissiveness and dependence which so governed female lives, made them all the more alluring. For men of wealth and power, such women were sought-after status symbols. To some extent the relationship was symbiotic: she needed his resources to maintain the extravagant lifestyle that underpinned her renown; he needed her to maintain his prestige. There was an expectation that a man of standing would possess such a woman, an expectation reinforced by the adulterous habits of royal princes. A courtesan was a form of conspicuous consumption that demonstrated the abundance of his social and financial capital. Some men for this reason financed courtesans with whom their relationships were entirely nonsexual. The Duke of Matalona was in this category, making it clear in an exchange with Casanova that he only loved his wife and kept a mistress for the sake of appearance. Sometimes binding contracts would be drawn up guaranteeing remuneration, such as a pension. Casanova records how a contract proposed by Lord Pembroke to a young countess whose family was penniless 'offered her fifty guineas a month guaranteed for three years, accommodation at St Albans, table and servants, if she would take him as her lover, not to mention what she should expect from his appreciation if she could come to love him.'[8] For comparison, it has been estimated that in the middle of the eighteenth century, only 2.5 per cent of families in England and Wales had an income of £200 a year or above.[9] The countess accepted.

If a courtesan had pleased her protector, he might pass her on to another wealthy man or organise an advantageous marriage for her. When Marie-Louise O'Murphy (Casanova's O-Morphi) fell out of favour with Louis XV, he married her off with a substantial dowry to an attractive young soldier of good pedigree. For some, one of the advantages of being a 'kept woman' was that it gave them a degree of freedom usually unavailable to other women. One such Casanova mentions was Camilla, an actress and a dancer whose patron was amenable to her taking other lovers. Her favourite, the Count de La Tour d'Auvergne, was not particularly rich so she made a present to him of a young girl she employed with whom he had fallen in love, along with money to cover the expense of maintaining her. In France, the association between actresses, courtesans and independence was underscored by the fact that a woman who was a member of an official theatre company was freed from parental authority, a circumstance which would normally come about only when that authority was transferred upon marriage to a woman's husband.

The term mistress was often used when referring to courtesans, which is hardly surprising given that their roles were so similar. Mistresses were more likely to be married, and any economic interaction was less overt, taking the form of gifts rather than money. Mistresses were more likely to be from the same social milieu as their benefactor, although their status and that of their husbands, if they had one, would be inferior. Husbands, being aware of the arrangement and probably a beneficiary of it in some way, would resign themselves to it with greater or lesser degrees of enthusiasm depending upon their particular circumstances and the nature of the couple's own relationship. Casanova recounts the Duke of Wurttemberg falling in love with the dancer Michelle dall'Agata. The duke 'petitioned her husband for her, who regarded himself as fortunate to be able to surrender her to him.'[10] Mistress relationships tended to be more discreet, stable and contain closer emotional bonds. For many years before her death, Madame de Pompadour and Louis XV had ceased to be lovers but both retained a strong affection for each other and she remained his official mistress.

For a number of women, becoming a courtesan or mistress was a deliberately chosen path. They could learn the trade by becoming assistants to courtesans who were already established or they could make the step up after being a prostitute at a brothel catering for high status men. A mother might have ambitions for her daughter to become an aristocrat's mistress. Casanova records the case of La Toscani. La Toscani had been planning for her young daughter to become the official mistress of the Duke of Wurttemberg even though that would involve displacing his present favourite Ursula Gardela. In the same way that many former servants became prostitutes, so did many female stage performers become mistresses and courtesans. It was hardly surprising. These were women who were willing to submit themselves to public gaze, women who possessed self-confidence and beauty to varying degrees, provocative women, entertaining, fashionable and accomplished; likely a very different kind of creature to a nobleman's pious and obedient spouse or spouse to be. They were also accessible, being of a lower status and either single or married to amenable husbands. Many women, such as Mimi, specifically went on the stage to advertise their wares and find a lover who would support them. Casanova encountered a 16-year-old Venetian, Mademoiselle Vesian, on his first stay in Paris. She was from a respectable family but upon the death of her father had become orphaned and penniless. The woman was pretty, so Casanova arranged for her to become a dancer and thereby ensnare a nobleman. After three months she succeeded, becoming the mistress of the Marquis d'Etréhan, and lived happily ever after according to Casanova.

The social acceptance of courtesans and mistresses was partly down to the nature of marriages, particularly marriages amongst the aristocracy. For many, as already mentioned, physical attraction, love and affection were not primary concerns in choosing a spouse. Courtesans and mistresses helped to meet men's unfulfilled desires. Women generally had to make do with liaisons that were more clandestine and ephemeral, although for women of means, particularly widows, gigolos were a possibility. One such was Tiretta, another young penniless Venetian whose amorous career Casanova launched. Tiretta's none-too-subtle nickname was Six Times, that being the number of times it was claimed he could perform in an evening. Casanova also records meeting a handsome young man in Bern who became the kept man of Madame de la Saône, the wife of a Lieutenant General.

The demand created for paramours as a result of marriage constraints can be seen nowhere more clearly than in Casanova's birthplace. The Serenissima had been governed for centuries by an oligarchy of patrician families numbering around 200 in the eighteenth century. Membership of the highest ruling councils was restricted to male representatives from these families. It had been an immensely stable form of government, which was jealously protected: patrician marriages were carefully recorded, regulated and supervised. Marriages outside the noble class were thus infrequent although permissible. For most of the higher levels of society, marrying below your status carried the danger of undermining the honour of your family and yourself. To conserve family wealth and status, both the nobility and the rich middling class were incentivised to keep legitimate offspring to a minimum. Many families limited themselves to marrying off one male per generation. More than half of Venetian noblemen in the eighteenth century remained unmarried, and significant numbers who did marry, did not do so until middle age. Widowers tended not to remarry, which was unusual compared to the rest of Europe. This prejudice against marriage was reinforced by a belief that for men who could expect to be in positions of authority, it would be a distraction from serving the best interests of the state. For families of higher rank, the cost of a daughter's dowry was another reason not to enter the marriage market. Unsurprisingly, many single men and men in marriages that did not meet their emotional and sexual needs sought alternative marriage-like arrangements.

Venetian authorities, families and the wider community generally accepted these relationships, particularly if they were stable, long-term and an alternative to marriages that would otherwise have crossed sensitive social divides. But the position of a concubine was precarious, relying so much as it did on the goodwill of her patron and being vulnerable to family politics. Illegitimacy did not carry the same degree of stigma as elsewhere in Europe, and illegitimate, or 'natural', children were often integrated into the father's households to be educated and raised within the family. 'Venetian law,' Alexander Cowan observes, 'made a generous provision for natural sons and daughters. They had the right to share in their father's inheritance, particularly if they were his only surviving children.'[11] Given the tightly regulated lives of the patrician class, having a natural son could offer some important benefits. They obtained citizenship rights that would have otherwise been out of bounds. They could more easily engage in trade or occupy certain official positions. But what to do with unmarried daughters? For many families the option they chose was to have them secluded in convents. Once enrolled there, the unmarried women would no longer have any claims to the family patrimony. While Venice was perhaps more extreme than most of the rest of Europe, similar underlying dynamics were at play – patriarchal societies governed through aristocratic lineage – leading to comparable outcomes.

Many non-marital relationships which existed across Europe fell under the broad category of concubinage, which can be regarded as a kind of consensual or irregular marriage. The term concubine commonly refers to women in relationships with elite men of the sort already discussed above. But it was in fact a phenomenon that was pervasive throughout society, and the term can relate to both men and women. Concubinal relationships were informal. They were not, like marriage, tightly prescribed according to law and religion, bound by sets of duties and rights. This gave them flexibility, allowing the participants to adapt to circumstances. Concubinage was negotiated, in the broadest sense of the word, by the individuals themselves, no doubt underpinned by the expectations of local custom and practice. Their conditions were not imposed by the state, Church or family. For the poor, struggling to find ways of simply surviving, such arrangements did not incur the costs and liabilities of marriage. Even the cheapest weddings imposed an unwanted burden requiring as they did funds for ceremonies, licences, entertainment, dowries, and so on. If a relationship did not work out, and the poor did tend to experience more itinerant working patterns and unsettled lives, those involved could move on without being entangled in complications such as divorce or bigamy; in marriage, if a woman's husband was cruel and abusive, there was little she could do except endure it. If a relationship succeeded, the benefits could be considerable: economically, by sharing resources and dividing labour; by supporting and protecting one another, an issue that was particularly important for women; and sexually and emotionally. Socially, too, longer term unions were valued more highly in the community and by the state, increasing the status of the participants over and above what might have been the case if they had remained single. Moreover, concubinal relationships were not only restricted to two adults. As we have seen, triangular relationships comprising a husband, wife and higher status patron, were well known.

Employment

Whatever the nature of women's personal relationships, most were expected to work, either for pay or subsistence or a combination of the two. Casanova records women participating in a wide range of economic activity as peasant farmers; street vendors; servants; landladies; shop owners and assistants; milliners; tutors; society hostesses-come-impresarios; investors; seamstresses; textile workers; midwives; healers; writers; stage performers; and, of course, sex workers and their procurers. Cultural norms and expectations, male determination to maximise economic advantages for themselves as well as discriminatory rules and regulations, all conspired to restrict economic possibilities for women. Laws ensured that most property remained under the control of men. Male-dominated guilds and professional associations, as well as the exclusion of women from universities, further depleted opportunities. The growth of capitalism and ideas of free trade opened up some opportunities for women while at the same time reducing others. There was an expansion in work related to shopping and consumption on the one hand, while on the other, the commercialisation of agriculture resulted in a decline in traditionally female work, such as dairying. The switch of land use to growing crops replaced such better paid jobs with more poorly paid employment like weeding and stone-gathering.

Women, like men, would begin work at 6 or 7 years of age, with the commonest forms of employment for women being agriculture and domestic service. Street selling and markets were also important. Throughout Europe, market women were famous for their forceful personalities and assertiveness. Mainly agricultural produce was sold but also cooked food and printed material such as pamphlets, newspapers, bawdy literature, magic spells and religious pictures. Many women were engaged in illegal activities like smuggling, thieving, making and selling alcohol, performing certain medical practices such as inducing abortions, witchcraft (often closely connected with the medical field) and prostitution. There are examples of women in work that required hard labour, such as coal carriers, oarswomen and rock breakers.

Although most women were employed in low paid and low status occupations, there were exceptions. Certain highly-skilled trades were dominated by women, especially those related to textiles, and female stage performers could become highly successful. Some women took over family businesses after their husbands had died, having already often been closely involved in their running, although they could face problems asserting their authority over male employees who were resistant to being directed or punished by a woman. Wives' dowries may well have been invested in these businesses, and, indeed, may have been used to establish the businesses in the first place. The famous Parisian hostess, Madame Geoffrin, had become the owner of the Saint-Gobain mirror and glass factory upon her husband's death, and spent over a decade managing it directly. Barbe-Nicole Ponsardin established Clicquot champagne after taking over her husband's wine business when she was widowed at the age of 27. Women can be found as merchants, clockmakers, carpenters, printers, publishers and booksellers as well as investing in stocks and shares.

Culture and education

Various barriers and restrictions limited women's cultural opportunities. As we have seen, female stage performers could attain widespread popularity but were stigmatised in the process. Certain types of art and musical instruments were regarded as less or more appropriate for women. Casanova's lover, Henriette, had mastered the violoncello in a convent but only after encountering strong resistance from the Abbess who claimed that she 'could only hold the instrument by assuming an indecent posture.'[12] It was felt more appropriate for women to play instruments such as the harp that were better suited for accompaniment than for solo performance; women who took centre stage could be criticised for lacking in modesty. Singing was permissible. Study by female painters of nudes was deemed inappropriate, effectively barring women from life-drawing classes. For a woman to hire her own male model was likely to damage her good name. There was even criticism in some quarters that it was immodest for women to display their painting skills publicly. The Royal Academy of Painting and Sculpture of Paris capped the number of women painters it admitted.

Despite these barriers, women did become recognised as talented actresses, singers, musicians, painters, writers and academics, in addition to being important patrons and cultural arbiters. Women such as Charlotta Dorothea Biehl, María Rosa Gálvez, Madame de Graffigny, Olympe de Gouge, and Susanna Centlivre rivalled men in the degree of success they achieved in writing for the stage. Reinforcing the importance of women in the theatre, it is worth noting that the role of women relative to men in the running of the Comédie Française was unusually egalitarian. Growing literacy and a market for printed texts allowed other women such as Lady Mary Wortley Montagu, Madame de Sévigné, Benedikte Naubert, and Sophie von La Roche to emerge as poets, novelists, epistolarians, essayists, biographers and spiritual autobiographers. Some could earn a living as writers of various kinds of instructional texts ranging from cookery to embroidery to midwifery to social etiquette. Women's writing focussed largely on topics deemed to be appropriate to female expertise. The commercialisation of the theatre and publishing incentivised businesses to encourage female playgoing and reading, with products that would appeal to women. Academic achievement for women was limited by their absence from universities but nonetheless even here you have examples such as Émilie du Châtelet, one of the most formidable intellects of the time and a foremost scholar on the works of Isaac Newton.

The extent to which women could play a part in cultural life was influenced, of course, by their education. There was an increasing recognition from the late seventeenth century onwards that educating girls was worthwhile. Typically, when they were educated, they were educated at home, taught by tutors or relatives. But circumstances did vary considerably. In some communities, convent schools were a valuable source of learning and instruction. Elsewhere, girls could attend village schools. In France, Madame de Maintenon established in 1684 the Saint-Cyr school for girls from impoverished noble families. In Russia, Catherine II set up boarding schools for girls as well as boys, and the first higher learning institute for women in Europe. Attempts at educational reform were made by Empress Maria Theresa, requiring both girls and boys between the ages of 6 and 12 to attend school. At the universities of Bologna and Padua, several women could be found lecturing in or studying traditionally male subjects such as philosophy, anatomy, mathematics and physics. Unsurprisingly, educational possibilities in rural areas and for the poor were more limited than for urban populations or the more affluent. For daughters of the elite, parental attitudes, particularly that of the father, could decisively affect the type of education that they would receive. Émilie du Châtelet's father was particularly supportive and progressive for the time.

Women were generally excluded or directed away from studying subjects such as science, politics, Latin, Greek and algebra, which were seen as unfeminine. Casanova himself admired intelligent women, and claimed that an intelligent but ugly woman was at an advantage over an unintelligent but beautiful one. Despite this, he did express the opinion that education in women could be taken too far: 'In a woman scholarship is out of place; she harms the essence of her sex and yet never goes beyond the boundary of what is already known. No scientific discoveries have been made by women. To go *plus ultra* ["further"] you need a vigour that the female sex cannot have. But in simple reasoning, and in delicacy of feeling we must defer to women.'[13] It was his belief that the undoing of the Marquise d'Urfé was down to her being too intelligent, although in this instance it may not have been the fact that she was a woman which was the issue. Casanova did believe that intellectual vanity, in man or woman, could lead people to behave stupidly and to hold ridiculous beliefs. On the other hand, in his satirical booklet *Goat's wool* (1772), Casanova argues that the sexes are fundamentally equal and puts differences between them down to women's subjugation to men.[14] Casanova makes a similar point in *Refutation* when defending Madame de Pompadour against those who blamed her rather than Louis XV or his generals for the disastrous conduct of the Seven Years War.[15] Casanova ends his case with a quotation from Ariosto's *The Frenzy of Orlando* (1516): 'And truly women have excelled indeed / In every art to which they set their hand.'[16]

More in favour, particularly among the nobility, was a curriculum that would enhance a woman's marriage prospects. It might include music, etiquette, domestic crafts such as embroidery, an understanding of the duties needed to be a good daughter or wife, religious virtue, enough literary and artistic knowledge to be able to converse coherently in polite company and so on. Further down the social scale the focus was upon literacy, although in some parts of Europe, such as in the east, even noblewomen were unable to read. On the lowest rung of the ladder, there were concerns that learning to write might make girls too proud and that it might be an impediment to marriage. Nonetheless, although there were marked variations across Europe, rates of literacy in women rose significantly during the eighteenth century, particularly in the west and in Protestant cities. In some areas of Scandinavia almost the entire population was able to read by the end of the century.

Religion and the Enlightenment

Given women's greater social and economic insecurity it is perhaps not surprising to learn that they pinned more of their hopes than men on religion and the supernatural despite the fact that the Abrahamic faiths were based upon a masculine God that legitimised patriarchal systems of government. Women had a significant presence both within established religion in the form of patrons, martyrs, and saints, and informally, as sources of authority on the occult. Unlike established religions the latter tended to be locally-based, with practices rooted in oral traditions and aimed at obtaining benefits in the here and now rather than the afterlife. There were exceptions, such as Rosicrucianism, the organisation of which was more male-dominated, formalised and international. But the overlapping domains of traditional medicine and the supernatural, in which women had such a prominent role, became increasingly marginalised, subject as they were to the hostility of the established Churches, attacks upon superstition by Enlightenment thinkers, and the emergence of science-based medicine controlled by men.

The central female figure in Catholicism was Mary, and veneration of her was particularly strong in the eighteenth and nineteenth centuries. Her sexual purity fed into traditions that prized female chastity. Encouraged by Jesuits, lay associations devoted to the Mother of God sprung up across Europe and attracted thousands of women. Other non-cloistered Catholic institutions, like the Daughters of Charity, saw many women devote themselves to charitable endeavours such as nursing, teaching or missionary work. Convents were still sources of female authority and outlets for religious piety. Within the Protestant faith the position of Mary was far less important: here the focus was not upon spiritual or institutional intermediaries but upon an individual's direct relationship with God. The main concern of any woman as far as Protestant reformers were concerned, was to be a good wife and mother. Attempts to establish female charitable associations similar to their Catholic counterparts were strongly resisted. But female Protestant mystics and theologians did contribute to religious debate and some questioned notions of maleness when considering the nature of divinity. In the Pietist and Methodist movements, opportunities were available for women to play leading roles. In the eighteenth century, the political power of the Churches began to wane with the emergence of centralised nation-states. The support of women in this context became more important, encouraging Churches to be more amenable to female concerns. Women were allowed to take a more active role in Church affairs, such as in their involvement in charity work and occupying official religious positions.

New Enlightenment discourses were not an unalloyed good for women. Rousseau argued that by their nature women were dependent upon men. Others used science to explain women's 'natural', and invariably more passive, role in society, viewing women overwhelmingly in terms of sexuality and reproduction. But space was opened up to question the older, ideological foundations supporting claims of male superiority. Eve was fashioned from Adam's rib and, hence, subordinate. If the symbolism was not clear enough, Genesis makes it explicit: 'he [your husband] shall rule over you.' Eve was also blamed for original sin by tempting man from the path of righteousness, a narrative that fitted in nicely with women's supposedly lusty appetites. Another long-standing justification for male supremacy was the Great Chain of Being, fundamental to Aristotelian scholasticism and for centuries at the core of most Christians' understanding of reality. For generations, scholars had fashioned it into an internally consistent theorem of seemingly enormous explanatory power that unified the natural and the spiritual, the material and the immaterial. The Great Chain of Being asserted that all entities in all their possible forms existed on a hierarchical continuum stretching from God downwards, each entity inferior to the one above. Men were placed above women, signifying that men were more complete beings than women.

Enlightenment thinkers were busily casting doubt on the Great Chain of Being, theism and the validity of the Bible, while feminists specifically critiqued the use of religion to undermine women's position in society. From Francis Bacon onwards, natural philosophy and empirical investigation began to dismantle traditional theoretical frameworks, while philosophers such as René Descartes and Baruch Spinoza devised their own rational systems to explain the relationship of God to man. John Locke's assertion that the human mind was essentially a blank slate ready to be shaped by the lessons of experience, offered a challenge to original sin and, therefore, Eve's culpability for human failings.

In the eighteenth century, Carl Linnaeus convincingly reclassified the biological world in terms of families, genera and species. Feminists took aim at male authority over the family and the exclusion of women from education. They argued that women were complimentary to men, not inferior to them, and that their souls were spiritually equal. Drawing on Descartes, they asserted that the capacity for reason was a quality that defined mankind generally, that the mind (the rational soul) was sexless, and bodily differences inessential. Mary Wollstonecraft and Mary Hays contested the idea that women were somehow intrinsically dependent upon men, arguing instead that any submissive behaviours they demonstrated were due to long years of socialisation.

This struggle to assert that men and women were equally deserving by dint of their common humanity was all very good but in everyday life it did not reflect women's attitudes towards each other. There was little sense of solidarity between a maidservant and her mistress. Just as men used their social and economic position to exploit and coerce others so did women. A woman's status was enhanced if she could supervise or consign menial work to other women, such as her daughters, daughters-in-law, servants or slaves. The freedom of a noblewoman or wealthy merchant's wife to play an active role in society was facilitated by the labour of other women and girls. If women exploited others less, it was probably more to do with limited opportunity than innate benevolence. There is little sign that women were more sympathetic than their menfolk to the tribulations of female slaves, nor any more tolerant of women of other faiths. Convent missionaries would happily kidnap and indoctrinate Protestant and Jewish children, while the women who rolled up to watch gruesome public executions, such as that of Robert Damiens, do not seem to have been particularly squeamish.

Chapter 10

The Meaning of Love

'As regards to women...when love gets involved, both sides are usually dupes.'

Giacomo Casanova, *History of My Life*

W hat did Casanova understand by the word 'love'? He describes it as 'a kind of madness', 'a sickness', 'incurable', 'a divine monster which can only be defined by paradoxes!'[1] This is something but it does not really take us very far. What was it for him to 'love' a woman? Did he understand romantic love to mean the same thing as it does for us? This is an important question if we are to avoid oversimplifying and perhaps becoming unduly cynical about his relationships with women.

First of all, let us start by getting an idea of what we are dealing with. Casanova had romantic and sexual encounters with scores of women, recorded and unrecorded. His memoirs refer to more than 130. Many of these are entirely anonymous, such as the twenty or more workers at his silk fabric workshop or the seamstresses at Casopo. The majority of women are identified with a name or label of some sort, such as Miss XCV (his code for Giustiniana Wynne). But we still have to be cautious. Casanova names five Hanoverian sisters with whom he had affairs. It turns out that two of the siblings were male. Make of that what you will. Then there is his undeclared love for the Duchess de Chartres. Should she be counted? Bearing that caveat in mind, by my estimation we are dealing with a ballpark figure of around 100 named or pseudo-named women who make up relationships which included those most significant to him in some way or other. Of these, he claims to the reader (as distinct to what he declared to the women themselves) to have been in love with just under half. On at least half-a-dozen occasions this love was unconsummated.

Other information worth having is how long these relationships lasted. Again, the answer is not precise. In the very large majority of cases, Casanova provides enough information to make it possible to work out the approximate length of his affairs but not always. A small number of the relationships were intermittent and extended over a period of years; brief resurrections as a result of chance. This was the case with Bellino, Donna Lucrezia and Teresa Imer.

That said, just over a third of Casanova's encounters lasted a week or less; just under a third were one to four weeks; about a dozen were one to two months; half-a-dozen were two to three months, and a similar number were three to four months. Outliers included Mimi in Paris (six months), Miss XCV (six months), MM (a year) and Manon (two and a half years). For relationships that lasted a week or less, Casanova does not claim to have been in love (perhaps with the exception of the Greek slave girl in Ancona). Beyond that there are plenty of relationships of less than two or three weeks for which Casanova does claim to have been in love, such as with the caretaker's daughter, Lucia, or the peasant, Cristina.

So what are we to make of this? There is no doubt that Casanova could be smitten very quickly. But to fall in and out of love that often, frequently for very short periods of time? A modern reader is likely to be sceptical. Surely this is merely lust in love's clothing. Before we look at the evidence in more detail, it is worth sketching out some of the ideas on the nature of love that were in circulation during this period and with which Casanova was likely to have been familiar.

One idea stretching back at least to Plato's *Symposium* (c 385–370 BCE) was that love is the expression of a desire to join with another as a way of resolving a lack of some sort. René Descartes suggests that love is an emotion of our soul which moves it to unite with objects that appear to be agreeable to it (this could be an individual, a town, a country, a ruler or the divine). This uniting of our soul with the love object creates a form of wholeness, but a wholeness of which we are only a part, not a complete merging. If we lose that love object, our soul will look to replace it with another. Depending upon the extent of our esteem for this object, we may describe our love as being of different types, ranging from friendship to devotion. In the latter case, our love might be such that we are even willing to sacrifice ourselves for it or, in the intensity of our passion, become disconnected from our individual selves and descend into madness. This raises the question of will and control. Is love a voluntary or involuntary condition? Can it be achieved through reason? Is falling out of love a voluntary or involuntary action? In his classification of basic human passions, love is placed after wonder and given primacy over hatred, desire, joy and sadness. Descartes also distinguishes between an intellectual love and a love which is sensuous or sensual.

Following along the lines of Descartes, Nicolas Malebranche develops the notion of natural love as an aspect of the soul which seeks that which is good, in turn connecting what is good with happiness. There are echoes here of Epicureanism. This was a philosophy which gave an important intellectual underpinning to libertinism, connecting together materialism, pleasure (in the sense of an absence of pain), happiness and the good, as John Locke was also to do. Originating from Aristotle, and in contrast to Descartes, is the idea that we love objects that are similar to ourselves. In his *Nicomachean Ethics* (c 340 BCE), Aristotle suggests that individual friendships are more likely to form amongst people who have things in common. For Spinoza, love is a form of joy inspired by an external cause. He comments on the empathy between a lover and their love object: if the latter feels joy or sadness, this will become mirrored in the feelings of the former. More than that, the lover will actively try to make their beloved love them in return. Damaris Masham defines love as pleasure in the being of another. She also argues that desire and benevolence can be compatible. Religious writers such as Jean Senault, influenced by Augustine, claimed that lovers became slaves to the objects of their love.

Turning back to Casanova we find that pretty much all of these notions are in some way exemplified by his relationships as described in his memoirs. There is love as a deep and persistent need. There is the natural desire to obtain and unite with an object of one's love, as well as to be loved in return. Love is portrayed as a moral good that is consistent with physical pleasure. There is the importance of empathy and mutuality, the compatibility of desire and benevolence, and love as a cause of happiness and sublime joy. There are different degrees of love. The closeness of the relationship between wonder and love is reiterated. Love is described as an involuntary impulse with the power of reason subjugated to the power of emotion. Lovers are presented as servants of their loved ones, so much so that they can become enslaved by their love to the point of madness.

Casanova makes an intriguing comment during his account of his lover, CC's, miscarriage, highlighting a theme that runs through his memoirs: the relationship between sex, pleasure, love and moral agency. As already mentioned, CC had been confined to a convent by her father but was by then already pregnant. She was able to keep the pregnancy and birth a secret with the help of a senior nun, MM, and a lay-nun called Laura, employed by Casanova. Receiving news of the miscarriage, and seeing the bloody linen that Laura had carried away from the scene, he was tormented by the fear that she would not survive. Casanova writes how he stays up all night: 'without having been able to sleep, or eat, or allowing Laura's daughters to undress me, for, although they were pretty, they horrified me. I viewed them as the instruments of my horrible incontinence which had made me the assassin of an angel incarnate.'[2]

On a number of occasions Casanova suggests that he is the victim of women: they sexually arouse him and make him fall in love with them. Sometimes they may intend to, sometimes not. It raises the question of accountability either way. Casanova's powers of reason and free will are displaced. He cannot help himself. He is acting under the influence of emotion, instinct, his soul or whatever we want to call it. Does this absolve him of responsibility? Morally, to some extent perhaps. But he is still the flawed being whose 'horrible incontinence' has brought about CC's suffering. Although CC was a willing partner in their relationship, and at one point embraced the possibility of her becoming pregnant as a way of getting leverage over her family, Casanova regards her as innocent. At 28 he was much older and far more experienced, after all. There is a tension here. Casanova seems to be reproaching himself but is that for who he is or what he has done?

Casanova found that sex devoid of emotional engagement was unsatisfying. Madly in love with a Signora F but unable to fully consummate the relationship, Casanova allows himself to be seduced by the beautiful courtesan, Melulla, much to his later disgust and self-loathing. Once again, he ascribes his behaviour to a moment of weakness. This was not pleasure for Casanova. It was a physiological compulsion, demeaning and repulsive. It explains his reluctance to resort to prostitutes. Drawing on his belief that animal nature is rooted in three basic drives tied to procreation, sustenance and revenge, he distinguishes sexual pleasure from sexual gratification. True pleasure for Casanova lay in the ability to employ reason, the quality that long distinguished man from beasts, to refine and enhance enjoyable feelings, whether that be from eating and drinking, sex or the subjugation of rivals. Moreover, it was a moral good. The Enlightenment had taught Casanova that only when encumbered by the absurd nostrums of religion could it be regarded as anything other than pleasurable.

It was a rare example of such an abstinence which led to one of the regrets of Casanova's life when he resisted the approaches of a young woman called Lucia, with whom he had fallen in love. Casanova was training for the priesthood and still a virgin. He blamed himself for her subsequently being seduced and running away from home. He was to meet up with her again years later, Lucia ravaged by prostitution and poverty, and in Casanova's view, a victim of prejudice against our natural God-given desires. In reality, sexual enjoyment could be liberating and educative as long as it was mutual. Casanova claimed that he derived 'four-fifths' of his own pleasure from the pleasure he gave to his lover.[3] The importance of mutuality and Casanova's strong sense of a duty of care was a good illustration of Damaris Masham's argument that desire and benevolence were compatible.

Sex was integral to love for Casanova, and it was unlikely that he could have been satisfied with a relationship of which it was not a central part, but love was so much more. Casanova hankered after romantic love throughout his life, or at least, its early, intense stages. He experienced melancholy and 'an unbearable emptiness'[4] in his heart when love was absent for any time. When Casanova describes his relationship with the mysterious Pauline (who turned out to be a Portuguese noblewoman), he reflects: 'I didn't need a woman to satisfy my temperament, but to love, and to find great merit in the object which interested me, both with regards to beauty and to the qualities of the soul; and my budding love grew stronger if I foresaw that the conquest would require some care.'[5]

'I didn't need a woman to satisfy my temperament, but to love.' It was not a matter of finding a woman with whom he could just get along. That was not what love was about for Casanova. It was something more dynamic. It was an adventure of discovery: physically, emotionally, psychologically. About all things, Casanova had an unquenchable appetite to explore and learn, 'to find great merit in the object which interested me.' Curiosity, Descartes' 'wonder', was part of love's pleasure and fascination for him. Casanova makes this point repeatedly. Curiosity was part of what drew him into love, and a number of times he comments upon the similarity between the two emotions. He delighted in the 'beauties' and 'qualities' of his lover's soul, and he wanted it to be reciprocal, to achieve two hearts which were in perfect harmony. That is what love was about. To be loved as well as to love was the conquest he sought. As for sex, as well as a delicious pleasure it was both love's confirmation and consummation.

Balancing hope with possibility, the challenge of winning over the object of his curiosity intensified the excitement of Casanova's quest and enhanced the enjoyment he would obtain from his anticipated success. There is more than an echo of courtly love here; the chivalrous knight proving himself worthy of his lady, solicitous to her every whim. Casanova was a devotee of the poet Ariosto and his knightly epic, the masterpiece *The Frenzy of Orlando*. Amidst his tests and trials, Casanova would suffer tormenting doubts, temporary rejections and unforeseen complications, for which he would have to devise strategies to overcome. Reason became the servant of love, its ingenuity harnessed to ensure victory and maximise pleasure. Curiosity, sex, reason, pleasure, courage and, ultimately, reciprocity and harmony. That was the package.

For Casanova, to be in love as opposed simply to having a light but nonetheless very enjoyable affair, involved commitment of some sort from both parties. The notion of commitment might sound odd given how brief were the majority of his relationships but beyond actual longevity this commitment could be expressed in different ways. There were, of course, verbal expressions about which Casanova promises his reader he was sincere at the moment he made them. Immediately upon the consummation of their love, Casanova assures the recently married Madame Baret of his eternal constancy. But the nature of love itself rendered such declarations worthless, as Casanova was the first to acknowledge. His relationship with Madame Baret lasted two to three weeks.

More substantial, if never realised, were Casanova's promises of marriage. Whereas declarations of eternal love could be dismissed as little more than a salesman's pitch, offers of marriage were very different. To seduce a woman on the basis of such a promise and then not follow through could incur severe reputational damage, as well as demands for satisfaction on the part of male relatives. After Casanova fell in love with Cristina, a respectable peasant girl from a well-to-do family, he raised with her uncle and herself the possibility of marriage and began making plans (at least, in his head). Shortly afterwards, the pair consummated their love and Casanova declared that they were married. But once the intoxication of love began to wear off, hand in glove with his curiosity no doubt, Casanova changed his mind. He decided instead to organise a match for Christina with someone else, a very good one, as it happened.

Ensuring that Cristina was provided for was not simply a shrewd protective measure against possible blowback but also tangible proof that his love was real. Likewise, it would have been evidence of his love to Madame Baret when he gave her 10,000 francs to enable her husband to get out of debt and carry on with his business. Today, qualities such as honour, piety and love are understood and experienced as subjective states which are primarily internalised. In the eighteenth century there was an element to them which was more performative and externalised, an outward show conformable to objectively understood conventions. To express one's experience of love to one's loved one, however heartfelt that might be, was not likely to cut the mustard without supplying something more tangible. The present of money or an expensive gift, or being prepared to undertake a task to demonstrate one's worth, was intrinsic to that love in a certain sense. This helps to explain why relationships of the time can often appear to be so transactional. The adventurer, Goudar, recounts to Casanova an incident in which he conveys to a courtesan (La Charpillon, as it happens) a message that an ambassador has noticed her while out strolling and 'was in love with her'. Goudar goes on to comment that this was a 'budding passion'.[6] It would be difficult to imagine the term 'love' being used in an equivalent context today. Here it feels like little more than the ritualised decorum of polite society, in this case one that probably foreshadowed a financial negotiation between a potential patron and mistress.

It is worth remembering that Casanova operated in a transitional world in which the business-like marriage arrangements of tradition were only starting to be displaced by ones rooted in notions of romantic love. Casanova's relationships with women reflect characteristics of both. Towards the end of his relationship with the aristocratic nun, MM, Casanova fell in love with his servant, Tonina. He records that the twenty-two days they spent together were amongst the happiest of his life. The Venetian-based British diplomat and friend of Casanova, John Murray, was also interested in Tonina, and given that Casanova's finances were not sufficient to support her, Casanova, her mother, and Tonina herself, agreed for her to become the diplomat's generously provided mistress. This does not look like love to us. Nonetheless, Tonina appeared to have little difficulty transferring her affections from one man to the other, perhaps influenced by the idea that for women, obedience was itself an aspect of love: 'Tonina embraced him, showing him the deepest gratitude, and assuring him that from that moment on she would love only him and would have only feelings of friendship for me.'[7]

Another indicator of Casanova's genuine love affairs, as opposed to relationships which were motivated by some combination of sexual desire and friendship, is the extent to which he suffered on account of them. This suffering was either during periods when Casanova's love was unrequited or when the affairs ended, notably those involving the ten to twelve women, at his estimate, whom he regarded as his greatest loves. Casanova would typically become melancholy and depressed, and on occasion, such as during his affairs with Signora F and Pauline, physically unwell. The day Henriette left him he describes as one of the saddest of his life. He compared the experience to when he was imprisoned under the Leads in Venice and at Buen Retiro in Madrid: 'This is the effect of great sadness. It deadens. It doesn't make the person it overwhelms want to kill himself, because it prevents thought. But it doesn't leave him the slightest ability to do anything towards living.'[8] For Casanova, each love was fresh and greater than any love he had experienced before; at least that is what he believed in the moment.

Once mutual love and harmony had been achieved, then what? There was the odd occasion when it seemed that Casanova was tempted by marriage but for the most part it was a prospect he shunned. Casanova valued his freedom too much. When his curiosity was sated and his conquest achieved, then his interest typically waned, particularly if another woman caught his attention as happened during his relationship with CC when he met MM. Love was stimulated by hope and fear, not certainty. It was an active and unstable substance that burned brightly and then faded, transmuting into something more predictable, more sustainable over the long term, perhaps – but far less thrilling. Sometimes economic reality intruded, as happened with his widowed housekeeper Madame Dubois. The wandering Venetian could not give her financial security. So when an offer of marriage from another suitor arrived, it made sense for Dubois to move on. In the case of Esther, whom he met during his stay in Amsterdam, Paris was too much of a pull for him to settle down. With Henriette, her own family commitments put an end to matters. A lost passport intervened to drive a wedge between himself and Bellino in something of a comic farce. Whiling away his time under custody until a replacement passport arrived, Casanova mounted a horse to see what it was like, having never ridden. The horse bolted across enemy lines, separating the two lovers who, despite their initial intentions, were unable to resume their affair until many years later. In the case of Marcolina, Casanova himself could not understand why he put an end to their relationship. He was madly in love with her, after all, and Marcolina was willing to travel anywhere with him.

To summarise, the progress of Casanova's relationships tended to follow a pattern. First of all, his interest was aroused by the beauty of a woman's face. It is a point Casanova makes several times. He likened it to a bill of fare or the cover of a book. A deeper curiosity then took over. About Maton in Dresden, he writes: 'I wanted to see if her qualities would make me fall in love with her, because as yet I was only curious.'9 Sometimes this would take him no further than a casual fling. On those occasions when he did find himself falling in love, he would set about trying to make his love object love him in return. This phase of the relationship was usually the most dramatic and intense, racked as he would be with hope, anger, frustration, humiliation, despair, guilt, dread and countless other emotions, sometimes tormented to near madness. Love-making itself would either take place as a consecration of the advent of mutual love or a little while afterwards, once any remaining reservations had been surmounted, such as religious prejudices. It would also coincide with a period of concord and happiness. Perhaps with the exception of Casanova's liaison with Francesca Buschini, which lasted several years but took place after the period of his life covered by his memoirs, this stage was the closest he got to conjugal love. Indeed, Casanova seemed to treat it as a form of marriage. In the eyes of the Christian church, marriage was, after all, the most complete form of love between a man and a woman. The relationship would end when Casanova began to lose interest or external events intruded. Very rarely would the woman put an end to the relationship, as in the case of Manon Balletti.

It is hard to read Casanova's accounts of his relationships with women and conclude that he treated love as no more than a cynical ploy to seduce them. One would have to be naïve to think that this was never the case; Casanova is quite open that at times he did lie to women about the nature of his interest in them (as, undoubtedly, they did to him). But for the most part, there's little reason to distrust him when he tells his reader that on this or that particular occasion, he believed himself to be in love, at least as love was understood in the eighteenth century. After all, Casanova comments upon a wide range of relationships, and for a significant number, probably more than half, he does not claim to have been in love. He was a libertine but a very soft-edged one. Possibly reinforced by his own superstitious nature, he gives the impression of navigating a compromise between his beliefs in a Christian God, and the freethinking deism of the Enlightenment that underpinned more radical libertine attitudes.

Towards the end of his life, Casanova's closest companion was a little dog called Finette. The dog was a gift from Princess Lobkowitz. In a letter to the princess in which he reflects on Finette's character, Casanova makes a comment revealing that even in old age he had a desire not just to be loved but for that love to be whole and unrestrained: 'I only need to raise my hoarse voice a little to see her obedient; and that's what displeases me a little, because I would like her to love me without the slightest shadow of fear.' He goes on to write: 'if Finette makes me happy for a few quarters of an hour, I will, on the other hand, make her happy every hour of the day and night. Woe to anyone who dares disrespect her.'[10] Even with Finette, his love was typically bound to duty; the duties of ensuring her happiness and of being her protector.

Chapter 11

Casanova's Lovers

'My housekeeper was too attractive and too intelligent. It was impossible for me not to fall in love with her.'

Giacomo Casanova, *History of My Life*

Eighteenth-century Europe was a world of prerogatives, ones defined by your position in society. Nobles protested against the government's attack on 'liberties' in the political tensions prior to the French Revolution. These nobles were not referring to broad liberties as we might understand them today, such as freedom of expression, movement or association, but specific privileges, such as tax exemptions. This mentality of exceptional rights extended to a sense of male sexual entitlement over women. In the case of husbands, this was legally enshrined. In the case of the unmarried Casanova, it took the form of a strong expectation, and one which seems to have been covertly endorsed by much of society – men and women – at least in the circles Casanova frequented.

Women as a form of property and sex as a form of transactional exchange, no doubt fed into this mentality. Casanova's new housekeeper at Soleure, Madame Dubois, complains about Casanova's manservant Leduc: 'He wanted to kiss me, I refused, and he, believing it was his right, became a little insolent.'[1] Casanova records several instances of high-status men who were perplexed and indignant when women of lower status declined to go to bed with them. The beautiful daughters of an impoverished aristocratic family living in London were regarded as 'fanatics' (excessively pious) for refusing to sleep with wealthy noblemen. In Avignon, the wealthy Marchese Grimaldi bemoans his failure to make headway with an adventuress called Madame Stuard: 'Given her poverty her attitude astounds me…it's a phenomenon that I can't explain.'[2] For Casanova, the strength of his sense of sexual expectation was strongly influenced by the status of the woman concerned. It shaped the manner of his initial overtures and the nature of the on-going relationship. An illuminating case study is Casanova's affair with Henriette.

The Venetian met the Frenchwoman, Henriette, in the summer or autumn of 1749 in Cesena, thirty miles south of Ravenna. She had disguised herself as a soldier, and in a union of convenience, had recently fallen in with a Hungarian military officer who had become her protector and lover, despite not sharing a common language. A disturbance at the boarding-house at which they were all lodged drew the Venetian's attention to them. The inn-keeper, along with several 'sbirri' (police) under the authority of the local bishop, were making their way into the couple's room. Local regulations forbade any man to sleep with a woman who was not his wife, and the inn-keeper was pretty sure that the Hungarian's companion was neither a man nor his wife. Casanova quickly discovered that the intrusion was not so much motivated by religious scruple but the opportunity to extort money. For a few sequins, the inn-keeper would have a word with the chief of police and the matter would be resolved.

Indignant at this stitch-up of a foreigner, and having an ingrained dislike of sbirri, along with his love for a good drama, Casanova allied himself with the Hungarian. Advising the officer to stay put, Casanova set off to see the bishop – not so much to resolve the matter but to be so unpleasant as to stoke the fires. Having been rebuffed by the bishop as planned, the next morning Casanova visited one General Spada, whose acquaintance Casanova had recently made. With a certain amount of embellishment, Casanova explained how disgracefully the Hungarian officer had been treated, and how the bishop had refused to intervene. With the General on side, the matter was quickly resolved. The bishop apologised and agreed to pay damages, while the inn-keeper and the sbirri had to beg for pardon on their knees.

Casanova's curiosity piqued by this Frenchwoman, who turned out to be witty and good company as well as beautiful, over the next day or so he fell in love and determined to supplant the Hungarian, who he guessed was about 60. Casanova expected his conquest to be straightforward. Ditching his plans to go to Naples, Casanova spoke to Henriette's protector, and offered to accompany them to Parma where they were headed. Casanova would take them in his own carriage which, he assured them, would be far more comfortable than a public coach. The officer agreed. In fact, Casanova did not own a carriage; a detail he soon resolved by going into Cesena and buying a particularly luxurious one. Before they left, Casanova had managed to confirm with Henriette that the officer was not her husband or her father, and he was growing confident that she would be prepared to exchange the older man for himself. Casanova appeared rich and was confident about what he could offer her physically, especially as the Hungarian seems to have been a bit of a disappointment.

As Casanova had intended, he was able to use the journey to find out more about the couple, conversing in French with Henriette, and Latin with her companion. It turned out that the Hungarian had a six-month sabbatical and was visiting Italy partly for pleasure and partly on business. He had come across Henriette in Civitavecchia where, disguised in military costume and in the company of an elderly man who was also an officer, she happened to be lodging at the same inn as himself. As seemed to have been clear to everyone, the Hungarian realised that Henriette was a woman. Interested in her, through an intermediary they arranged to meet in Rome, the Hungarian offering her ten sequins for her company. Henriette refused the money, asking him instead to take her to Parma, where she claimed to have some business. That was all he knew.

During a stopover at Bologna, Henriette made it clear to the Hungarian, via Casanova, that once they had arrived at Parma they were to go their separate ways. Casanova made his move the following morning. He spoke to the Hungarian to receive his blessing in attempting to obtain Henriette as his mistress. After all, the officer had demonstrated himself to be a decent man and, what's more, he and Henriette seem to have developed a fondness for each other. The Hungarian agreed to leave her in the Venetian's custody and Casanova went away to declare his undying love, proposing that she become his mistress. The tone of his proposal was rather imperious, and to Casanova's discomfort, Henriette's initial response was to laugh at him. But after more desperate pleading, she consented.

The behaviour of both men towards Henriette was rooted in their perceptions of her place in society. Her actions were not those of a respectable woman. She had dressed as a soldier and moved on from the protection of one man to another in exchange for sex. Henriette was on the run. Perhaps from an unhappy lover, husband or father. Or maybe she was being pursued by creditors. But what to make of the fact that she was beautiful, witty, confident and generally charming? Perhaps she had a background as a stage performer. That would also account for her promiscuity. Such a woman would likely be open to a contractual arrangement as a mistress. While playing the role of a besotted but noble saviour, the conditions of the relationship Casanova outlined were clear: he would provide for her and keep her safe in return for him becoming her lover and enjoying exclusive access to her charms. The tetchiness of the manner in which Casanova made his offer gives the impression that he felt he was dealing with a woman of little consequence, someone who was in no position to turn him down. Certain aspects of Henriette's behaviour did not quite add up, notably her refusal to take money from the Hungarian officer. But after reflecting on her circumstances the night before he makes his proposal, Casanova brushes these aberrations aside: 'She may have virtues but not the one that could have prevented me from claiming the normal reward a woman owes to the desires of a lover.'[3] The assumptions of both men were unexceptional for their time.

In fact, Henriette was well bred, most likely a Provençal aristocrat fleeing to Parma from an unhappy marriage. It appears they were threatening to put her in a convent, possibly for having had an affair. Ian Kelly summarises the situation: 'She was waiting for some sort of rapprochement with her in-laws or her husband, perhaps the granting of an official separation or the right to see her children [she may have left small children in France] without bringing further scandal on the family.'[4]

Henriette's status became clear in Parma. There had already been clues: she was highly educated and something of an epicure. But it was upon appearing for the first time in fashionable dress, rather than in a soldier's uniform, that the truth became evident. The attitude of the two men changed dramatically, recognising as they now did their failure to show the respect due to a woman of such rank. The Hungarian in particular was mortified.

For Casanova, who was already madly in love with her, he was now the cat who had got the cream. Under normal circumstances a woman such as Henriette would have been out of his reach. Casanova was still only 24, and with no secure income or career prospects. His celebrity; Paris; his initiation into the dissolute habits of its nobility; his making (and losing) of fortunes; his numerous connections amongst the great and the good of Europe – all of this lay in his future. In a skilfully constructed narrative, Casanova records the three months they spent together in Parma. He depicts this new stage of their relationship in idealised terms, reflecting not only his love for Henriette, but his reverence for the noble class into which she was born.

The story Casanova tells is of soulmates whose sublime love was doomed by fate. It should not be a surprise if there are echoes of ancient Greek tragedy woven into his account; Casanova had translated Homer's *Iliad* after all. You can struggle against your destiny, possibly delay it, but eventually you will succumb. A characteristic of the working out of fate in Greek tragedy is irony, the decisions and actions of the protagonists bringing about the fate they are trying to avoid.

The theme of star-crossed love is communicated to the reader in different ways. There is the mystery of Henriette herself, in flight from some unresolved predicament. Never a good sign. The revelation that she had been escaping from her father-in-law and an unhappy marriage deepens the reader's apprehension. Then there is the social mismatch: Casanova born into a family of performers; Henriette an aristocrat. Henriette is making her way, as Casanova points out, to the most Frenchified city in Italy; not the place to be if you do not want to be spotted by your French relatives or any of their associates in the small world of the European aristocracy. In a foreshadowing of events, Casanova records Henriette's concern about being seen in public. Then there is the issue of money. Dialogue between the two makes it clear on their first day in Parma that despite all his show, extravagance and reassurance, Henriette is shrewd enough to realise that Casanova does not possess an endless supply of funds – when she leaves, she slips him 500 sequins. Another bad omen.

Casanova and Henriette remain cocooned for much of their stay in Parma, the future pushed aside, their love an amulet to protect them as long as it is not exposed to the outside world. But meanwhile, the reader understands that fate is busily at work. Their demise begins when they re-enter society. Casanova overcomes Henriette's prophetic reservations and convinces her to take a box at the opera, an odd decision given that you go to the opera precisely to be seen. Nonetheless, they seem to get away with it. They begin to socialise more widely until, eventually, a chance encounter with the French ambassador gives the game away. Approaches are made and a deal is done. Henriette returns to Provençal, the threat of being consigned to a nunnery lifted.

While there is little reason to question the events that took place as described by Casanova, there are some aspects which are unconvincing. In recreating this blissful time, and in his desire to construct a story of doomed love, Casanova has shied away from addressing issues that might cast some doubt on the motivations underpinning their romance. References to fate leave the purity of their love unsullied by baser interests. Henriette's determination to travel to the most French city in Italy made little sense unless she was intending to be found. It made even less sense to stay there if she did not want to endanger her relationship with her new-found love. And then, once they had been spotted, there was nothing to stop them leaving. Both she and Casanova were too astute to imagine there could be any other outcome. If fate was at work, they did not put up much of a struggle against it. Playing the honourable man, Casanova took responsibility for the events that lead to the ending of the relationship, but his histrionics, full of regrets, questions and exclamation marks, ring hollow.

But there are other ways of reading Casanova's account. It may be that he has idealised the nature of his relationship with Henriette in order to illustrate a deeper concern. This would be consistent with the idea that his memoirs are as much a philosophical project as a personal history. It may be that Casanova is exploring here the question of whether it is possible to attain happiness through libertinism. As discussed in the previous chapter, the conception of love that existed when Casanova was in his pomp was different to that of today. Romantic love was regarded as unstable and transitory, rooted in passion rather than reason. It was not something upon which to establish a lasting relationship. Marriage was traditionally arranged on the basis of economics and politics, not necessarily love. Is Casanova suggesting that love can only exist as a temporary state of happiness? If their relationship had been diluted by more worldly concerns from the start, then it would be hard to judge whether love itself was intrinsically unstable. It is also worth asking to what extent Casanova's older self is endorsing or satirising the sentiments of his younger self. We should not assume that when the older Casanova records the speech and thought of the younger, with all its pomposity, arrogance and vanity, that he is doing so uncritically.

Casanova records how years later their paths were to meet again, although he did not realise at the time that the woman whose company he was in was Henriette, as she did not reveal her face to him. It so happens that she took a liking to his bisexual female companion, Marcolina, and the two had a one-night fling. By a curious coincidence, a few years before Casanova embarked upon his memoirs, a drama entitled *Henriette* was written and performed in 1782 by Mademoiselle Raucourt (1756–1815), a famous tragedienne of the Comédie Française. Raucourt herself was famously bisexual, and her play featured a woman who dressed as a soldier.

Casanova's affair with Henriette highlights the importance of considering his lovers' place in society if we are to understand the nature of his relationships with them. Factors such as affluence, age and the degree to which a woman was a free agent, all had an impact. A small percentage of women were sufficiently independent and in control of their own property to be able to decide their own fates. These tended to be widows, courtesans and stage performers. The overwhelming majority of women were under the direct authority of others: fathers, brothers, husbands, mothers, mothers-in-law, employers, patrons and institutions such as convents. Given this was the case, and given how closely women were supervised, Casanova had to take into account the extent to which the authority of these others might help or hinder his quest.

Casanova's memoirs contain numerous examples. Take the family of CC: Casanova generally found mothers more trusting than fathers and CC's was no exception. He had managed to win over the mother to his side but CC's father rejected Casanova's request to marry his daughter. Then there was her wastrel brother who endeavoured to sell her virginity to him, much to Casanova's disgust. Husbands could be accommodating or jealous. The much older lawyer and husband of Donna Lucrezia seemed relaxed about the 19-year-old's friendliness with his wife. It is not certain that her husband knew the two were having an affair but it seems likely that he did. An ulterior motive for the husband's easy-going disposition might have been the fact that the couple had yet to produce any offspring after almost a decade of marriage; a problem which Casanova was able to resolve. For Monsieur ..., a husband who did not appear to be quite so understanding, Casanova contrived to do an important favour. He obtained a pardon from Choiseul for Monsieur's cousin who had killed a man in a duel. This enabled him to become a trusted friend and opened up opportunities to socialise with the wife of Monsieur … . Casanova cultivated the image of being a rich and generous nobleman, which was appealing to families searching for a suitable marriage or in need of money. Both situations were the case with the family of Count Ambrosio of Milan. It took just seven hours for Casanova to fall in love with the countess' sister Clementina, and in less than two days the family were openly welcoming the prospect of marriage. In the case of Zaire, Casanova simply bought her from her peasant father for the small sum of one hundred roubles. The father was delighted at his good fortune, it appears. Casanova records well over a dozen encounters with male and female guardians who were willing to allow, or actively encouraged, him to pursue their womenfolk on the basis of some kind of economic remuneration.

Casanova enjoyed a range of different kinds of relationships. The majority were ephemeral love affairs and several were concubinal, such as that with Henriette. He had formal or quasi-formal economic arrangements with a handful of women. This was a diverse bunch from hardened professionals, such as La Charpillon, to stage performers, such as La Renaud, to novices, such as Rosalie, whom Casanova took pleasure in educating and transforming. Casanova was also a client of prostitutes. Of his roughly one hundred lovers who are not more or less anonymous, around seventy were subject to the authority of guardians, and around twenty were independent (a high number). Some women, such as Bellino or Donna Lucrezia, who renewed their relationships with him years after their initial affairs, fell into both camps. Casanova does not provide information either way for the remainder. About thirteen of his lovers were married and another ten were already in entanglements with fiancés, lovers or sweethearts. In terms of their individual or family status, twenty-three were stage performers; twenty-five were noblewomen (many of whom were not particularly well off); sixteen were servants; twelve could be described as affluent commoners (from professional, financier, merchant families); five were from an artisan or small business background; four were courtesans; four were peasants; two were slaves and one was a high-class prostitute. There are here, as always, categories that overlap or are a little fuzzy, and there will be women who we do not know anything about. So it is not the precise figures that are interesting, so much as the broad profile.

The first thing to notice about Casanova's lovers is that they are not representative of women in society as a whole: around 25 per cent of his lovers are stage performers, with a similar percentage who are noblewomen. In a country such as France, if you put both of those categories together, they probably would not make up more than a couple of per cent of the population as a whole. They were also unusually sexually active, particularly in Paris. Casanova was taken aback on his first visit to the French capital. Meeting the popular actress, Le Fel, he commented upon how different each of her children looked. She explained, unabashed, that each of the three were fathered by a different man. Casanova went to meet a ballet master on another occasion and came across a group of girls who were between 13 to 14 years-old along with their mothers. One of the girls was not feeling well. When her friend inquired why, she replied that she thought she was pregnant. After Casanova expresses to her his surprise that she is married, 'she looks at me, then turns to her friend, and they both fall about laughing. I went away utterly ashamed and resolved in the future not to assume the modesty of young women of the theatre.'[5] Rates of illegitimacy in the eighteenth century were generally very low compared to today, although growing. But the cities were a different matter, dominated as they were by royal courts, aristocrats and all the services required to support them. The illegitimacy rate in the countryside in France was 1 or 2 per cent by 1789. It was 20 per cent in Paris.[6]

The disproportionate number of stage performers and noblewomen is a reflection of Casanova's upbringing and adopted lifestyle. On the one hand, he was raised amongst performers and felt at home amongst them. The stage gave him a network of friends and contacts who were typically on the move around Europe like himself. On the other hand, Casanova's favoured habitat was that of the court or the residence of the aristocrat; a world of gambling, the opera, fashionable dress, fine dining, witty conversation and flexible morality. He lived the life of an itinerant courtier, immersing himself in the concerns of his well-bred hosts, part of an entourage of individuals who toured these cultured centres of power and wealth, moving from nobleman to nobleman, and from court to court, in the hope of official advancement or a business opportunity. Casanova was employed in various capacities to do with court or government business. As we have seen, he had been a secretary to diplomats, a financial agent, a spy, and would have represented the interests of Portugal at the European Congress of Augsburg had it not been cancelled. Works for the stage that he had either written, re-worked or translated were performed at the court theatres of Dresden and Madrid. He was a man of cities and towns and urban elites. This also explains the third largest category of lovers: servants. These were a numerous, ever-present and vulnerable group amongst the lives of the better off – as much a public statement of the prestige of their masters as a practical necessity.

So how did Casanova interest women? Why did they become his lovers? To start with, he was fascinating. He had achieved a degree of fame across

Europe by his mid-30s. Contemporaries recognised him as extraordinary, if not entirely respectable. He was well-connected and a traveller with many tales to tell. He was a man who was generous, courageous and empathetic. He was a libertine, uninhibited by stifling moral constraints. And he was available. For many women – more experienced, more independent – this was enough. For other women, perhaps cautious or younger and inexperienced, sensitive to possible dangers, Casanova at least posed the question 'why not?' and to every rational objection they might think of this intelligent and quick-thinking man was likely to have a persuasive answer. Pleasure was a gift from God, a good in itself, he would be able to explain. The unforgivable crime was to reject this gift, to sacrifice happiness on the altar of superstition and misguided prejudices. For young women in their teens, under constant supervision, perhaps having been sequestered in a convent for some time, experiencing growing sexual curiosity and longings while being denied even the most rudimentary sexual education, Casanova must have offered an unbearable temptation.

Then there was the money. The allure of the most unprepossessing of men (or women) can be transformed if their bank balance is healthy enough. From his early 20s to his late 30s, Casanova was either rich or appeared to be rich. If we divide up his life into four periods, from the time of his first love, Bettina, until his return to Venice from exile at the age of 49, Casanova's success with women appears to correlate with his wealth, at least in the cases of the approximately one hundred women he specifically records in his memoirs. From the age of 11 to 21, when Casanova was adopted by Bragadin, he mentions around sixteen love interests. From 21 to 29, up until he was incarcerated in the Leads, there are around twelve. From 30 to 38, the most affluent phase of his life, until he nearly bankrupted himself in London, there are around fifty-five (not including the twenty women at his silk workshop in Paris). From 38 to 49, there are around twenty-two. The period when he was richest, therefore, he records as having more love interests than the other three periods put together.

Casanova was clear-sighted about the power of money: 'a theatre girl in love with someone is invincible unless you know how to conquer her with gold.'[7] It was a point made by his favourite poet, Ariosto: 'And not for love, but for their pockets' sake / The old, the ugly, the deformed they take.'[8] In Turin, when Leah objects that she is not for sale, Casanova retorts, 'all women, honest or not, sell themselves. When a man has time he buys them with his attentions, and when he's in a hurry like me he uses presents and gold.'[9] As ever in the eighteenth century, the relationship between affection, love and money was more nuanced and pragmatic than today. Casanova is using the words 'sale' and 'buy', not as one might with regards to a prostitute but as a short-cut to winning a woman's affection. All women are for sale in the sense that they are open to a romantic liaison, if time, money or both is spent on them. After London, now having to husband his resources more carefully, Casanova finds himself less able to pursue romantic affairs so freely.

One of the most common strategies Casanova used to obtain a woman's affection was to put them or their family under some sort of obligation. It would involve presents, favours or services of various kinds. He could provide a dowry or pay off a debt. In the case of Henriette, Casanova rescued her and her lover from an attempt at extortion. For the benefit of the wife of Burgomaster X from Cologne and the family of Count Ambrosio, he put on lavish entertainments. While this was sometimes a straight-forward quid pro quo for sex, as it was when Casanova agreed to pay for Zenobia's wedding to a poor tailor, more typically Casanova was aiming to engender a sense of gratitude. It was love that was his goal, not begrudged submission. After helping to cure a young woman of a debilitating ailment, Casanova notes how she 'was touched by a gratitude which in women is distant from love only by the smallest of steps.'[10] A more subtle version of this obligation routine was when he declared to his love object that she was responsible for making him fall in love with her because of her beauty and charms. Her indebtedness to Casanova was framed in this case as a sort of promise which he had accepted.

There were exceptions but, broadly speaking, the poorer and lower in status the woman, the more Casanova was open and direct; conquering 'with gold'. To the attractive widow and daughter of a French officer called d'Aché, Casanova was blunt: 'I will give you enough to redeem your belongings [from a pawnbroker] … but you must consent to me giving your charming daughter evidence of my love.' After initially rejecting his 'dreadful proposal', Casanova writes, 'Soon the widow of Aché, forced by need, found herself having to give me her Mimi.'[11] The richer and higher in status the woman, the more Casanova was courtly, proving his worth in ways beyond the simple provision of gifts, and being more in tune with the chivalric code of honourable service, self-sacrifice and love tests. The wife of Burgomaster X, who was the mistress of the General Kettler who accused Casanova of spying, insisted that he attend a large company supper provided by the General, even though he was not invited. This was dangerous, duel-making territory. Casanova refused initially but acceded when she maintained that it would be proof of his affection and esteem for her.

A quality typical of Casanova's wooing was persistence. If one strategy failed, he would try another, probing the character of his adored, and searching for ways to obtain an encouraging response. He appealed to the head and to the heart. He seemed to understand the contagious nature of emotions, using his passionate declarations of love to help kindle love in return. He would be attentive, playful, tender, compose love poems, promise marriage, make pledges of eternal devotion and proclaim his desperation and torment. He might show 'proofs' of his affection, sometimes explicit ones in order to arouse his love object sexually. For the same purpose, Casanova carried around with him a collection of pornographic miniature paintings. He might 'attack her', albeit 'politely and gently', to test a woman's resistance.[12] Perhaps drawing upon his experience with Marta and Nanetta when he was 16, Casanova had discovered that it was often easier to overcome the inhibitions of two women together, rather than of one of them individually, especially if they were friends, cousins or sisters, with the bolder having the effect of leading on the more timid, as in the case of Hedwig and Helena in Geneva. Casanova had also learned that one way for a man to win over a woman was for him to introduce her to a new kind of pleasure.

The one type of relationship which was absent from Casanova's life was marriage. When asked by Pauline why he detested the sacrament of marriage, he replies 'Because it is the tomb of love.'[13] Yet despite regular similar pronouncements, Casanova's attitude was perhaps more ambivalent. On at least one occasion he appears to have come close to tying the knot and he frequently made promises of marriage. Now it is true that most of those promises were probably lures, while in the case of others Casanova was carried away by love. Nonetheless, one is left with the impression that marriage might not have been entirely out of the question for him. He appears in some ways to have seen this cultural institution as the ultimate legitimation of his love, which is ironic given his libertine beliefs. Casanova talks on a number of occasions of a lover as his 'wife', himself as her 'husband' and sexual consummation of a relationship as marriage.

Casanova's attachment to the sexually active but commitment-free life of a bachelor, may not seem strange today but this was not the case at the time, which may help to explain his flirtation with the prospect of settling down and enjoying the respectability of a love that was socially sanctioned. Men were expected to take on their proper role as guardians of women, children, property and the family name. It was the way society was regulated. Marriage was a state that was much sought-after by most men. Not only did it allow them to enjoy guilt-free sex but they acquired status, purpose and a companion to share what were usually the very onerous burdens of survival. Bachelors, by contrast, were loose cannons, often viewed as sources of social instability. It was understandable as a temporary condition. They might, in preparation for marriage, want to establish a career or business, or perhaps accumulate some savings. But there was little sympathy for the man who persisted in his bachelorhood without good reason.

The appeal of marriage or some sort of concubinal arrangement was not lost on Casanova. He experienced its benefits during his relationship with Tonina, one of the rare occasions when he lived with his lover. He considered her 'my wife, my mistress, and my servant all at the same time' and a little later he declares, 'I spent twenty-two days with the girl, which I count today, when I remember them, among the happiest of my life.'[14] Excluding Casanova's volatile relationship with his slave girl, Zaire, the occasions when he lived with women – as in the cases of Tonina, Henriette, Pauline and Madame Dubois – he regarded as periods of unusual happiness. Henriette and Casanova spent their time together under the guise of husband and wife, and it is worth noting that he settled down for two or three years with a woman called Francesca Buschini when he returned to Venice from exile. Reflecting on his relationship with Madame Dubois, whom he regarded amongst the ten or twelve women with whom he was most in love, he laments: 'If I had married a woman shrewd enough to guide me, to govern me without my being able to notice my subjugation, I would have taken care of my fortune, I would have had children, and I would not have been as I am, alone in the world and having nothing.'[15]

When Leo Damrosch declares, 'In reality, Casanova's treatment of women was manipulative,'[16] it is a statement which is simultaneously true, over-generalised and misleadingly simplistic. It ignores the extent of female agency even within the restrictions of a patriarchal society. Casanova's relationships with women involved quite a number who were either instigators or open-eyed collaborators, especially those connected to the theatre. It is likely that many women were using him for agendas of their own, including Bettina, Nanetta and Marta, Donna Lucrezia, Cattinella, Henriette, MM of Venice, Teresa Imer, Giustiniana Wynne, La Charpillon, La Renaud, Signora F, Nina, Leonilda and Leah of Ancona. On several occasions Casanova was knowingly given the pox by women who were trading sex for some service or financial benefit they wanted from him. On one occasion he was physically coerced by a woman into penetrative sex, and on another, he was deceived into sex by a woman pretending to be someone else.

Chapter 12

What Kind of Man was Casanova?

'As far as I am concerned, always recognizing myself as the principal cause of all the misfortunes that have befallen me, I have congratulated myself on being my own pupil and acknowledging my duty to love my teacher.'
Giacomo Casanova, *History of My Life*

Few of us are able to remain consistent as we manoeuvre through life, our behaviours and beliefs occasionally falling out of tune with each other in the face of events. The best that most of us can do is set ourselves broad parameters that we try to respect, but even those parameters shift as we age, change, recognise our insuperable biases, and encounter the unanticipated. There is, of course, a temptation to use our powers of rationalisation and selective memory to gloss our more egregious inconsistencies, especially ones that might trouble our conscience or our sense of who we are. This is a temptation to which autobiographers and writers of memoirs are prone, sensitive to projecting a coherent and defensible portrayal of who they are and how they came to be that person. They search for forks in the road and describe how they chose to travel one way rather than the other. Those descriptions will incorporate their own agency, the agency of others, of society, its institutions, as well as of God and the metaphysical. Autobiographers, like all story-tellers, will construct lines of narrative through which this agency will flow. Chance will also play a part but this feels less satisfactory. Humans are meaning seekers, alert to intentions. With chance, the trail goes cold. This preference for narrative and agency encourages people to look deeper and further, and to diminish the significance of coincidence.

It is one of the striking features of Casanova, in contrast, that he is able to resist this temptation. Casanova refers to fate but so little does he read into it that it is no more than a synonym for chance. Likewise, although Casanova does not rule out notions of destiny and providence, he regards them, if they do exist, as inscrutable. He believes he has a daemon that at times has kept him out of trouble (and, more rarely, gets him into it) but in the grand scheme of his life its significance was minor. Casanova embraces a qualified form of free will, rejecting the idea that the course of his existence is pre-determined.

The causal chains of the events Casanova describes in his memoirs are typically short and chance happenings are common. At the outset of each new episode, fate may deal him the cards but he is the one who plays them. His memoirs read more like a collection of incomplete short stories than a novel with its defined plots and sub-plots, its carefully explored themes, its balance of characters, conflicts and timely resolutions. In Casanova's world, people are just getting on with their own lives. Again and again Casanova comes across old lovers, friends and enemies as he criss-crosses Europe. Such coincidences entertain him and sometimes set off new escapades but he does not read anything more deeply into this. He sees no guiding hand, no divine author. There is nothing inevitable. *History of My Life* is the work of a man who is describing life as it unfolds moment to moment, sensitive to people's present motivations and behaviour.

The result is that when we read Casanova's memoirs we are confronted with human complexity. His character does possess predictable patterns of behaviour, attitude and self-serving rationalisation but there are also conflicts that defy simple formulae. He has, of course, provided us with so much material that it is always possible, by being selective, to construct different Casanovas, ones which are more consistent. These Casanovas might be tidier but they might also be more reflective of the preoccupations and filters of those who construct them.

The Venetian was imposing: tall, muscular, dark-skinned, with a large nose, strong chin and heavily lidded eyes. He was 'built like a Hercules' according to his celebrated friend, the Prince de Ligne.[1] Frederick II remarked that Casanova was 'a fine figure of a man' although he himself did not think that he was handsome.[2] He fizzed with energy and ideas to the end of his life, and possessed an enormous appetite and an incredible constitution. Travelling long distances by road or sea was notoriously onerous as well as hazardous, particularly in the winter, but Casanova seemed to manage it with little difficulty.

Casanova had a strong need to be liked and accepted. It is no doubt the reason he fell in with rather dubious company in his early teens, and later when he was a penniless musician. Casanova loved to be the centre of attention, to be able to surprise and astonish. He was a brilliant conversationalist. He charmed and ingratiated himself with the rich and powerful. It delighted him to be recognised in some way by those in authority. When Casanova had the honour of being employed as a financial agent for the French government, he was so pleased that he could hardly sleep. He was overjoyed when Pope Clement XIII awarded him the Order of the Golden Spur, an award which had been granted so liberally that it had lost much of its prestige. He celebrated the honour by spending 1,000 scudi on a cross set with precious stones (a sum that was five times the annual wage of Giovanni Righetti, a servant who swept the pope's rooms and whom Casanova befriended). Casanova wanted to be recognised as a man of letters and respected by polite society. But whatever literary and scholarly ambitions he may have harboured, in his 20s and 30s he was enjoying adventure, women and the good life too much. Only when the sources of finance required for his lavish existence started to dry up and he began losing the appeal of youth, did he seriously turn his attention to writing.

Integral to Casanova's social acceptance was being a highly educated man who was well-read but not a pedant; as we know, a gentleman or courtier wore his learning lightly. Reading was a core aspect of sociability and identity. For a start, it required leisure time and resources. In his analysis of La Morlière's satire of French society, *Angola, Indian History* (1751), Thomas Kavanagh lists reading alongside the theatre, opera, receptions, hunting, gambling and the bedroom as typical pursuits of Parisian elites.[3] What you read; who you read; knowing what was fashionable in the moment; being adept, when called upon, to comment on this or that poem or play or book, or this or that writer, said a great deal about you. It was an image the Venetian was careful to promote. 'There was nothing he did not know,' observed de Ligne.[4]

But reading was about more than acquiring knowledge, and it was by no means a solitary pursuit. Family, friends, guests and acquaintances would read to each other selected pieces of prose and verse, literary and non-literary, which they would discuss and critique. It was a common entertainment and a great deal of attention was given to the performance both on the part of the reader and the listener. In Britain there was a brisk trade in elocution and other advice books to help the reader to maximise the clarity and emotional impact of their delivery. Sometimes people chose to read their own work. Casanova read extracts of his memoirs to friends as did Jean-Jacques Rousseau. On one occasion in 1770 the latter read for 17 hours with only two short breaks. 'When he came to the subject of the abandoned children,' Damrosch comments, 'he stared at his audience challengingly, and no one made any response; at the end they kissed his hand and tried to console him. He wept, and all of us wept hot tears.'[5] As can be imagined, Casanova was in his element. At his visit to Voltaire, he was called upon by Madame Denis, the *philosophe's* niece and lover, to recite in front of the assembled guests a thirty-six-stanza section from Ariosto's *The Frenzy of Orlando*. He did so, from memory it would appear, and was a great success. Tears flowed all round and Voltaire rushed to embrace him.

Famously, Casanova rejected conservative and religious injunctions against non-marital sex. They were irrational conventions, tyrannical and contrary to nature. The ability to experience sensual pleasure was a gift from God to make the effort of survival worthwhile and should be enjoyed to the full. In his seduction of the pious Dona Ignacia, he railed against the oppressiveness of religious ideas which lead to her resisting physical intimacy. She confessed to loving him but wished she could love him in a 'different way' (that is, in a way that did not arouse her sexually). 'A monstrous desire,' the old librarian at Dux exclaims to his reader, 'which can only exist in an honest soul if it's enslaved to a religion which makes it see crime where nature cannot allow one to be.'[6] At first sight, this rejection of sexual social norms, Casanova's criticisms of the Church, along with his humble background, regular collisions with authority, and his philosophically materialist leanings, might lead us to suppose that he would be politically progressive, perhaps in the mould of a Baron d'Holbach or a Diderot. In fact, Casanova's politics were conservative. He justified despotism in theory but was critical of its excesses, and was in favour of a regulated, aristocratic-based government such as that of Venice. He had little time for anything democratic. He may have been critical of the Church and the priesthood but so were plenty of others who professed themselves to be Christian. He believed the Church was essential for the maintenance of social cohesion, for all its faults. Neither was his promiscuity in itself particularly remarkable or indicative of a forward-thinking mindset. Casanova rubbed shoulders with many an aristocrat who was as equally debauched, if not more so, such as his friend Lord Pembroke.

Casanova was knowledgeable of the lineages of European nobility and would sometimes use it to curry favour with this or that well-born host. He was sensitive to the niceties of aristocratic behaviour and custom. He defended the Venetian penal system as well as the Republic's general system of governance despite his incarceration in the Leads. He wrote character portraits of the various European rulers he came across during his travels, and while these were not always uncritical, they did tend to range from sympathetic to effusive to downright sycophantic. Given that his esteem for monarchs and the aristocracy was far more Burke than Robespierre, it is unsurprising that Casanova had no sympathy for the French Revolution, although he well understood the abuses of the Church and the defects of monarchical rule that had contributed to it.

If Casanova was politically conservative, in the spheres of economics and administration his attitude was more typical of the Enlightenment. He favoured innovation, and for a period in the 1760s he devised and proposed various projects to governments around Europe. James Rives Childs notes: 'While in Russia, he submitted a project...for the establishment of a silk industry, and in Warsaw he suggested a project for a Polish soap factory. In Spain...he proposed a tobacco manufactory.'[7] He also encouraged Catherine II to replace the old Julian calendar with the Gregorian, which was more closely aligned to the solar year, and he took an interest in a Spanish scheme to revitalise the Sierra Morena through colonisation.

'Anger had the same power over me as love,' the old librarian records.[8] De Ligne observes: 'He had feeling and gratitude; but if you displeased him he was malignant, peevish, and detestable; a million ducats could not buy back the smallest little jest made upon him.'[9] If at all possible, Casanova would seek retribution against anyone he thought had harmed or offended him. He believed that revenge (in the form of defeating a rival) was one of three motivating desires common to all creatures (the others being procreation and subsistence). Casanova translated Voltaire's play *The Scotswoman* (1760) but became his enemy when he discovered that the great man had disliked the translation. On one occasion, when a trick had been played upon him which left him a drenched laughing stock, Casanova dug up a recently buried corpse, cut off its arm near the shoulder and hid under the bed of the culprit. When the man himself retired to bed, Casanova pulled at the bedcovers. After some to-ing and fro-ing, the man reached down, grabbing at the presumed prankster, and found himself taking hold of the detached arm. The shock induced a debilitating stroke from which the victim never recovered. Casanova was unrepentant. His anger was abetted by his pride and a prickly sense of honour. One symptom was his desire always to win an argument. It was his insistence on proving a point with regards to the value of a ring that led to one of his many duels.

Any form of embarrassment or public disrespect affected Casanova badly, his sensitivity partly rooted in the fact that he was the son of an actress. We find him repeatedly striving to capture the esteem of elite society. Casanova records how his conduct during his duel with Count Branicki 'did me an immortal honour,' and how afterwards out of a misplaced sense of pride, he refused offers of financial help.[10] During one ridiculous encounter, Cardinal Passionei, a man as proud as the Venetian, gave Casanova a book, to which Casanova responded by presenting Passionei with a book in return. But the Cardinal insisted on paying for the book he had been given, which Casanova refused to accept, indignant that he should be treated as a bookseller. Consequently, they returned the books back to each other. It was as a reward for donating to the Vatican library the book that he had offered to Passionei that Casanova received the Order of the Golden Spur.

Casanova's pride was such that at times it could degenerate into childish bravado, petulance or spite. When he was arrested by the Venetian Inquisition, he dressed in his finest clothes almost as though he was going to a wedding. Unable to win over a beautiful dancer who was in love with another man, he stole from her a miniature portrait of herself. He became jealously annoyed with a man who was engaging in polite conversation with a woman who, unbeknownst to everyone else including herself, he had taken a shine to. If Casanova received a snub of some sort, he was not below engineering circumstances that enabled him to snub that person in return.

Casanova was a gifted man in many ways but his birth meant that he would always be regarded as an inferior. It was an impossible bind. More than once did his origins undermine, or threaten to undermine, his social position and career prospects. As a young man in Naples, Casanova had the opportunity of becoming a well-paid tutor to the 10-year-old nephew of the Duke of Matalona. By coincidence, he had met Don Antonio Casanova, a man of some influence, who upon comparing genealogies turned out to be a distant cousin. But the Venetian Casanova had not told Don Antonio about his mother. When his friends were determined to introduce him to the Queen of Naples, he felt that he had to leave the city because he was aware that the Queen knew of his mother's profession, and he would be humiliated if this became known.

For much of his life Casanova did in fact present himself to the world as a nobleman. He gave himself titles, dressed fashionably and expensively, took mistresses and attended the typical watering holes of good society. These included casinos, courts, salons, spas, theatres, fashionable gardens, literary academies, masonic lodges, and so on, where nobility and elite commoners mingled. Running alongside this desire to pass himself off as an aristocrat was his ambition to become famous. And he was successful, to a degree and for certain lengths of time. The type of fame he achieved was that of a celebrity, someone whose renown was neither due to their rank by birth, nor to their pre-eminence in some or other career or field of endeavour. Celebrity culture was long considered to be a modern phenomenon but the study of sources such as *History of My Life* has traced its emergence back to the eighteenth century and earlier. 'Casanova is the historical celebrity *par excellence*, 'writes Nicola Vinovrški. 'He was not, at any point,' she says, 'well known because of, or at least primarily because of, his occupation or ascribed status. He was not a famous person whose private life then became a matter of public interest.'[11] So what were the foundations of this celebrity?

The development of the public sphere began to break down the barriers between court and commoner. At the same time the broader emancipationist impulse of the Enlightenment encouraged individualism and the transgression of established social roles and norms, seen most notably in libertinism. Individuals and their personal lives became a source of fascination in themselves, evidenced by the growing popularity of such content in periodicals and novels. This left room for an adventurer like Casanova. He was an opportunist and something of a polymath. He wanted to be famous but was not too concerned about the foundations upon which this fame was to be built. One feature of Casanova's personality was that he became easily intoxicated by the idea of something. As he was intoxicated by the idea and experience of love as much as any specific love object themselves, likewise he was intoxicated by the idea and experience of being famous, rather than becoming famous for a specific reason. Vinovrški observes: 'He claimed that he wanted to be at various times a famous preacher, famous astrologist, famous conversationalist, famous writer, or famous in the arts.'[12] Casanova was also very competitive. His mother and brothers, Francesco and Giovanni, had achieved varying degrees of fame in their own right, and it may be that this further motivated him to acquire a bit of limelight for himself.

It was Casanova's escape from the Leads that propelled his name into the consciousness of European polite society through word of mouth, correspondence and periodicals. Wherever he went, Casanova would be asked to give an account of the affair, and he did so superbly. It would take him at least two hours, and the account became something of a fashionable social event. He produced a written version at the request of Madame de Pompadour, which no doubt would have been copied and circulated far and wide. His duel with Branicki created a similar stir across Europe nine years later. Casanova's arrival in a town or city would be recorded in local gazettes, and there was sufficient public interest in the Venetian that governments would compile reports on him and keep tabs on what he was up to. Throughout much of his life, Casanova helped to cultivate his celebrity by searching out and keeping the company of famous people as well as wooing listeners with a wide array of well-honed anecdotes about himself. On occasion he would write and circulate copies about an incident in which he may have been involved, to exonerate or justify himself or to undermine his critics. Vinovrški comments: 'By writing circulars for distribution and telling his stories at length before society audiences, he ensured that his own version of events was the one instilled in the public consciousness.'[13]

It is perhaps because Casanova was effectively an imposter for so much of his life, mimicking the persona of an aristocrat, that a sense of inadequacy lurked within: 'In the most brilliant company, if only one person looks me up and down, I'm lost; I become bad-tempered and stupid. It is a failing.'[14] In his 1797 Preface, Casanova notes: 'I have always had a dread of being hissed.'[15] Men or women of the highest status could intimidate him. Despite falling in love with the royal princess, the Duchess de Chartres, the social gulf between them was too great for him to dare make an approach, and he let the opportunity pass. At Casanova's first meeting with Frederick II, he was so overawed that his mind went blank.

Despite Casanova's pride, proneness to anger and occasional insecurity, he was a man frequently overcome by his softer emotions, whether they be sad or happy. Either one could move him to tears. Casanova regularly wept when taking leave of friends (and, it seems, so did they). Likewise when he was reciting literature (along with his audience), as we have seen above. On one occasion he was at an elegant social gathering, when his lover, Henriette, unprompted, took centre stage and revealed that she was an accomplished violoncello player. Casanova, who had no idea that she could even play, was overwhelmed: 'I disappeared to go and weep in the garden.'[16] Casanova's emotion in this case was due to his pride in the talent, courage and beauty of Henriette, and that this extraordinary woman was his lover.

In his romantic relationships Casanova generally sought harmony. The slightest discord, real or imagined, could be a torment to him. Here he is reflecting on an unspoken moment of dissonance between himself and his love object, Sara: 'I spent a cruel night. It was the first time in my life that I found myself loved and yet unhappy on account of a whim of the strangest kind. Weighing the reasons she gave me, and finding them frivolous, I ended up concluding that my caresses had upset her.'[17] At the end of an intense love affair, it was not unusual for Casanova's mood to swing towards melancholy and ruminations on death.

Evident throughout his memoirs, is Casanova's emotional and social awareness, a product of his fascination with people and human nature. He travelled extensively, was curious about everything, and met and interacted with numerous people across the social spectrum. He was continuously recording and reflecting upon his experiences and the experiences of others. When Casanova depicts people, he generally tries to portray them as they are – their strengths, weaknesses and idiosyncrasies – whatever his own relationship with them might be, good or bad. It is clear from his descriptions of his lovers that they are more to him than notches on a bedpost. He represents them as unique individuals. Take Rosalie: she had been a servant at a brothel, whom he was to transform Pygmalion-like into his mistress:

She was a tall brunette with black eyes, fine eyebrows, a delicate face without much colour, and white as a lily. Her cheeks had two dimples that you only saw when she laughed, and there was another on her chin. Her bottom lip, of the brightest crimson, protruding a little beyond the top lip, seemed designed to catch a kiss and keep it from falling. All this made an elegant portrait: one of those faces which are arresting because they speak and make you want to know what they are saying.[18]

Casanova's memoirs are peppered with psychological insights into men, women, specific nationalities, human nature in general and, above all, himself. It was his knowledge of the psychology of gamblers that in part enabled him to convince the French government to establish the Paris lottery. This understanding of his own character and that of others is one of the reasons Casanova was not only successful in seducing women but also in charming those around him whomever he met. Here is one of the ways he would get people on his side at moments of misfortune: 'The strategy that I used for this was to tell the story truthfully without omitting certain circumstances that one cannot say without having courage. That's the secret which, because most of the human race is made up of cowards, not all men can put into effect.'[19]

Casanova's awareness of the complexity of human motivation is well illustrated by his response to Giustiniana Wynne's appeal to him for help regarding her unwanted pregnancy. Casanova highlights the interaction of vanity, ego, reason and emotion and, in particular, how impulses of chivalrous self-sacrifice and opportunistic sexual exploitation can co-exist: 'I was very happy that she thought of me instead of anyone else, even if I had to perish along with her. Can we think otherwise when we love?' Casanova could see that Giustiniana was counting on and exploiting his love for her, while also recognising that for his part, he was almost pleased at her misfortune because it had encouraged her to contact him: 'If I could succeed in remedying it, I was sure of my reward.'[20] Elsewhere he observes how at times he deceived himself, pretending that the motives behind some or other of his actions were virtuous when in reality they were selfish. Rescuing a woman from her fraud of a lover he writes:

> But was it virtue that prompted me to act? Was it for love of the innocent beauty whom I had before my eyes and whose affliction pierced my soul? That was all a part of it; but as it was plain that if I had found her ugly and sullen I might have left her to die of hunger, then it followed that I worked only for myself. ... I was playing a false role in good faith, which I could only play well by convincing myself that I was not playing it.[21]

Into his 40s Casanova was a man who lived in the moment, not for the future. Possessing a low boredom threshold, he was frequently rash and governed by impulse. To some extent this may have been due to the precarious conditions of eighteenth-century life. The benefits of deferred reward may be attractive to those of us brought up in modern societies, which are largely stable, safe and predictable, but in centuries gone by horizons were by necessity more short-term. To forego a benefit in the present in the expectation of reaping more in the future was not such a straight-forward calculation. Circumstances could change rapidly. You may not be around to collect, or the promised reward may be impossible to deliver. A bird in the hand was the preferred option for many. 'In life nothing is real but the present,' Casanova writes.[22] 'Eat, drink and be merry, for tomorrow we die,' was pretty sage advice in the eighteenth century, especially if you were poor.

Casanova's propensity for living in the moment manifested itself in various ways. He was, for a start, skilled at improvisation. Drawing on his capacious memory and facility with language, he was a blagger of the first order: in front of the three noble senators, Barbaro, Bragadin, and Dandolo, he becomes a medical expert; in front of Parisian financiers, he becomes an expert on how to establish a successful lottery; in front of Frederick II, he becomes an expert on taxation; in front of Spanish politicians and reformers, he becomes an expert on land colonisation. At the court of the Duchy of Kurland, he even becomes an expert on mining. Casanova made such a positive impression upon the duke, that he subsequently embarked upon a two-week tour of the Duchy's iron and copper mines, writing up a report on how to improve them. It turned out that he had something of a talent for the work despite admitting he knew very little about the subject, and he received a handsome 200 zecchini reward for his efforts.

Time and again, Casanova would use his wits either to get out of a tricky situation or to entertain himself and others. A pretty woman with a speech impediment was having trouble reading her part in some amateur theatricals. Casanova announced that he would devise a spell that would cure her problem by the morning without the woman needing to do anything. True to his word, the next day the woman was able to deliver her script flawlessly. Casanova had spent the night re-writing her lines to remove the words that had caused the difficulty. One time when he arrived at his lodgings in Ferrera, Casanova came across a dancer called Catinella, who, as soon as he entered the dining room, introduced him to the assembled company as her cousin. Without missing a beat, despite having never met the woman before, he went along with what he realised was a scam. As part of his plan to escape from the Leads, he manufactured an oil lamp from disparate and hard-to-obtain materials to help him work at night. To communicate with his fellow conspirator, Father Balbi, he let the nail of his little finger grow, then sharpened it to a point to make a pen, using mulberry juice for ink. Casanova's first attempt to break out of the Leads was uncovered after he was unexpectedly moved to a better cell as a consequence of an intervention by his patron, Senator Bragadin. Shrewdly, Casanova implied to his jailer that the attempt to escape from his previous cell had been made possible by the jailer's own incompetence, ensuring that it was never reported. Close to exhaustion during a marathon fifty-hour game of cards with a gambler called d'Entragues, Casanova deliberately instigated a quarrel over how long his rival had taken for a break. So disconcerted did the accusation make d'Entragues that shortly afterwards he collapsed, handing Casanova victory.

Casanova's focus on the here and now meant that decisions he made affecting his future could be somewhat arbitrary. When he was reluctantly dismissed from the service of Cardinal Acquaviva in Rome, the cardinal asked the budding churchman, Casanova, where he would like to go. Acquaviva had important contacts throughout Europe and would supply him with letters of recommendation. Much to the cardinal's surprise, Casanova chose Constantinople, an unlikely place to carve out a successful career in the Church, or pretty much any career if you were a Christian. Similar whims led him to become a military officer, and then a professional gambler (very briefly; he lost too much). At one point, he thought of giving up his worldly possessions to become a monk, and was taking steps to do so, when he got side-tracked by yet another beautiful woman. Casanova was not a fool, of course. He understood that financially his lifestyle did not bode well for the future. Occasionally he gave some thought to making investments that would provide for him in the longer term but little materialised or, as in the case of his silk fabric workshop in Paris, it backfired.

Casanova's decision to go to Constantinople was typical of moments when his judgement-making was so bafflingly antithetical to his interests as to be wilfully self-destructive. The best example was his affair in London with 18-year-old La Charpillon (Marie-Anne Genevieve Augspurgher) who lived with her mother, grandmother and two aunts, all of whom, presently or in the past, had been courtesans or mistresses. Casanova had met the women in Paris several years earlier, when they passed on to him a false bill of exchange worth 6,000 francs, a considerable sum. He could have had no illusions as to the kind of women with whom he was dealing. When Casanova began to show an interest in La Charpillon, Lord Pembroke warned him against the idea, as he had had dealings with her himself. La Charpillon even told Casanova in advance that she had the power to make him fall in love with her and to suffer for it. Despite all this, over the ensuing weeks, he was manipulated, tormented and fleeced, repeatedly resolving to give up the woman, and then inexplicably going back to her. Eventually, after his abortive suicide attempt, he ended up in court. According to Casanova, the blind magistrate, Sir John Fielding (Henry Fielding's half-brother), sentenced him to life imprisonment without testing the evidence or even informing him of his crime. Two witnesses had been procured to support trumped-up charges that Casanova was intending to attack and disfigure La Charpillon. Once he was told of the accusations, he denied them, and was released on bail (he fled from London before the date set for trial). In reality, it is doubtful that Fielding had pre-emptively condemned him. It is more likely that Casanova had misunderstood the niceties of English court procedure.

Unsurprisingly, travel, gambling, socialising and endless love affairs appealed to Casanova's taste for novelty and short-term gratification. When he had funds, he spent the large bulk of them on what gave enjoyment to himself and others (which, for Casanova, was tantamount to the same thing), his extravagance simultaneously broadcasting the nobility of his character. Returning to Paris from Amsterdam, having made a lot of money from his financial dealings there, Casanova bought lavish gifts for his friends, the Balletti family. His aim was always to dazzle. After one particularly successful entertainment that he had organised, he observed: 'Happy with it all, I paid the worthy pastry chef everything he wanted. I loved, I was loved, I was in good health, I had a lot of money and I spent it. I was happy and I told myself so, laughing at the stupid moralists who say that there is no true happiness on earth.'[23] To count the cost of his pleasures was to diminish his enjoyment of them. In his final weeks in England, he refused to budget, despite rapidly running out of cash, continuing to spend generously on his love interests to the point of bankruptcy. When arranging a high-society luncheon in Brühl, near Cologne, he was asked how much he wished to spend. His response was typical: 'As much as possible'.[24]

Casanova's material generosity reflected the spirit of a fundamentally compassionate man. He described the slave trade as 'horrible merchandise', and unlike many of his contemporaries, he was sensitive to the suffering of animals.[25] He was sceptical of the widespread belief that animals were little more than soulless machines operating on instinct, devoid of thought and consciousness. For the likes of Descartes, animals did not feel pain despite appearances to the contrary. Casanova called bull fighting a 'barbarous spectacle' and was particularly distressed by the fate of the horse which 'was always sacrificed, murdered by the coward who rode it.'[26] In his *Examination of the 'Studies of Nature' by Bernardin de Saint-Pierre* (1788/9), Casanova describes being deeply moved by the cries of a dolphin that was dying having been stranded on a beach: 'If the cries of this fish did not come from genuine sensitivity and great pain, it was the cleverest charlatan of all the fish in the sea.'[27]

Casanova was a man who liked to do people good. Given that pleasure-seeking was so central to his character, we should perhaps not be surprised. Acts of kindness can be profoundly satisfying. There are many examples of Casanova aiding others when he had an opportunity to do so, even enemies who had repeatedly caused him grief. True, when women were involved, and they were mostly women, there was often an ulterior motive. But there are plenty of times when he received nothing from his good deed other than the satisfaction of having helped another human being. Casanova successfully intervened to transform the oppressive and impoverished conditions suffered by poor girls who had been packed off by their families to a 'pious foundation' near Rome to prevent them from succumbing to sin. The foundation, probably the Istituto di Santa Caterina dei Funari, contained 100 women and girls, and had existed for over a century. They could leave what was essentially a prison, if they were able to contract a marriage for which they would be provided a dowry. The secluded conditions of the women's and girls' confinement meant that only a few managed to marry, leading Casanova to suspect that funds intended for the provision of dowries were being siphoned off elsewhere. They could otherwise leave once they reached the age of 35. Fear of destitution meant that virtually all chose to stay. It appeared that only four women in total had left in the previous twenty years. Drawing on the support of influential friends, including Cardinal de Bernis and a princess, Casanova submitted a petition to the pope, who then instituted an investigation and implemented reforms.

In the light of this, moments of callousness strike the reader as all the more puzzling. There was Casanova's desire to humiliate a noblewoman over that 1,000 zecchini dress. He was surprisingly non-judgemental about the violent and sadistic conduct of an officer called O'Neilan, whom he befriended in Mantua in his early 20s. Casanova found him entertaining company even though he recognised that the man was particularly debauched. Any kind of novelty interested Casanova, so perhaps O'Neilan's excessiveness appealed to him, along with his respect for soldiers. Another piece of cruelty with which Casanova appeared to have no problem was perpetrated by the King of Naples. The 19 year-old forced two terrified young Florentine noblemen, both hunchbacks, to strip naked in front of spectators and be tossed into the air in turn. 'How could anyone resist bursting into laughter seeing this malformed body flying three times in the air at the height of ten or twelve feet?' asks the Venetian.[28] But such examples of indifference to the suffering of others were unusual. Towards the end of his memoirs, feeling melancholy, Casanova was cheered by the thought that 'apart from La Corticelli, I had conferred happiness on all the girls that I had loved.'[29]

For all his brilliance Casanova was quintessentially a child of Venice; a city addicted to its pleasures. Its people were singers, dancers, story tellers, bon viveurs and, of course, gamblers. It was a place of endless festivals, and for more than six months of the year you could venture out concealed, perhaps donning your long domino-cloak and baùta, the latter comprising a mask, black hood and mantle. This provided you with not quite anonymity – there could be tell-tale signs that gave you away to your more vigilant compatriots – but, at least, plausible deniability. In this discreet environment, you were free to experiment with different identities irrespective of rank or sex; a skill that Casanova mastered effortlessly and was to exploit throughout his life. Venice's patricians, Casanova's role-models, were famous for their geniality and silky courtesy. Highly cultivated, they engaged easily with anybody of whatever status. Most noblemen attended the university of Padua, Zanetta's precocious outcast rubbing shoulders alongside them. No doubt there were plenty of lessons learned.

The Venetians as a whole were reported to be good natured and practised in easy virtue; the Church and its killjoy instincts were kept firmly under control. Venetians lived in an eternal present, a society resistant to change, reassured in their conservatism by a millennium of political stability. They did not have too many complaints. Ordinary people did not suffer from the same levels of poverty that existed elsewhere in Europe: the state, the guilds and the wealthy patrician families generally took care of them. On day-to-day affairs, authorities avoided voluntarily intruding into people's lives, despite being well informed on what they were up to through an extensive network of spies and informers. A light touch was preferred except where an individual's behaviour was deemed to be excessive or liable to undermine good order. If people indulged their sins with tact and moderation, all was well. For the most part the state played the role of the ineffectual parent, forever remonstrating with the behaviour of their charges but rarely doing anything. Regulations were routinely ignored, such as those to do with dress or gambling. Paradoxically, despite the close supervision, Venetian commoners enjoyed a degree of liberty and freedom from oppression unusual in much of Europe. But politics, which also included anything related to the patrician caste, were different. Then, the government could act decisively.

Venice was Casanova's sandpit, and his preoccupations were those of his birthplace: the love of freedom, books, seduction, the theatre, food, improvisation, risk-taking. Everything except music, oddly, given how central it was to Venetian culture and the fact that he himself was a violinist.

'Casanova is not usually described as a *philosophe* but the similarities between himself and that renowned category of French intellectuals are striking. Casanova was steeped in learning, a man of letters, and a skilful and versatile author who could be pugnacious and witty. He was a sociable urbanite who engaged with some of the foremost Enlightenment minds and influencers of the time, along with many lesser lights. He met the likes of d'Alembert, Fontenelle, Albrecht von Haller, Voltaire - of course - Winkelmann, possibly Diderot and possibly Rousseau. His intellectual interests mapped closely on to those of the *philosophe* tradition. There was his attraction to pagan writers and ideas, his eclecticism, and his high regard for reason and education. He advocated tolerance and moderation. He questioned prevailing moral norms and was critical of the Church and religious doctrine. His own philosophical and historical writing is infused with a spirit of critical enquiry, coupled with a preference for knowledge founded upon empirical investigation and human experience rather than abstract systems that were tortuously deductive. Casanova was politically conservative, but this was not untypical either. Most Enlightenment figures of any stature, although progressive in some ways, were closely aligned to the established social order.'

Extract from Dave Thompson's forthcoming
Casanova & Enlightenment: His Study of Life and other Writers,
due to be published in 2024.

Notes

My primary resource for *Casanova's Life and Times* has been Willard R Trask's authoritative English translation of Casanova's memoirs which is now over fifty years old. I have supplemented it with the recent Bouquins French edition (2013–2018). Using Bouquins I have produced my own translations of material I have taken from the memoirs. I have toned down the formality of Trask a little but not too much. To help guard against the dangers of presentism it is useful to maintain something of the more formal register typical of educated elites of the past. In his preface, Casanova is explicit that he wrote for a 'well-bred audience'.

For the most part the variations between my translations relative to Trask's are minor and make little difference to the informational content. But this is not always the case. An example would be Casanova's homosexual encounter with Ismail. In the French we have: 'je n'ai pas trouvée de mon goût…je n'étais pas amateur de la chose.' (*HV* 1:377) In Trask: 'it was not to my taste…I was not of that persuasion.' (*HL* 2:83) And in mine: 'I didn't find it to my taste…I wasn't a fan of it.' Trask's use of the word 'persuasion' could signify homosexuality in the modern sense of being an identity whereas across most of Europe, for most the eighteenth century, it was seen as a behaviour. Trask's translation here could complicate our understanding of Casanova's perception of homosexuality. Likewise with women. Casanova thought highly of women who were intelligent and well-read, yet in Trask we have him complaining that 'In a woman learning is out of place' from the French 'Dans une femme la science est déplacée.' (*HL* 3:50, *HV* 1:631) In reality, for Casanova it seems that the issue was not with women who were educated but with women who engaged in academic study, hence my translation, 'In a woman, scholarship is out of place.'

I have used short abbreviations to indicate where the material can be found in both the Trask and Bouquins editions. For Trask I have used *HL* (*History of My Life*) and for Bouquins *HV* (*Histoire de Ma Vie*). In the notes, references such as the above would look like: 'I didn't find it to my taste': *HL* 2:83 / *HV* 1:377, where the first number is the edition volume and the second number is the page reference.

Introduction
'I will leave it to others': *HL* 1:31 / *HV* 1:11

1. 'This [teacher of morals] must know': Casanova, cited in Denieul's 'L'essai de critique,' trans. author, 138
2. 'It is difficult to arrive': Casanova, *Soliloque d'un Penseur*, trans. author, 16
3. 'make moral reflections': Casanova, cited in Vescovo's 'Ruffiano e messegero di Talia', *Casanova: tra Venezia e l'Europa*, Gilberto Pizzamiglio (ed), trans. author, 287
4. 'Comedy was created': Goldoni, *The Comic Theatre*, 31
5. 'moderation is recognised': Casanova, *Confutazione della* 'Storia del Governo Veneto' *d'Amelot de la Houssaie*. Divisa in tre parti (I parte), trans. author, 32
6. 'needs nothing but moderation': Bernardini, 'Politica e filosofia', trans. author, 9
7. 'He [Casanova] investigated human nature': Cerman, *Casanova: Enlightenment Philosopher*, 47
8. 'Moreover, his narrative strategies': Vitelli, '"Dark Matter" in Casanova's memoirs', *Casanoviana 3*, (2020), 16
9. 'My misfortunes': *HL* 1:26 / *HV* 1:5
10. 'after the death': Bernardini, 'Politica e filosofia', trans. author, 11
11. 'They invented descriptions': Cerman, *Casanova: Enlightenment Philosopher*, 43
12. Casanova's claim that the Marquise d'Urfé died in 1763: *HL* 9:245
13. 'he [that is, himself] who is writing': Casanova, *The Duel*, 27

Chapter 1: A different country
'I have written my history': *HL* 1:28 / *HV* 1:6

Making ends meet
1. Income spent on diet: Shammas, 'Food Expenditures', 91
2. Estimate of beggars in London who were women: Hunt, *Women in Eighteenth-Century Europe*, 200
3. 'Help!': *HL* 4:135 / *HV* 1:1114
4. 'Women's consumer goods': Hunt, *Women in Eighteenth-Century Europe*, 159
5. Cost of a court dress: Greig, 'Faction and Fashion', 17
6. Cost of living estimate: Melton, *The Rise of the Public in Enlightenment Europe*, 127
7. Empress Elizabeth's dresses: Szabo, *The Seven Years War in Europe (1756–1763)*, 335
8. 'spent a soldo on a good stick': *HL* 1:185 / *HV* 1:164
9. 'It will be said at Versailles': *HL* 11:158 / *HV* 3:720
10. 'In this new life': *HL* 1:95 / *HV* 1:77
11. 'I saw before my eyes the inevitable gallows' *HL* 10:32 / *HV* 3:241

Law enforcement
12. The lantern maker: *HL* 9:128–9
13. 'either per week': *HL* 11:186 / *HV* 3:750

Violence

14. Rousseau's corporal punishment: Rousseau, Jean-Jacques. *The Confessions*, 29
15. 'I then felt rain down': *HL* 1:172 / *HV* 1:152
16. 'Twenty-three years of fighting': Blanning, *The Pursuit of Glory*, 670

Personal freedom

17. 'I have found this common': *HL* 2.246 / *HV* 1:531
18. 'In polite society': *HL* 8:243–4 / *HV* 2:1056–7
19. 'I find my name': *HL* 11:149 / *HV* 3:709
20. Permission to travel: Hunt, *Women in Eighteenth-Century Europe*, 25

Sexuality

21. 'the scandalous morals of the times': *HL* 3:193 / *HV* 1:845–6
22. 'according to Tim Hitchcock': Hitchcock, 'Sex and gender: Redefining sex in eighteenth-century England', 79
23. 'an even greater crime than unlawful copulation': *HL* 2:84–85
24. 'Europeans began to think that most men': Trumbach, 'The transformation of sodomy...', 832
25. 'It has been convincingly argued': Kozul, 'Casanova and the undifferentiated body', *Casanova in the Enlightenment*, Malina Stefanovska (ed), 55–67
26. Casanova's homosexuality: Masters, *Casanova*, 226
27. 'Petronio was a real Giton': *HL* 2:6 / *HV* 1:301
28. 'I didn't find it to my taste': *HL* 2:83 / *HV* 1:377
29. 'He was a Ganymede': *HL* 7:72 / *HV* 2:617

Medicine

30. 'The physician Zambelli': *HL* 1:47–48 / *HV* 1:29
31. 'Casanova, in accordance with': Lovett, *Casanova's Guide to Medicine*, 234
32. Importation of leeches: Morabia, 'Pierre-Charles-Alexandre Louis and the evaluation of bloodletting', 158
33. Smallpox mortality: Blanning, *The Pursuit of Glory*, 62
34. 'all her foul pustules turned black': *HL* 1:89 / *HV* 1:71
35. 'had no need to fear it': *HL* 1:88 / *HV* 1:70
36. 'those who die killed by doctors': *HL* 1:91 / *HV* 1:73

Taboo

37. 'The *Encyclopedia* entry for "Viol" (Rape)': Brin, '"Triompher par la force"', Malina Stefanovska (ed), *Casanova in the Enlightenment*, 21
38. 'Evidence from rape trials': Levack, 'The Prosecution of Sexual Crimes', 179
39. 'sexual intercourse': Childs, *Casanova: a biography based on new documents*, 40
40. 'The discovery of adolescence': Hall, *Adolescence* (1904)
41. 'In the eighteenth century': Lovett, *Casanova's Guide to Medicine*, 88
42. 'Sir John Acton': online Dictionary of National Biography, 1885–1900, vol 1
43. 'A 12-year-old female': Leneman, 'Wives and mistresses in eighteenth-century Scotland', 673

44. 'In Russia': Ottenheimer, *Forbidden relatives*, 90–91
45. 'In England': Ibid, 74
46. 'violation of not only biblical': Levack, 'The Prosecution of Sexual Crimes', 176
47. 'It was also a capital offence in Sweden': Bonnie, *Incest in Sweden, 1680–1940*
48. 'in open discourse': Lovett, *Casanova's Guide to Medicine*, 73
49. 'in sexual intercourse each person': Kant, *Lectures on Ethics*, 168
50. 'free-flowing compendium': Bergreen, *Casanova: the world of a seductive genius*, 449
51. 'such relationships were not uncommon': Pearson, *Voltaire Almighty*, 188
52. 'I have never been able to conceive': *HL* 10:19 / *HV* 3:229
53. 'If the father seizes his daughter': *HL* 7:229 / *HV* 2.772
54. 'He is not jealous': *HL* 11:311 / *HV* 3:876
55. 'Research has revealed': Musi, 'I viaggi di Casanova nel regno di Napoli', *Casanoviana 2*, (2019), 29

Chapter 2: Giacomo Casanova: 1725 to 1798
'At dawn the following day': *HL* 4:199 / *HV* 1:1174

Early life
1. 'For the greater part of the century': Norwich, *A History of Venice*, 584
2. 'In terms of trade': Ibid, 591
3. 'That was how they got rid of me': *HL* 1:51 / *HV 1:34*
4. 'The Paduan records make clear': Kelly, *Casanova: Actor, Spy, Lover, Priest*, 36
5. 'The Inquisition files': Ibid, 108
6. 'His conviction': Iordanou, *Venice's Secret Service: Organising Intelligence in the Renaissance*, 175

The wanderer
7. Income of labourers and barristers: Lindert, "English workers' living standards', 4

Later years
8. 'Helmut Watzlawick': Watzlawick, 'Les Tristesses de Dux: critique d'un mythe' in *Giacomo Casanova: tra Venezia e l'Europa*, Gilberto Pizzamiglio (ed)

Chapter 3: Connections
'It was then that the pope': *HL* 7:188 / *HV* 2:732

Social networks
1. 'These productions': Rousseau, *Politics and the Arts: Letter to M. D'Alembert on the theatre*, 27
2. 'to please corrupt minds': Ibid, 45
3. 'the more the comedy is amusing': Ibid, 34

4. 'imbecile audiences': Ibid, 49
5. 'I ask how an estate': Ibid, 90
6. 'a perversion of natural relations': Ibid, 49
7. 'ascendancy': Ibid, 49
8. 'Every young man who travels': *HL* 3:116 / *HV* 1:696

Freemasonry
9. Numbers of masonic lodges: Blanning, *The Pursuit of Glory*, 332
10. 'I had supper with a company': *HL* 6:25 / *HV* 2:287

The occult
11. 'the origins of his interest': Kelly, *Casanova: Actor, Spy, Lover, Priest*, 217
12. 'I told her to ask in writing': *HL* 5:153 / *HV* 2:146
13. 'Cabbala, its associated disciplines': Ibid, 220
14. 'It is perhaps not too much to say': Childes, *Casanova: A Biography Based on New Documents*, 54

Chapter 4: The gambler, the duellist and the gentleman
'I loved gambling': *HL* 4:109 / *HV* 1:1091
'I craved a duel': *HL* 2:279 / *HV* 1:561

1. 'a man could gain reputation': Walker, 'Gambling and Venetian Noblemen', 49–50

The gambler
2. 'Nowhere was the social mix': Johnson, *Venice Incognito*, 25
3. 'This casino': *HL* 4:46 / *HV* 1:1033
4. 'is a capable gambler': cited in Kelly, *Casanova: Actor, Spy, Lover, Priest*, 113
5. 'Such [losing] is the fate of every man': *HL* 2:66 / *HV* 1:360

The duellist
6. 'the duel became a working mechanism': Reyfman, 'The Emergence of the Duel in Russia', 26
7. 'The honest man who bears a weapon': *HL* 8:55 / *HV* 2:886
8. '[Schmit] fired his first shot into the air': *HL* 8:57 / *HV* 2:888
9. 'by putting the point of my sword to his throat': *HL* 2:277 / *HV* 1:559
10. 'kill without discourtesy': Casanova, *The Duel*, 8
11. 'Branicki, taking the other' *HL* 10:185 / *HV* 3:409
12. 'it [Torriano's shifty behaviour]': *HL* 12:233 / *HV* 3:1123

Chaper 5: The political landscape
'It is a fancy common to all nations': *HL* 9:161 / *HV* 3:6

The west
1. 'I admired the beauty of the carriages': *HL* 9:161 / *HV* 3:6
2. 'nothing's more beautiful than the roads of England': *HL* 9:257 / *HV* 3:107
3. Edinburgh to London travel times: Blanning, *The Pursuit of Glory*, 11
4. 'With us, paying with hard cash': *HL* 9:180 / *HV* 3:28
5. 'By this policy': *HL* 9:182 / *HV* 3:31
6. Dutch trade: Blanning, *The Pursuit of Glory*, 96
7. Number of French government offices: Woloch, *Eighteenth-Century Europe*, 14
8. 'a monstrous indiscretion': *HL* 11:103 / *HV* 3:664

Chapter 6: The Seven Years War: 1756–1763
'The last struggle had exhausted her': *HL* 4:70 / *HV* 1:1056

1. 'the Venetians were astonished': Bernis, *Memoir and Letters of Cardinal de Bernis*, Vol. 1, 177
2. Evidence of De Bernis' affairs in Venice: Childes, *Casanova: A New Perspective*, 69–70

Prelude to war
3. 'Frederick was an opportunist and risk taker': Szabo, The Seven Years War in Europe, 426
4. 'All the court': Bernis, *Memoir and Letters of Cardinal de Bernis*, Vol. 1, 200
5. 'I saw at Dresden the most brilliant court in all Europe': *HL* 3:218 / *HV* 1:894
6. 'ruin of Saxony': *HL* 3:218 / *HV* 1:894
7. 'the same intrigues': Bernis, *Memoir and Letters of Cardinal de Bernis*, Vol. 1, 307

1756 and 1757
8. 'One sees by this on what ridiculous considerations': Ibid., 301
9. Annual wage in Paris in 1760 was around 450 livres. Milanovic, 'Level of income and income distribution', 8, note 15
10. 'Money which cost them nothing': *HL* 5:98 / *HV* 2:82

1758 and 1759
11. 'it was madness': Bernis, *Memoir and Letters of Cardinal de Bernis*, Vol. 2, 34
12. 'I have always had more difficulty': Ibid, Vol. 1, 232
13. 'fatal obligation': Ibid, 299

1760 and 1761
14. 'he suspects him': cited in Childes, *Casanova: A Biography Based on New Documents*, 119

Chapter 7: Religious Life
'However it acts': *HL* 2:17 / *HV* 1:312

1. Income of the Archbishop of Paris: Blanning, *The Pursuit of Glory*, 371
2. Land ownership of the Catholic Church in France: Ibid, 364
3. Church tithe: Woloch, *Eighteenth-Century Europe*, 83
4. 'It's raining bombs on the house of the Lord': Diderot, *Lettres à Sophie Volland*, 212
5. 'a man of thirty, with red hair' *HL* 1:220–221 / *HV* 1:201–202
6. 'His Rhine wine was exquisite': *HL* 6:92 / *HV* 2:356
7. Statistics for growth of Methodism: Field, 'The social composition of English Methodism', 153
8. Statistics for monasteries and monastics: Beales, *Prosperity and Plunder*, 2–3
9. St Sergius-Trinity: Blanning, *The Pursuit of Glory*, 379
10. 'They possessed farms and forests': Beales, *Prosperity and Plunder*, 4
11. 'What! You have no monks instructing and disputing': Voltaire, *Candide or Optimism*, 47
12. Involuntary monastics: Schute, 'Between Venice and Rome: the dilemma of involuntary nuns.' 149
13. 'An Englishman,' he notes, 'as a free man': Voltaire, Letters on England, 37
14. 'No one can know for certain': *HL* 9:344 / *HV* 3:193
15. 'False zeal is a tyrant': Frederick II, *Memoirs of the House of Brandenburg*, 242
16. Gordon riots: Blanning, *The Pursuit of Glory*, 326
17. 'I don't want anyone, let alone a Jew': *HL* 12:159 / *HV* 3:1049
18. 'Because…out of religious duty': *HL* 12:159 / *HV* 3:1050
19. 'While waiting for the maid': *HL* 12:161 / *HV* 3:1051
20. 'What a difference between the cold reception': *HL* 12:187 / *HV* 3:1077

Chapter 8: The Public Sphere
'The true man of letters': *HL* 11:153 / *HV* 3:714

Origins
1. 'representative publicness': Habermas, *The Structural Transformation of the Public Sphere*, 7
2. 'dyed a true Son of the Church of England': 'The London Gazette', Issue 24, 1

Politics
3. 'The favourite': Walpole, *Memoirs of the reign of King George III*, Vol. 1, 11
4. 'the *North Briton* proceeded with an acrimony': Walpole, *Memoirs of the reign of King George III*, Vol. 1, 116
5. 'ignominious peace': Wilkes, *The North Briton*, Issue 45, 261
6. 'Every friend of his country': Ibid, 263
7. 'responsible to his people': Ibid, 368

8. 'His image could be found': Cash, *John Wilkes: The Scandalous Father of Civil Liberty*, 119
9. 'A man dressed for court': *HL* 9:174 / *HV* 3:22

Books
10. The relative cost of bibles: Gawthrop and Strauss, 'Protestantism and Literacy in Early Modern Germany', 40 (n.41), 49
11. Journal topics: Addison, *The Spectator*, Vol. I,
12. 'appears to have seen and read a prodigious amount': *HL* 6:321 (appendix: Bernard de Muralt's letter to Albrecht von Haller)
13. 'I had about thirty of them [books], all enemies of religion': *HL* 7:178 / *HV* 2:722
14. 'over one hundred books': *HL* 8:249 / *HV* 2:1062
15. 'They [the books] were few but choice': *HL* 4:57 / *HV* 1:1044

People of letters, salon culture and writers
16. 'a subject of the Republic of Venice': *HL* 11:30 / *HV* 3:590
17. 'The man of letters was distinguished': Lilti, *The World of the Salons*, 109
18. 'the function of salons': Ibid, 5
19. 'The supper was like most suppers in Paris': Voltaire, *Candide*, 63
20. 'He has gained admittance': cited in Robilant, *A Venetian Affair*, 169
21. 'these estimates situate the Paris salons': Lilti, *The World of the Salons*, 32
22. 'There are many men of letters': *Encyclopedia*, Voltaire entry, 'Gens de Lettres', trans. author, Vol. 7, 600
23. 'Ten to twelve that I like': *HL* 6:225 / *HV* 2:486
24. 'I felt that writing for a living': Rousseau, *The Confessions*, 375
25. 'I was thought to be above a poet' : *HL* 11:56 / *HV* 3:616

The theatre
26. 'Early modern Spanish drama': Greer, 'Playing the palace', 79
27. Theatre riots: Gorrie, *Gentle Riots?* 4

Chapter 9: Men and Women
'Sorrow and joy': *HL* 5:224 / *HV* 5:224

Male guardianship and marriage
1. 'among peasants and others': Shute, 'Society and the Sexes in the Venetian Republic', 370
2. 'Because men depended on': Shoemaker, *Gender in English Society, 1650–1850*, 144

Sex
3. 'adultery is the highest invasion of property': Kesselring, 'No greater provocation?', 214

4. 'the lack, especially among very young girls': Hunt, *Women in Eighteenth-Century Europe*, 120

Children
5. Women dying in childbirth: Hunt, *Women in Eighteenth-Century Europe*, 144
6. 'I laughed at myself': *HL* 10:35 / *HV* 3:245
7. Swedish child mortality; https://ourworldindata.org/parents-losing-their-child

Non-marital relationships
8. 'offered her fifty guineas a month': *HL* 10:21/ *HV* 3:231
9. Income of top 2.5% of families: Hume, 'The value of money', 377
10. 'petitioned her husband for her': *HL* 6:67 / *HV* 2:330
11. 'Venetian law': Cowan, *Marriage, Manners and Mobility in Early Modern Venice*, 131

Culture and education
12. 'could only hold the instrument': *HL* 3:65 / *HV* 1:642
13. 'In a woman scholarship is out of place': *HL* 3:50 / *HV* 1:631
14. 'the sexes are fundamentally equal': Casanova, *Lana Caprina*, Kindle locations 286–300
15. '*Refutation*': *Della* 'Storia del Governo Veneto' *d'Amelot de la Houssaie*. Divisa in tre parti (I parte), 152–156
16. 'And truly women': Ariosto, *Orlando Furioso, Part One*, 20:2:1–2

Chapter 10: The Meaning of Love
'As regards to women…when love gets involved': *HL* 1:27 / *HV* 1:6

1. 'A kind of madness': *HL* 2:152 / *HV* 1:441–2
2. 'without having been able to sleep': *HL* 4:7 / *HV* 1:997
3. 'four-fifths': *HL* 2: 25 / *HV 1:319*
4. 'an unbearable emptiness': *HL* 11:7 / *HV* 3:568
5. 'I didn't need a woman to satisfy my temperament': *HL* 9:202 / *HV* 3:53
6. 'was in love with her': *HL* 9:285 / *HV* 3:134
7. 'Tonina embraced him': *HL* 4:176 / *HV* 1:1152
8. 'This is the effect of great sadness': *HL* 3:78 / *HV* 1:654
9. 'I wanted to see if her qualities': *HL* 10:214 / *HV* 3:441
10. 'I only need to raise': Ravà, *Lettere di donne à Giacomo Casanova*, trans. author, 255

Chapter 11: Casanova's Lovers
'My housekeeper was too attractive': *HL* 6:159 / *HV* 2:420

1. 'He wanted to kiss me, I refused': *HL* 6:127 / *HV* 2:391
2. 'Given her poverty her attitude astounds me': *HL* 7:60 – 61 / *HV* 2:607

3. 'She may have virtues': *HL* 3:32 / *HV* 1:613–4
4. 'She was waiting for some sort of rapprochement': Kelly, *Casanova: Actor, Spy, Lover, Priest*, 121
5. 'She looks at me, then turns to her friend': *HL* 3:139 / *HV* 1:744
6. Rates of illegitimacy: Blanning, *The Pursuit of Glory*, 46
7. 'a theatre girl in love': *HL* 3:231/ *HV* 1:922
8. 'And not for love': Ariosto, *Orlando Furioso, Part Two*, 43: 4
9. 'all women, honest or not, sell themselves': *HL* 7:269 / *HV* 2:810
10. 'was touched by a gratitude': *HL* 4:185 / *HV* 1:1161
11. 'I will give you enough.' *HL* 8:63–64 / *HV* 2:892
12. 'attack her' *HL* 11:9 / *HV* 3:570
13. 'Because it is the tomb of love': *HL* 9:208 / *HV* 3:59
14. 'my wife, my mistress': *HL* 4:153–4 / *HV* 1:1132–3
15. 'If I had married': *HL* 8:94 / *HV* 2:917
16. 'In reality, Casanova's treatment of women': Damrosch, *Adventurer*, 3

Chapter 12: What kind of man was Casanova?
'As far as I am concerned': *HL* 1:38 / *HV* 1:19

1. 'built like a Hercules': Ligne, *The Prince de Ligne*, 2:160
2. 'a very handsome man': *HL* 10:70 / *HV* 3:282
3. 'In his analysis of La Morlière's satire': Kavanagh, *Enlightened Pleasures, 32*
4. 'There was nothing he did not know': Ligne, *The Prince de Ligne*, 2:161
5. 'When he came to the subject': Damrosch, *Jean-Jacques Rousseau*, 474
6. 'A monstrous desire': *HL* 11:86 / *HV* 3:647
7. 'While in Russia': Childs, *Casanova: a new perspective*, 230
8. 'Anger had the same power over me as love': *HL* 9:100 / *HV* 2:1209
9. 'He had feeling and gratitude': Ligne, *The Prince de Ligne*, 2:161
10. 'did me an immortal honour': *HL* 10:190 / *HV* 3:414
11. 'Casanova is the historical celebrity *par excellence*': Vinovrški, 'Casanova: A Case Study', 100
12. 'He claimed that he wanted': Ibid 103
13. 'By writing circulars': Vinovrški, 'Casanova's Celebrity', 140
14. 'In the most brilliant company': *HL* 1:247 / *HV* 1:227
15. 'I have always had a dread of being hissed': *HL* 1:34 / *HV* 1:16
16. 'I disappeared to go and weep in the garden': *HL* 3:62 / *HV* 1:640
17. 'I spent a cruel night': *HL* 9:362 / *HV* 3;210
18. 'She was a tall brunette': *HL* 7:88 / *HV* 2:631
19. 'The strategy that I used': *HL* 1:176 / *HV* 1:156
20. 'I was very happy': *HL* 5:186–7 / *HV* 2:181–2
21. 'But was it virtue': *HL* 11:230–1 / *HV* 3:798
22. 'In life nothing is real but the present': *HL* 7:92 / *HV* 2:634
23. 'Happy with it all': *HL* 8:274 / *HV* 2:1085
24. 'As much as possible': *HL* 6:49 / *HV* 2:311

25. 'horrible merchandise': Bernardini, 'Politica e filosofia', trans. author, 10
26. 'barbarous spectacle': *HL* 11:88–9 / *HV* 3:650
27. 'If the cries': cited in Hauc, 'Casanova et la souffrance animale', *Casanoviana*
    4, (2021) trans. author, 9
28. 'How could anyone resist': *HL* 11:299 / *HV* 3:865
29. 'apart from La Corticelli': *HL* 12:94 / *HV* 3:984

Bibliography

Specialist Texts and Primary Sources

Addison, Joseph and others. *The Spectator*, vol. I. J M Dent & Co, 1897.

Aleksić, Branko. 'Casanova et D'Alembert.' *Recherches sur Diderot et sur l'Encyclopédie*, 42 (2007): 83–94.

Aleksić, Branko. 'Effets des Passions (Anon, 1776): la source de "Delle Passioni, Traduzione di Giacomo Casanova".' *Topique* 1 (2012): 151–165.

Allen, Douglas W., and Clyde G. Reed. 'The duel of honor: screening for unobservable social capital.' *American Law and Economics Review* 8, no. 1 (2006): 81–115.

Andrews, Charles M. *Ideal Empires and Republics*. 1901.

Antony, Robert, Stuart Carroll, and Caroline Dodds Pennock, (eds). *The Cambridge World History of Violence: Volume 3, ad 1500–ad 1800*. Cambridge U P, 2020.

Augustine. *The Confessions of St Augustine*, trans. E B Pusey. J M Dent & sons, 1939.

Bacon, Francis, *The New Organon: and related writings*. Liberal Arts Press, 1960.

Bateman, J. Chimène. 'Amazonian Knots: Gender, Genre, and Ariosto's Women Warriors.' *MLN* 122, no. 1 (2007): 1–23.

Beales, Derek. *Prosperity and Plunder: European Catholic monasteries in the Age of Revolution, 1650–1815*. Cambridge U P, 2003.

Bellamy, Elizabeth J. 'Alcina's Revenge: Reassessing Irony and Allegory in *Orlando Furioso*.' *Annali d'italianistica* 12 (1994): 61–74.

Bernardini, Paolo, and Diego Lucci (eds). 'Politica e filosofia in Giacomo Casanova. Quattro inediti.' First published in *Annali dell'Università di Ferrara. Sezione di Storia 2* (2005), 251–270.

Bernis, François-Joachim de Pierre de. *Memoirs and Letters of Cardinal de Bernis*, trans. Katherine Prescott Wormeley. Hardy, Pratt & Co, 1902.

Boros, Gábor, and Herman De Dijn. *The concept of love in 17th and 18th Century Philosophy*. Martin Moors (ed). Leuven: Leuven U P, 2007.

Bregoli, Francesca, and Federica Francesconi. 'Tradition and transformation in eighteenth-century Europe: Jewish integration in comparative perspective.' *Jewish History* vol 24, no. 3–4 (2010): 235–246.

Brown, Alison. 'Lucretius and the Epicureans in the Social and Political Context of Renaissance Florence.' *I Tatti Studies in the Italian Renaissance* 9 (2001): 11–62.

Brown (ed), John, Russell. *The Oxford Illustrated History of Theatre*. Oxford U P, 1995.

Byars, Jana. *Informal Marriages in Early Modern Venice*. Routledge, 2019.

Buck, Mitchell. *The Life of Casanova from 1774–1798: a supplement to the memoirs*. Nicholas Brown, 1924.

Buckley, Theodore Alois, (ed) *The works of Horace*, trans. C Smart. HG Bohn, 1856.

Casanova, Giacomo. *Confutazione della* 'Storia del Governo Veneto' *d'Amelot de la Houssaie*. Divisa in tre . parti (I parte), Amsterdam, presso Pietro Mortier, 1769.

Casanova, Giacomo. *Della filosofia e de' filosofi*, (1780?).

Casanova, Giacomo. *Histoire de ma fuite des Prisons de la République de Venise*. Éditions Allia, 2018.

Casanova, Giacomo, Jean-Christophe Igalens, and Érik Leborgne. *Histoire de ma vie*. Vols. 1–3. Bouquins, 2013–2018.

Casanova, Giacomo. *History of My Life*, trans. W R Trask. Vols. 1–12. Johns Hopkins U P, 1997.

Casanova, Giacomo. *Lana Caprina*. I edizione eBook: giugno 2014.

Casanova, Giacomo. *Philocalies sur les Sottieses des Mortels* (1794)

Casanova, Giacomo. *Soliloque d'un penseur*. Vol. 1. Editions Allia, 1998.

Casanova, Giacomo. *The Duel*, trans. J.G. Nichols. Hesperus Press, 2003.

Cavaillé, Jean-Pierre. 'Libertine and libertinism: polemic uses of the terms in sixteenth- and seventeenth-century English & Scottish literature.' *Journal for Early Modern Cultural Studies* 12, no. 2 (2012): 12–36.

Cavallo, Jo Ann. 'Orlando Furioso'. *The Literary Encyclopedia*. 30 December 2014.

Cerman, Ivo, Susan Helen Reynolds, and Diego Lucci (eds). *Casanova: Enlightenment philosopher*. Voltaire Foundation, 2016.

Childs, James Rives. *Casanova: a biography based on new documents*. George Allen & Unwin Ltd, 1961.

Childs, James Rives. *Casanova: a new perspective*. Paragon House, 1988.

Childs, James Rives. *Casanoviana: an annotated world bibliography of Jacques Casanova de Seingalt and of works concerning him*. CM Nebehay, 1956.

Clay, Lauren. 'Provincial actors, the Comédie-Française, and the business of performing in eighteenth-century France.' *Eighteenth-century studies* (2005): 651–679.

Clementsson, Bonnie. *Incest in Sweden, 1680–1940: A history of forbidden relations*. Lund U P, 2020.

Coleman, James K. 'Translating Impiety: Girolama Frachetta and the first vernacular commentary on Lucretius.' *Quaderni d'italianistica* 35, no. 1 (2014).

Collins, Nancy W. *The problem of the Enlightenment salon: European history or post-revolutionary politics 1755–1850*. University of London, University College London (United Kingdom), 2006.

Cowan, Alexander. *Marriage, Manners and Mobility in Early Modern Venice*. Ashgate, 2007.

Cryle, Peter and Lisa O'Connell (eds). *Libertine Enlightenment: sex, liberty and licence in the eighteenth century*. Palgrave, 2003.

Davenport, Guy. *7 Greeks*. New Directions Paperbook 799, 1995.

Davis, Gregson (ed). *A Companion to Horace*. Wiley-Blackwell, 2010.

Delon, Michel (ed). *Encyclopedia of the Enlightenment*. Fitzroy Dearborn, 2001.

Denbo, Seth J. 'Speaking relatively: a history of incest and the family in eighteenth-century England.' Thesis submitted for the degree of Doctor of Philosophy at University of Warwick, 2001.

Denieul, Séverine. 'Essai de critique sur les sciences, sur les mœurs et sur les arts de Casanova: un dictionnaire raisonné de la sottise?' In *Casanova à tort et à travers*, 123–142. Classiques Garnier, 2014.

Denieul, Séverine. 'Casanova lecteur et critique de Voltaire.' In *Voltaire philosophe: regards croisés*. Textes réunis par Sébastien Charles et Stéphane Pujol. Publications de la Société Voltaire (2017): 125–139.

Descartes, René, and Laurence Julien Lafleur. *Discourse on Method: Translated, with an Introduction, by Laurence J. Lafleur*. Bobbs-Merrill, 1956.

Diderot, Denis. *An Essay on Blindness in a Letter to a Person of Distinction*, trans. unknown. Richard Dymot, 1895.

Diderot, Denis and Jean-Baptiste le Rond d'Alembert. *Encyclopédie, ou dictionnaire raisonné des sciences, des arts et des métiers*. Collaborative Digital Edition of the Encyclopedia (1751–1772).

Diderot, Denis. *Les éleuthéromanes: avec un commentaire historique*. Paris: [s.n.] 1884.

Diderot, Denis. *Lettres à Sophie Volland: textes publiés d'après les manuscrits originaux avec une introd., des variantes et des notes*. Vols. 1 & 2. Gallimard, 1950.

Diderot, Denis. *Sur la peinture*. Moritz Diesterweg, 1909.

Ducheyne, Steffen. *Reassessing the radical enlightenment*. Taylor & Francis, 2017.

Dupré, Louis. *The Enlightenment and the Intellectual Foundations of Modern Culture*. Yale U P, 2004.

Emery, Ted. 'Queer Casanova: Subversive Sexuality and the (Dis) embodied Subject in History of My Life.' *Italian Culture* 24, no. 1 (2007): 23–44.

Evans, Lewis. *The Satires of Juvenal, Persius, Sulpicia and Lucilius*. HG Bohn, 1861.

Faubert, Michelle. 'Romantic Suicide, Contagion, and Rousseau's Julie.' In *Romanticism, Rousseau, Switzerland*, pp. 38–53. Palgrave Macmillan, London, 2015.

Fee, Jerome. 'Maupertuis and the principle of least action.' *American Scientist* 30, no. 2 (1942): 149–58.

Field, Clive D. 'The social composition of English Methodism to 1830: a membership analysis.' *Bulletin of the John Rylands Library* 76, no. 1 (1994): 153–178.

Force, Pierre. 'Helvétius as an Epicurean political theorist.' *Epicurus in the Enlightenment* 12, Neven Leddy and Avi S. Lifschitz (eds), (2009): 105–118.

Frederick II. *Memoirs of the House of Brandenburg*, trans. unknown. J Nourse, 1758.

Gaisser, Julia Haig. 'Poggio and Other Book Hunters.' Ricci, Roberta. *Poggio Bracciolini and the Re (dis) covery of Antiquity: Textual and Material Traditions: Proceedings of the Symposium Held at Bryn Mawr College on April 8–9, 2016*. Firenze University Press, 2020.

Gawthrop, Richard, and Gerald Strauss. 'Protestantism and literacy in early modern Germany.' *Past & present* 104 (1984): 31–55.

Gay, Peter. *The Enlightenment: An Interpretation*. Alfred A Knopf, 1966.

Gliozzo, Charles A. 'The Philosophes and Religion: Intellectual Origins of the Dechristianization Movement in the French Revolution.' *Church History* 40, no. 3 (1971): 273–283.

Goodman, Dena. *Marriage Calculations in the Eighteenth Century: Deconstructing the Love vs. Duty Binary.* Ann Arbor, MI: Michigan Publishing, University of Michigan Library, 2005.

Gorrie, Richard. *Gentle Riots? Theatre Riots in London, 1730–1780,* thesis submitted for the degree of Doctor of Philosophy, University of Guelph, 2000.

Goulemot, Jean-Marie, and Arthur Greenspan. 'Toward a definition of libertine fiction and pornographic novels.' *Yale French Studies,* no. 94 (1998): 133–45.

Greenstone, Gerry. 'The history of bloodletting.' *BC Medical Journal* 52, no. 1 (2010): 12–14.

Greer, Margaret R. 'Playing the palace: space, place and performance in early modern Spain.' *A History of Theatre in Spain*: 79–102. Cambridge U P, 2012.

Greig, Hannah. 'Faction and Fashion: the politics of court dress in eighteenth-century England' in I Paresys & N Coquery (eds), Se Vêtir à la Cour en Europe (1400–1815). IRHiS, 2011.

Gregory, Mary. *Diderot and the Metamorphosis of Species.* Routledge, 2006.

Gregory, Tobias. *From Many Gods to One: Divine Action in Renaissance Epic.* Chicago U P, 2009.

Gregory, Tullio. "Libertinisme érudit' in seventeenth-century France and Italy: The critique of ethics and religion.' *British journal for the history of philosophy* vol. 6, no. 3 (1998): 323–349.

Habermas, Jurgen. *The Structural Transformation of the Public Sphere,* trans. Thomas Burger. MIT Press, 1991.

Harrison, Stephen (ed). *The Cambridge Companion to Horace.* Cambridge University Press, 2007.

Harvey, Karen. 'The century of sex? Gender, bodies, and sexuality in the long eighteenth century.' *The Historical Journal* 45, no. 4 (2002): 899–916.

Hitchcock, Tim. 'Sex and gender: Redefining sex in eighteenth-century England.' In *History Workshop Journal,* vol. 41, no. 1, 72–90. Oxford U P, 1996.

Hitchcock, Tim. 'The Reformulation of Sexual Knowledge in Eighteenth-Century England.' *Signs: Journal of Women in Culture and Society* 37, no. 4 (2012): 823–832.

Holbach, Paul Henri Thiry. *The System of Nature,* trans. W Hodgson. W Hodgson, 1795.

Hume, Robert D. 'The value of money in eighteenth-century England: incomes, prices, buying power – and some problems in cultural economics.' *Huntington Library Quarterly* 77, no. 4 (2014): 373–416.

Huzzey, Richard. 'Contesting Interests: Rethinking Pressure, Parliament, Nation, and Empire.' *Parliamentary History* 37 (2018): 1–17.

Huzzey, Richard, and Henry Miller. 'Petitions, Parliament and Political Culture: Petitioning the House of Commons, 1780–1918.' *Past & Present* 248, no. 1 (2020): 123–164.

Iordanou, Ioanna. *Venice's Secret Service: Organising Intelligence in the Renaissance.* Oxford U P, 2019.

Jacob, Margaret. 'The Nature of Early Eighteenth-Century Religious Radicalism.' *Republics of Letters: A Journal for the Study of Knowledge, Politics, and the Arts* 1, no. 1 (2009): 1–11.

Johnson, James H. 'Deceit and Sincerity in Early Modern Venice.' *Eighteenth-Century Studies* 38, no. 3 (2005): 399–415.

Johnson, Marguerite. 'Witches in time and space: "Satire" 1.8, "Epode" 5 and landscapes of fear.' *Hermathena* 192 (2012): 5–44.

Johnson, Monte Ransome. 'Was Gassendi an Epicurean?' *History of Philosophy Quarterly* 20, no. 4 (2003): 339–60.

Kant, Immanuel. *Lectures on Ethics*, trans. Infield Louis. Methuen and Co, 1930.

Kavanagh, Thomas M. *Enlightened Pleasures: Eighteenth-Century France and the New Epicureanism.* Yale U P, 2010.

Kavanagh, Thomas M. *Esthetics of the Moment: Literature and Art in the French Enlightenment.* Pennsylvania U P, 1996.

Kelly, George Armstrong. 'The Point of Honour.' *Historical Reflections/Réflexions Historiques* (1986): 103–125.

Kennedy, William J. 'Ariosto's ironic Allegory.' *MLN* 88, no. 1 (1973): 44–67.

Kerhervé, Alain, and Valérie Capdeville. *British Sociability in the Long Eighteenth Century. Challenging the Anglo-French Connection.* Boydell Press, 2019.

Kesselring, Krista J. 'No greater provocation? Adultery and the mitigation of murder in English law.' *Law and History Review* 34, no. 1 (2016): 199–225.

Klein, Daniel. *The Art of Happiness*, trans. George K Strodach. Penguin, 2012.

Kruckeberg, Robert D. 'The wheel of fortune in eighteenth-century France: The lottery, consumption, and politics.' Thesis submitted for the degree of Doctor of Philosophy at University of Michigan, 2009.

Lahouati, Gérard. 'Être ou ne pas être matérialiste?' *Avec Casanova. Penser, songer et rire*, Classiques Garnier, 2020 157–167.

Leneman, Leah. 'Wives and mistresses in eighteenth-century Scotland', *Women's History Review*, (1999), 8:4, 671–692.

Levack, Brian P. 'The Prosecution of Sexual Crimes in Early Eighteenth-Century Scotland.' *Scottish Historical Review* 89, no. 2 (2010): 172–193.

Levi, Peter. *Horace: a life*. Gerald Duckworth & Co, 1997.

Ligne, Charles Joseph. *The Prince de Ligne: his memoirs, letters, and miscellaneous papers*, trans. Katherine Prescott Wormeley. Hardy, Pratt & Co 1899.

Lindert, Peter H., and Jeffrey G. Williamson. "English Workers' Living Standards during the Industrial Revolution: A New Look." *The Economic History Review* 36, no. 1 (1983): 1–25.

Lolordo, Antonia. *Pierre Gassendi and the birth of early modern philosophy.* Cambridge U P, 2006 *London Gazette*. Authority, Est 1665.

Marrone, Gaetana, Paolo Puppa and Luca Somigli. Encyclopedia of Italian Literary Studies. Routledge, 2007

McCall, Brian. 'The New Protestant Bargain: the influence of Protestant theology on contract and property law'. In C Rao (ed), *Luther and His Progeny: 500 Years of Protestantism and Its Consequences for Church, State, and Society.* Angelico Press (2017), Kindle Edition.

McDonald, Christie V. 'The Utopia of the Text: Diderot's "Encyclopédie".' *The Eighteenth Century* 21, no. 2 (1980): 128–144.

McPherson, Heather. 'Theatrical riots and cultural politics in eighteenth-century London.' *The Eighteenth Century* 43, no. 3 (2002): 236–252.

Milanovic, Branko. 'Level of income and income distribution in mid-18th century France, according to Francois Quesnay.' *World Bank Policy Research Working Paper* 10545 (2010).

Milton, John R. 'Locke and Gassendi: a reappraisal.' In MA Stewart (ed), *English Philosophy in the Age of Locke*. Oxford U P. (2000): 87–109.

Mitsis, Phillip (ed). *Oxford Handbook of Epicurus and Epicureanism*. Oxford University Press, 2020.

Morabia, Alfredo. 'Pierre-Charles-Alexandre Louis and the evaluation of bloodletting.' *Journal of the Royal Society of medicine 99*, no.3 (2006): 158–160.

Muravyeva, Marianna. '"A king in his own household": domestic discipline and family violence in early modern Europe reconsidered.' *The History of the Family* 18, no. 3 (2013): 227–237.

O'Connell, Lisa. 'The Libertine, the Rake, and the Dandy: Personae, Styles, and Affects.' *Cambridge History of Gay and Lesbian Literature*, edited by EL McCallum and Mikko Tuhkanen, Cambridge U P (2014): 218–238.

Ohsumi, Megumi. *Pope and Horace: Imitation and Independence*. Doctoral dissertation. Université de Neuchâtel, 2013.

O'Rourke, James. *Sex, Lies and Autobiography: The Ethics of Confession*. Virginia U P, 2006.

Ottenheimer, Martin. *Forbidden relatives: The American myth of cousin marriage*. University of Illinois Press, 1996.

Pascal, Blaise. *Thoughts*, trans. W F Trotter. P F Collier, 1910.

Peltonen, Markku. 'Francis Bacon, the Earl of Northampton, and the Jacobean anti-duelling campaign.' *The Historical Journal* 44, no. 1 (2001): 1–28.

Pizzamiglio, Gilberto (ed). *Giacomo Casanova: tra Venezia e l'Europa*. Firenze: Leo S. Olschki, 2001.

Quint, David. 'The Figure of Atlante: Ariosto and Boiardo's Poem.' *MLN* (1979): 77–91.

Quint, David. 'Duelling and Civility in Sixteenth Century Italy.' *I Tatti Studies in the Italian Renaissance* 7 (1997): 231–278.

Ravà, Aldo. *Lettere di donne à Giacomo Casanova*. Milano: Fratelli Treves, 1912.

Reyfman, Irina. 'The emergence of the duel in Russia: corporal punishment and the honour code.' *The Russian Review*, 54, no. 1 (1995): 26–43.

Robertson, Ritchie. *Mock-epic poetry from Pope to Heine*. Oxford U P, 2009.

Rosenberg, Daniel. 'An Eighteenth-Century Time Machine: The "Encyclopédia" of Denis Diderot.' *Historical Reflections/Réflexions Historiques* (1999): 227–250.

Roth, Ben. 'Confessions, excuses, and the storytelling self: rereading Rousseau with Paul de Man.' In *Re-thinking European politics and history: IWM Junior visiting fellows' conferences*, vol. 32. 2012.

Rousseau, Jean Jacques. *Eloisa, or a series of original letters*, vol 2 trans. William Kenrick. Samuel Longcope, 1796.

Rousseau, Jean-Jacques. *Politics and the Arts: Letter to M. D'Alembert on the theatre*, trans. Allan Bloom. Cornell U P, 1959.

Roustang, François. *The Quadrille of Gender: Casanova's Memoirs*, trans. Anne C Vila. Stanford U P, 1988.

Rudé, George E. 'Prices, wages and popular movements in Paris during the French Revolution.' *The Economic History Review* 6, no. 3 (1954): 246–267.

Sarasohn, Lisa T. 'Motion and morality: Pierre Gassendi, Thomas Hobbes and the mechanical world-view.' *Journal of the History of Ideas*, vol 53 no. 3 (1985): 363–379.

Shammas, Carole. 'Food expenditures and economic well-being in early modern England.' *The Journal of Economic History*, 43, no.1 (1983): 89–100.

Scherr, Arthur. 'Jews in Voltaire's "Candide".' *Romance Notes* 46, no. 3 (2006): 297–308.

Schutte, Anne Jacobson. 'Society and the sexes in the Venetian Republic.' In *A Companion to Venetian History, 1400–1797*, pp. 353–377. Brill 2013.

Schutte, Anne Jacobson. 'Between Venice and Rome: the dilemma of involuntary nuns.' *The Sixteenth century journal* (2010): 415–439.

Sciascia, Leonardo. 'L'utopia di Casanova.' *Belfagor* 34, no. 5 (1979): 505–11.

Sha, Richard. 'Medicalizing the Romantic Libido: Sexual Pleasure, Luxury, and the Public Sphere.' *Romanticism on the Net 31* (2003).

Shoemaker, Robert B. *Gender in English Society, 1650–1850*. Longman, 1998.

Shoemaker, Robert B. 'The taming of the duel: masculinity, honour and ritual violence in London, 1660–1800.' *The Historical Journal* 45, no. 3 (2002): 525–545.

Simonton, Deborah (ed). *The Routledge history of women in Europe since 1700*. Routledge, 2006.

Singh, Christine M. 'The Lettre sur les aveugles: Its Debt to Lucretius.' *Studies in Eighteenth-Century French Literature Presented to Robert Niklaus* (1975): 233–42.

Skipp, Jenny. 'Masculinity and Social Stratification in Eighteenth-Century Erotic Literature, 1700–1821.' *Journal for Eighteenth-Century Studies* 29, no. 2.

Spencer, Jane. '"The link which unites man with brutes": Enlightenment Feminism, Women and Animals.' *Intellectual History Review* 22, no. 3 (2012): 427–444.

Stefanovska, Malina. *Casanova in the Enlightenment: From the Margins to the Centre*. Vol. 30. Toronto UP, 2021.

Symons, Arthur. 'Casanova at Dux: An Unpublished Chapter of History.' *The North American Review* vol. 175, no. 550 (1902): 329–346.

Tague, Ingrid H. 'Love, honor, and obedience: Fashionable women and the discourse of marriage in the early eighteenth century.' *Journal of British Studies* 40, no. 1 (2001): 76–106.

Thomas, Chantal. 'Casanova and the Revolution', trans Nicole Santilli. *Public* (1994).

Thysell, Carol. *The Pleasure of Discernment: Marguerite de Navarre as Theologian*. Oxford U P, 2000.

Traer, James F. *Marriage and the Family in Eighteenth-Century France.* Cornell U P, 1980.

Trampus, Antonio (ed). (2018–2021). *Casanoviana.*

Trumbach, Randolph. 'The transformation of sodomy from the renaissance to the modern world and its general sexual consequences.' *Signs: Journal of Women in Culture and Society* 37, no. 4 (2012): 832–848.

Turner, James G. 'The Properties of Libertinism.' In *'Tis Nature's Fault: Unauthorized Sexuality during the Enlightenment.* Cambridge U P 1988.

Veen, Mirjam van (ed). *Ioannis Calvini Scripta didactica et polemica, Volume 1.* Librairie Droz, 2005.

Vinovrški, Nicola. 'Casanova: A Case Study of Celebrity in 18th Century Europe.' *Historical Social Research / Historische Sozialforschung. Supplement*, no. 32 (2019): 99–120.

Vinovrški, Nicola. 'Casanova's Celebrity: A Case Study of Well-knownness in 18th Century Europe.' Thesis submitted for the degree of Doctor of Philosophy at the University of Queensland (2015).

Voltaire, *Sentiment des citoyens.* In *Oeuvres completes de Voltaire*, Louis Moland (ed), vol. 25. Garnier Frères, 1877–1885.

Voltaire. *Memoirs of the Life of Voltaire*, trans unknown. G Robinson, 1784.

Voltaire. *A Philosophical Dictionary, Vol 2.* W Dugdale, 1843.

Voltaire. *Toleration and other essays*, trans. Joseph McCabe. G P Putnam's Sons, 1912.

Voltaire. *The Works of Voltaire: a contemporary version*, trans. William F Fleming. E R Dumont, 1901.

Walker, Jonathan. 'Gambling and Venetian noblemen.' Past & present 162, no. 1 (1999): 28–69.

Walpole, Horace. *Memoirs of the Reign of King George III.* Yale U P, 2000.

Weidinger, H E. 'The "Dux Drafts". Casanova's Contribution to Da Ponte's and Mozart's Don Giovanni.' *Maske und Kothurn* 52, no. 4 (2006): 95–130.

Wilkes, John. *The North Briton: revised and corrected*, vol. 1 (1766).

Williams, David Lay. *Rousseau's Platonic Enlightenment.* Penn State U P, 2007.

Wolfe, Charles T. 'A happiness fit for organic bodies: La Mettrie's medical Epicureanism.' in *Epicurus in the Enlightenment* 12, Neven Leddy and Avi S. Lifschitz (eds), (2009), 69–83.

Wright, D. G. 'Rousseau's Confessions: The Tragedy of Teleology.' *Journal of Social and Political Thought*, vol. 1 no. 4 (2003).

Yack, Bernard. 'Popular Sovereignty and Nationalism.' *Political Theory* 29, no. 4 (2001): 517–36.

Yona, Sergio. *Epicurean Ethics in Horace: The Psychology of Satire.* Oxford University Press, 2018.

Zweig, Paul. *The Adventurer.* Akadine Press, 1999.

Texts for the General Reader

Andrieux, Maurice. *Daily Life in Venice at the Time of Casanova*, trans. Mary Fitton. Praeger, 1972.

Ariosto, Ludovico. *Orlando Furioso, Part One*, trans. Barbara Reynolds. Penguin, 1973.

Ariosto, Ludovico. *Orlando Furioso, Part Two*, trans. Barbara Reynolds. Penguin, 1977.

Bergreen, Laurence. *Casanova: the world of a seductive genius*. Simon and Schuster, 2016.

Blanning, Tim. *The Pursuit of Glory*. Penguin, 2008.

Blanning, Tim. *Frederick the Great: King of Prussia*. Allen Lane, 2015.

Blom, Philip. *Wicked Company: freethinkers and friendship in pre-revolutionary Paris*. Phoenix, 2011.

Bloom, Allan, and Adam Kirsch. *The republic of Plato*, trans. Allan Bloom. Basic books, 2016.

Casanova, Giacomo. *The Story of My Life* (abridged), trans. S Hawkes and S Sartarelli. Penguin 2001.

Cash, Arthur H. *John Wilkes: the scandalous father of civil liberty*. Yale U P, 2006.

Curran, Andrew S. *Diderot and the Art of Thinking Freely*. Other Press, 2020.

Damrosch, Leo. *Jean-Jacques Rousseau: restless genius*. Mariner Books, 2007.

Damrosch, Leo. *Adventurer: the life and times of Giacomo Casanova*. Yale U P, 2022.

Diderot, Denis. *Rameau's Nephew and D'Alembert's Dream*, trans. L W Tancock. Penguin, 1976.

Flem, Lydia. *Casanova: the man who really loved women*, trans. Catherine Temerson. Farrar, Straus and Giroux, 1997.

Goldoni, Carlo. *The Comic Theatre*, trans. J W Miller. Nebraska U P, 1969.

Greenblatt, Stephen. *The Swerve: how the Renaissance began*. Vintage, 2012.

Holme, Timothy. *A Servant of Many Masters: The Life and Times of Carlo Goldoni*. London: Jupiter, 1976.

Hunt, Margaret. *Women in Eighteenth-Century Europe*. Routledge, 2014.

Ilchman, Frederick, Thomas Michie, C D Dickerson III and Esther Bell (eds). *Casanova: the seduction of Europe*. MFA, 2017.

Johnson, James H. *Venice Incognito: masks in the serene republic*. California U P, 2011.

Kelly, Ian. *Casanova: actor, spy, lover, priest*. Hodder & Stoughton, 2008.

Lilti, Antoine. *The World of the Salons: sociability and worldliness in eighteenth-century Paris*, trans. Lydia G Cochrane. Oxford U P, 2020.

Lovett, Lisetta. *Casanova's Guide to Medicine: 18th-century medical practice*. Pen & Sword History, 2021.

Lucretius. *The Nature of Things*, trans. A E Stallings. Penguin, 2007.

Masters, John. *Casanova*. Michael Joseph, 1969.

Melton, James Van Horn. *The Rise of the Public in Enlightenment Europe*. Cambridge U P, 2001.

Norwich, John Julius. *A History of Venice*. Vintage Books, 1989.

Parker, Derek. *Casanova*. Sutton, 2003.

Pearson, Roger. *Voltaire Almighty: a life in pursuit of freedom*. Bloomsbury, 2006.

Robilant, Andre di. *A Venetian Affair*. Harper Perennial, 2005.

Rousseau, Jean-Jacques. *The Confessions*, trans. J M Cohen. Penguin, 1977.

Rousseau, Jean-Jacques. *Emile or on Education*, trans. Allan Bloom. Basic Books, 1979.

Rousseau, Jean-Jacques. *The Social Contract, or Principles of Political Right*, trans. C M Sherover. Meridian Books, 1974.

Sollers, Philippe. *Casanova the Irresistible*, trans. Armine Kotin Mortimer. Illinois U P, 2016.

Shank, J B. *The Newton Wars and the Beginning of the French Enlightenment.* Chicago U P, 2008.

Summers, Judith. *Casanova's Women.* Bloomsbury, 2007.

Szabo, Franz A. J. *The Seven Years War in Europe (1756–1763).* Routledge, 2013.

Voltaire. *Candide, or Optimism.* Penguin, 2005.

Voltaire. *Letters on England*, trans. Leonard Tancock. Penguin, 2005.

Williams, Abigail. *The Social Life of Books.* Yale University Press, 2017.

Woloch, Isser & Gregory S. Brown. *Eighteenth-Century Europe: tradition and progress, (1715–1789).* W W Norton & Co, 2012.

Useful on-line resources

ARTFL Project: https://artfl-project.uchicago.edu/

Digital Encyclopedia of British Sociability in the Long Eighteenth Century – https://www.digitens.org/en

Édition Numérique Collaborative et Critique de l'Encyclopédie: http://enccre. academie-sciences.fr/encyclopedie/

Encyclopedia of Diderot & d'Alembert, collaborative translation project: https:// quod.lib.umich.edu/d/did/

Internet Encyclopedia of Philosophy: https://iep.utm.edu/

Internet Archive: https://archive.org/

Johnson's Dictionary Online: https://johnsonsdictionaryonline.com/

JSTOR: https://www.jstor.org/

OpenEdition Books: https://books.openedition.org/

OpenEdition Journals: https://journals.openedition.org/

Project Gutenberg: https://www.gutenberg.org/

Répertoire des oeuvres de Giacomo Casanova conservées au chateau de Dux: https://app.lib.uliege.be/casanova/

Stanford Encyclopedia of Philosophy: https://plato.stanford.edu/

Index